Royalty Inc.

Royalty Inc.

Britain's Best-Known Brand

By Stephen Bates

Aurum
Press

First published in Great Britain
2015 by Aurum Press Ltd
74–77 White Lion Street
Islington
London N1 9PF
www.aurumpress.co.uk

A catalogue record for this book is available from the British Library.

ISBN 978 1 78131 356 5

1 3 5 7 9 10 8 6 4 2
2015 2017 2019 2018 2016

Typeset in Dante MT Std by SX Composing DTP, Rayleigh, Essex
Printed and bound by CPI Group (UK) Ltd, Croydon, CR0 4YY

For Alice

Oh philosophers may sing
Of the troubles of a king,
But of pleasures there are many and of worries there are none;
And the culminating pleasure
That we treasure beyond measure
Is the gratifying feeling that our duty has been done.

Gilbert and Sullivan: *The Gondoliers*, Act II

(The first Gilbert and Sullivan operetta that Queen Victoria saw, at Windsor on 6 March 1891. She apparently enjoyed the experience and rather thought she might have given them the idea for the plot.)

Contents

Chapter 1

'I have to be seen to be believed'

(Said to be the Queen's private motto)

Whoever wrote the original words to the National Anthem, the signature tune of Britain, probably at some time in the first half of the eighteenth century, could not have known how apposite they would still be two and a half centuries later. Our noble Queen has certainly lived long – longer than any previous monarch in the nation's history – and she has long reigned over us too, generally happily and graciously, though gloriously may be more a matter for debate. You have to be in your seventies now to remember a time when she was not the monarch. Indeed, if you were born on the day she became Queen you can't be far off reaching retirement and collecting your state pension.

The Queen's longevity is a tribute to her robust health, but how is it that the institution she represents, based on some very quaint traditions and dated assumptions, tracing its origins back more than a thousand years, has not only managed to survive but to flourish well into the twenty-first century? There are very few enduring monarchies in the world in democratic countries: they are basically restricted to a fringe of western Europe, and the British monarchy is by far the best known of them. More than a governmental system, an ancient flummery or a tourist trap, it is, arguably, the most famous non-commercial brand in the world. Our small, sprightly, octogenarian Queen, after more than sixty-three years on the throne, is one of the most famous women anywhere on earth, as recognisable to someone in Tokyo or Tulsa, or even Timbuktu and Tuvalu, as in Tooting or Truro. Everything about her on the surface is familiar, from her dress sense – pastel colours, off-the-face hats – to her voice, reminiscent of a different era and class. We know she likes dogs and horses and Scotland, that in private she is a good mimic and sometimes sardonic, that she hates being late, that she is strongly religious and is very conscientious and stoic. What we don't know is what she thinks about almost anything: her opinions are unknown and unknowable, a blank. Her inscrutability is the secret of her success. If we really knew anything about her thoughts, the monarchy would rock: its apparent impartiality is its greatest strength, for almost any opinion held by the sovereign would divide the country, whereas having none publicly goes a long way towards uniting it.

For a journalist it is the greatest frustration: how do you report on someone you cannot talk to? With the possible exception of Kim Jong-un, the Supreme Leader of North Korea, the Queen is the only person on the planet who cannot be interviewed – even Pope Francis regularly chats to the media these days. We can guess what she is like and speculate for all we are worth, the Queen even occasionally shows passive emotion, but ultimately the mask never slips. We may think we know what she is really like, but do we? As Lord Fellowes, her former private secretary, told a new member of staff: 'Just because she is friendly, it does not mean she is friends with you.'

Everyone knows (or thinks they know) her family, too. The royal soap opera trundles on, less thrilling perhaps than twenty years ago, but still fulfilling all the requirements of an ongoing weekly saga: the matriarch with an ageing husband apt to speak his mind too freely and put his foot in it; the frustrated eldest son with the turbulent lovelorn backstory; the young married couple with babies; the dull and grasping younger children. Characters come and go, some die off, others arrive and plots emerge, then peter out, but the story continues. It is a seeming anachronism which remains incredibly popular – much more so than most other institutions in Britain or abroad, shining bright in public affection, untarnished like politicians, or the church, the media, the bankers or big business. This is one company that has somehow pulled off the trick of seeming never to change, but yet it always manages to evolve, quietly, inconspicuously but firmly: as familiar in its way as a Coca-Cola bottle or a Marmite jar. A new label here, a new ingredient there, a plastic bottle instead of a glass one, a new taste sensation. We think iconic brands do not change, but they do and if they do it too drastically or obviously, they suffer. Equally, if they do not change, they decline and die. Royalty is a bit like that. It has been changing successfully for years, centuries even, without most people really noticing. It is not the same institution it was when the Queen came to the throne in 1952; in many ways it has changed out of all recognition and so it sails on. This book seeks to track the changes and explain how the monarchy has achieved its transformation. How has it pulled it off? And will it continue to do so?

The parameters are easy to discern, as are the changes to the lives of those she governs. Queen Elizabeth II is not the longest-reigning sovereign in history. She'll have to last nearly another twenty years to beat King Sobhuza of Swaziland's eighty-two years and 254 days between 1899 and 1982, until 2024 to whizz past Louis XIV of France and 2019 to beat the Emperor Franz Josef of Austria and who knows when the reign of the King of Thailand, Bhumibol Adulyadej, who has been on the throne there since June 1946, will end? Unlike the Queen, he is perhaps not a world-renowned figure, possibly not even in Bangkok[1]. But in Britain the sixty-three years and 216 days that Queen Victoria was on the throne will be eclipsed on 9 September 2015. Remarkably, at the time of writing, Britain has had a female head of state for 127 of the past 180 years. The British Empire has long gone – partly assembled in the reign of Queen Victoria, it has been completely dismantled in the time of her great-great-granddaughter – but she still remains sovereign of sixteen realms, from the United Kingdom and Northern Ireland, Canada, Australia, New Zealand, Jamaica, Barbados, the Bahamas, Grenada, Papua New Guinea, the Solomon Islands, Tuvalu, St Lucia, St Vincent and the Grenadines, Belize, Antigua and Barbuda to St Christopher and Nevis, and about 130 million people are her subjects. Any proposed change in the monarch's constitutional position in the UK requires their agreement as independent states too. The Commonwealth has replaced the empire: fifty-three independent nations, encompassing a third of the world's population, and the Queen is at its head. Even countries that were never ruled by the British, such as Mozambique, have joined and those thirty-one member states that are now republics still acknowledge her: they recognise the organisation as a useful and beneficial international association, bound together by a colonial history, mainly a common language and shared traditions. In the words of the then Australian prime minister Julia Gillard in 2011, in a country that has strong republican traditions, not least in Gillard's party: the Queen remains 'a vital, constitutional part of Australian democracy'. If the Queen sometimes seems the most enthusiastic member of the Commonwealth, she also gives it something that other

---

1 He may not be as well known as the Queen, but he is considerably richer, with a fortune of £35 billion.

transnational bodies lack. 'She distinguishes us from the United States,' as one Canadian commentator said to me during a royal trip. 'She's something they don't have.'

Not only a constitutional monarch, Elizabeth II is also the Supreme Governor of the Church of England, the mother church of the world's fourth-largest Christian denomination, the worldwide Anglican communion and, following a quirk of sixteenth-century diplomatic intrigue just before the Reformation, has inherited Henry VIII's title, bestowed on him by a then grateful pope, of being Defender of the Faith. Anglicanism's reach, too, extends to the farthest, smallest Pacific islands.

During her reign, Elizabeth II has met a very roughly-estimated one million people, including many of the most significant figures on the planet: not least, a quarter of all the American presidents who have ever lived, five popes and just about every famous starlet from Marilyn Monroe (who was born six weeks after the Queen) to Dame Angelina Jolie and Daniel Craig, and from Frank Sinatra to Kylie Minogue. 'Met' of course is a comparative term: very many of those presented to her have been tongue-tied, or effusive, or have just babbled foolishly in the presence of someone so famous and important; and their conversations will have been fleeting and superficial: a gentle, anodyne question awaited from the Queen, a gasped reply from the subject.

What did she say, for instance, to Pope Benedict XVI in September 2010 when she met him on his arrival at Holyroodhouse in Edinburgh at the start of his official visit? As one who was in the room at the time, I can report there was an exchange of gifts: a reproduction set of Hans Holbein prints of Tudor worthies from her to him and a replica eighth-century German Bible from him to her. 'Oh lovely,' said the Queen as if she was accepting a pair of socks at Christmas, 'thank you very much indeed. Lovely.' Then, 'Where would you like to sit?' pointing to one

of three chairs in the room. And: 'It was a very small car you arrived
in, wasn't it? Very tight squeeze? But you have got your own car here,
haven't you, the Popemobile?' The Pope, a trifle deaf and perhaps not
one of the world's great conversationalists, indeed looking a little like
the Addams family's Uncle Fester, dressed in white, shifted uneasily and
silently in his seat. Thus, one great Christian leader to another. Sadly,
we were ushered out before the discussion grew theological.

But it is not just a shy German pope. Even a hardened television
interrogator like Jeremy Paxman admits to having shied away from
speaking to her when he had the chance at a palace reception: 'The
truth was that I had been overcome by nerves . . . "a certain tension
which is akin to awe" fitted the mood well enough . . . What was it
about this diminutive grandmother that induced paralysing tension?'
Even those who work for her experience something similar. One
former senior official who found himself being interviewed for his job
by the Queen, who he had not met, seen before or ever considered
working for, said: 'It is surreal. You are sitting there thinking: "This is
the woman whose head is on the ten pound note." Then you start
looking harder and thinking, hmmm, curls are tighter. The surprising
thing was she was actually quite teasing: it was just a chat, more than
an interview. She asked me where I came from and it turned out she'd
just been there and knew it better than I did. In meetings with her after
I joined the palace you would sit around a table, with tea and
sandwiches. I realised that my interview had been about whether I
would fit in. The Queen herself was always quite detached: it was as if
she was in another world.'

Some would say the nerves come from the sense of being in the
presence of majesty – the divinity that doth hedge a king, as Shakespeare
said – or of magic; a sense of nerves at standing next to one of the most
famous people on earth. It is not power – the Queen cannot order you

to the Tower, or to execution, change a government or decide what constitutes the law in her own courts like some of her predecessors tried to do. It is not, particularly, charisma; perhaps not even a sense of history. But there is definitely an aura. People dream about the Queen, they imagine what they might say to her and what she might say to them (allegedly, it is often something about a cup of tea. And she's usually wearing a crown). Possibly it is an awareness of just who else she has met and shaken hands with and a consciousness of making a fool of oneself by saying something utterly banal or foolish when what one wants to say ought to be memorable, original and witty. She will have heard it all before. She can't answer any really interesting questions. There won't be a *real* conversation (not that you would have that perhaps with any other famous person you met briefly). Best not to say anything. Maybe turning your back and taking a selfie would be safer. As the Queen herself said to someone whose mobile phone went off just as he shook her hand: 'Better answer that. It might be someone important.' So she does have a sense of humour.

And, more importantly, she has been around for a very long time. She has seen more confidential government documents, intelligence reports, foreign and diplomatic assessments, and heard more crucial gossip than anyone else alive. Twelve prime ministers have come and gone – a fifth of all the prime ministers of the past three hundred years – starting with Sir Winston Churchill, born in 1874, to David Cameron, born ninety-two years later, who is younger than all her children. Prime Minister Cameron did not see the light of day until she had already been on the throne for fourteen years. Her governments have required her to meet tyrants such as Nicolae Ceaușescu and Robert Mugabe; heroes like Nelson Mandela and Václav Havel; former terrorists including Martin McGuinness who might once have tried to kill her and now says he likes and admires her; to heads of state of every stamp and status. There are very few countries she has not visited: North Korea, Cuba, the Congo – turbulent states or ones where they do not appreciate a monarch, even if they are ruled by a dynasty themselves; a dynasty much more controlling, autocratic and tyrannical than Britain has ever had.

It is an extraordinary feat in the twenty-first-century world of instant fame – fame for fame's sake – and sliding celebrity that the Queen should still be one of the most recognisable and photographed people on the planet. Her voice has modified its timbre over the years but is still redolent of another era, her sensible dress sense has remained much the same for decades and her interests – dogs, especially corgis, horses, racing and church – are mundane or esoteric to many of her subjects. We understand that she does not like opera much, or the ballet; she has given up attending film premieres and Royal Variety Performances with relief – those endless pleasures have devolved on Prince Charles; and she does not often read books. Her reading is the paperwork from the daily red boxes, and the *Racing Post* and *Sunday Telegraph*, whose crossword she enjoys. She has admirably succeeded in passing through the world, meeting its most interesting and important people while scarcely saying a memorable or opinionated word to any of them in reply. Her self-restraint and discipline have been heroic. The nearest she comes to criticism is the blank stare when told something disagreeable or wrong: impassive and inscrutable, but devastating. When it comes to annoyance, if circumstances have made her late for an engagement: 'She does get stroppy then,' says a former aide. 'She doesn't like keeping people waiting.'

Almost her whole life has been lived without ever mingling on equal terms with anybody: an ultimately lonely and exposed state. She did not go to school, but was privately tutored and the only other children she met were the Girl Guides recruited to join the specially set up Buckingham Palace group who were all drawn from aristocratic backgrounds – her father feared that otherwise she might meet 'the wrong types'. She has never lived in a house without servants; her first appearance on the cover of *Time* magazine was at the age of three and the first biography about her was published when she was four. No wonder that as she was posing for Pietro Annigoni's famous portrait of her in Garter robes in 1954, she recalled gazing out of the palace window as a child and wondering what the people outside in the Mall were really like and what they thought of her. Only on one heady evening, VE night in May 1945, is she known to have slipped out of Buckingham Palace incognito to join the crowds celebrating in the Mall; and she has very occasionally popped into shops, or driven a car – though at Balmoral and Sandringham, not in the middle of London.

You will not see her getting out of a taxi in front of the palace, carrying her shopping, as Denmark's Queen Margrethe, cigarette usually in hand, does from time to time. Queen Elizabeth has occasionally taken scheduled train services in recent years. There are also sometimes scheduled airline flights. She has had tea with pensioners in their council flats and mingled with winning sportsmen and women at receptions. Even journalists have sometimes been invited en masse to the palace, but never for a press conference by the Queen. She meets all sorts of people, but from the outside looking in, as it were, and she rarely hears someone disagreeing with her to her face.

Even now she ploughs on, making royal visits, holding investitures, attending and giving dinners, seeing her prime minister every week, dutifully working on endless boxes of documents for several hours a day, just as she has done since 1952, keeping herself informed, hearing, but not repeating, the gossip and the assessments of her private secretary and other staff, her ministers, the government's mandarins and diplomats. She knows no other way and could not imagine stopping: it has been what her whole life has been dedicated to doing. There is still a relentless annual round: regular excursions through the year, the Maundy service at Easter, trooping the colour and Buckingham Palace garden parties in the summer, the Order of the Garter gathering at Windsor in June in the week of Royal Ascot (when the Queen fails to attend the latter we will know something is really wrong), a week at Holyroodhouse in Edinburgh before the annual summer holiday at Balmoral, the State Opening of Parliament, November's Remembrance Sunday ceremony at the Cenotaph, then the Christmas broadcast. There are religious services and commemorations, meetings with ambassadors, both British and foreign, heads of states to meet and entertain on their official visits to Britain. Then there are also state visits abroad – the most recent to Germany in June 2015 – though they are fewer than previously, and also Commonwealth heads of government gatherings every second year. These are increasingly brief affairs, a few days at a time, compared with the 1950s when the Queen embarked on a leisurely but gruelling tour of the Commonwealth lasting six months. Having gone all that way – the first reigning monarch to visit the Antipodes – she spent two months in Australia and New Zealand during the trip in 1953–54. Her sixteenth visit to Australia in 2011 lasted just over a week, including flights from Britain and then back again. If it all sounds like fun, into a seventh decade the routine must have grown wearing at an age when many are putting their feet up – not that there are many outward signs of this happening with the Queen. There are fewer engagements and they are spaced out more to give her and her nonagenarian husband, who often accompanies her, time to recover. There tends to be one engagement a day these days, or one in the morning and another in the afternoon, with a break to catch breath in between – but to all appearances the Queen still seems to enjoy herself and, as many have commented, certainly smiles more genially and frequently in public than formerly.

Everywhere she goes the Queen – and other members of the royal family – are given presents: a deluge of gifts for the family that already has everything, a sort of permanent Christmas without the possibility of saying: 'Oh, you shouldn't have' and meaning it. Recently the royals have started filing a public annual account of what they have received. In January 2015, the list for the Queen included several bronze equine statuettes, from the president of Ireland, the president of France and two from the Emir of Qatar to take account of her interest in horses and racing – you can see how their minds worked – together with a dressage crop from the governor-general of Canada and a bristled boot-scraper from Felsted public school in Essex. For her bedside table at the same time came *Who's Who in Australia*, the story of Eurotunnel and a history of accountancy in Ireland, which sounds like a good cure for insomnia. This was just a selection of the odder items: the published list goes on for nine pages. However, even the Queen's list was outdone by that of her great-grandson, the baby Prince George, whose gifts from Australia and New Zealand included soft toys, a polo mallet, a surfboard, a skateboard, a cricket bat, a rocking horse, a miniature amphibious boat and a possum-skin cloak. Meanwhile, his grandfather Prince Charles returned from a tour to North America with a Stetson, a Metis fur hat from Canada, and a Panama hat and sombrero from Mexico, not to overlook a woollen poncho, a boxed football shirt, a pair of maracas and two slingshots. The twelve jars of honey from Saudi Arabia following a visit there may have come in useful, however, and the twelve boxes of mangoes received by Prince Andrew from the president and prime minister of Pakistan would not have been unwelcome, providing they could be consumed before going bad. The more evanescent presents such as bouquets and posies are discreetly distributed to local old people's homes, and the more substantial are catalogued and stored: the royals do not sit submerged by presents like the winners of a game show. Some, as became clear during a court case in 2002, find their way quietly to salerooms, but most have served their purpose merely by being given as public tokens of esteem and regard. Maybe some do indeed become useful around the palace. It may be wondered, however, whether the Irish accountancy book or the maracas will ever be seen in public again.

The Queen's reign is a triumph of endurance and not just of longevity. In all those years, she has never acted impetuously nor capriciously, never lost her temper – it seems – nor retreated for years from her public duties as Victoria did. The age will not be named after her, as Victoria's was. Her reign has not defined the country Britain has become. Attempts at the start in the early 1950s to speak of a new Elizabethan era and a young Gloriana were quickly abandoned: it has not been a time for heroics or conquering the world. And yet despite, and perhaps because of, her apparent benign passivity, this woman, whose interests and life experiences are so different from the vast majority of the inhabitants of her realms, remains hugely popular. It is an irony, as well as an achievement, that while most other institutions of the state have declined in popularity, prestige and influence: the landed aristocracy, politics and politicians, government and the church, trade unions and police, banks and lawyers, even the National Health Service and the armed forces, the monarchy not only endures but flourishes: the one unimpeachable, uncompromised and untarnished institution in the land, generally held in as high regard now as in 1952.

In opinion polls, a constant two-thirds to three-quarters of those questioned admire the Queen, with the number rising at times of royal events and celebrations. The figure drops when they are asked about the institution as opposed to the person, but there are still solid majorities for the monarchy and indifference rather than hostility to it among most of the rest[2]. Impressionistically, the monarch seems to offer a sense of tradition and spiritual continuity between the past and the present. In a largely religiously unobservant, often ignorant country there is a sort of sentimentality about the institution as well as the person.

Maybe the history feeds into a sort of colourful national mythic past. Despite the best efforts of historians to focus on a range of historic narratives and themes: economic history, social history and ethnic minority history, the story of our past is still largely narrated through our kings and queens. They form a sort of backbone on which the rest of our history is hung. It is a vibrant story, replete with incidents real, imagined and exaggerated: good kings, bad kings, wise kings, foolish kings, deposed kings, an executed king, a mad king, a profligate king and even a queen or two, who have done rather better than any of their male counterparts. The character of the monarchs and the office they held informs and shapes our knowledge of our past. They personify the nation's history and are some of its most distinctive characters. Why else would 35,000 people crowd the streets of a Midlands provincial town on a spring Sunday to hurl white roses on the cortege carrying the twisted bones of Richard III to a revered resting place in the local cathedral? Admittedly, the story of the unearthing of the fifteenth-century king's corpse from under a council car park and the forensic work to identify him was extraordinary and fascinating, and the story of his brief, contested reign and ghastly death is compelling. It made for

---

2 A ComRes online poll of 2,000 Britons in April 2015, carried out for the *Daily Mail*, showed 77 per cent 'liked' the Queen, while 79 per cent 'liked' Princes William and Harry. Asked whether Britain should remain a monarchy, 70 per cent thought so, the figure rising to 84 per cent for older respondents. Those questioned were much more ambivalent about whether Prince Charles should succeed to the throne: 40 per cent were in favour of him giving up the succession, 43 per cent were against; and 55 per cent were opposed to his wife Camilla becoming Queen.

a sort of true-life *Game of Thrones,* a television series whose popularity coincided with the discovery of the body; but the last Plantagenet, the last English king to die in battle, still has a decidedly chequered reputation even by the standards of Medieval royalty. The fascination may be obvious and even worthy if it stimulates interest in a remote and complicated period of English history, but why throw flowers? Whoever he was, Princess Diana he wasn't. Despite the best efforts of the obsessives of the Richard III Society, he was never the People's Prince.

Nowadays, lacking a solid and agreed alternative, let alone a rival, or much pressure for change from its subjects, the institution sails serenely onwards, largely because of what it represents rather than who the monarch is. As her subjects hardly know her, she incurs respect for her dutifulness rather than love for her person. Even republicans, in Australia and New Zealand as well as Britain, do not demand that she should stand down. They recognise her popularity and the hopelessness of either expecting her to abdicate – that's not in her DNA after what happened to her uncle Edward VIII – or the hopelessness of drumming up a popular majority against her. Even in the United States, President Obama appeared to recognise the monarchy's popularity among his fellow citizens, if his mumbled words to Prince Charles during the latter's visit to the White House in March 2015 were anything to go by. The muttered aside – not heard by the assembled media in the Oval Office but picked up on a boom microphone – had the president saying: 'I think it's fair to say that the American people are quite fond of the royal family. They like them much better than they like their own politicians.' The words may have been avuncular and there is no sign of America petitioning to have the Windsors back as heads of state, but there is a small sliver of truth in there. Americans remain proud of having divested themselves of King George in the War of Independence – their great founding narrative – but, as anyone knows who has ever met an American, they remain fascinated by the royal family their country escaped and many seem more interested in the minutiae of their lives than most Britons are. The US networks send aircraft-loads of camera crews and television anchors to cover royal weddings and funerals, the US London correspondents write up their activities, celebrity authors tap away at biographies, supermarket magazines lap up the latest gossip, film-makers churn out royal fairy tales and American tourists peer through the railings of Buckingham Palace every day of the week. Popular, yes – in a sort of appalled, obsessive, baffled, prurient way.

The first duty of a monarch is to preserve the family line and inheritance, so the Queen may well have done that for a century to come, perhaps even longer than the United Kingdom itself, as things stand. If her great-grandson Prince George, born in 2013, lives as long and as robustly as she has, he will see in the next century as King George VII – and, barring accidents of fate and unforeseen upheavals, who would bet against that happening? The future succession seems all mapped out: after the Queen's death, an inevitably short reign by an elderly King Charles III, followed by a longer one by a middle-aged William V and then, hopefully many decades hence, the seventh George. Recent changes in the law of succession – the Succession to the Crown Act 2013 – to remove gender inequality have been symbolic, but possibly a century premature: the Windsor male line now stretches for decades ahead. Vicissitudes, political, popular and constitutional, may conceivably change things, but the current family firm has at least done its best to preserve its dynastic longevity into the distant, unforeseeable future for decades to come. It will be a middle-aged to elderly monarchy, perhaps lacking the Camelot sparkle, but the family firm has grown wary of that sort of thing. The royal soap opera is here to stay: daylight has truly been let in on the magic and interest across the world will remain intense, but the next two monarchs at least look set to be boringly and resolutely unglamorous. And that, maybe, is how it should be too. Raciness is not a recipe for longevity.

The Windsor royal family has not survived this far by accident. In the twentieth century, through two world wars, social change, revolutions and economic upheavals when other European monarchies were toppling, they and their advisers devised and developed strategies for endurance and continuing popularity. The Bourbons learnt nothing and forgot nothing, and the Kaiser lost his place in the sun, the Hapsburgs faded away and the Romanovs were shot, but those have not been mistakes made by the Windsors. It has not happened just by osmosis, but by a mixture of guile, pragmatism, common sense and public relations. It has been planned and worked upon, as this book aims to show: the result of subtle and continuous rebranding of a sort that should be the envy of many more supposedly savvy and up-to-date organisations.

Chapter 2

'It is a great inheritance – and a heavy burden – on the girl who becomes Queen'

(*Manchester Guardian*, February 1952)

The British monarchy has changed enormously over the past sixty years, to keep pace with the evolution of a country that has itself changed perhaps more in the past sixty-five years than at any other time in its history: from a grey, deferential and widely impoverished, drab, post-war society to one bursting with life and colour, whatever one thinks of modern life. Consider the changes that have taken place in Britain during the decades since the young Queen came to the throne in 1952. In that year, the average wage was a little over £8 a week, only one household in twenty had a fridge, one in ten had a telephone installed, just a third had a washing machine, only one in five had access to a car and just 29 per cent of families were buying their own homes. Only about half a million households had a television set, though that figure would multiply by eight around the time of the Coronation, which was broadcast live for the first time. The transmission of black-and-white pictures had only recently spread as far as the Midlands, sets were expensive at about £100 each – the equivalent of ten weeks' pay for a middle-class household – the technology was primitive, programming was unexciting and broadcasting hours were limited. Most still relied exclusively on the radio for entertainment and broadcast information. Nevertheless, about 20 million people are thought to have watched the coronation on television in Britain on that day, as people with sets invited their neighbours in to see the event. Most of the remainder listened to the commentary on the wireless. It was not only the first time that some people had seen a television broadcast, but also the first time that such an undertaking – transmitting live for more than twelve hours – had been attempted by a broadcasting organisation. Film of the event was carried round the world, too, so it was seen by many millions from Australia to the United States.

During this period, there were no motorways in Britain and only four million cars, compared with more than 35 million today. Seven years after the end of the Second World War (and only half a century since the death of Queen Victoria) there was still food rationing, bombsites littered the cities and much sub-standard, grimy and dilapidated housing disfigured urban areas. Many houses still had outside toilets and most, still lacking central heating, relied on coal fires. In the so-called Great Smog of December 1952 – when cold weather and anticyclonic conditions caused London to be blanketed with a thick, coal-particle-infused fog for five days, reducing visibility to a few feet in places – an estimated 12,000 people died of respiratory diseases. The Clean Air Act four years later finally ensured that cities were unlikely to be polluted in quite the same way ever again, though it would be many years before public buildings lost their Victorian blackness.

When Princess Elizabeth succeeded her father George VI, a third or more of the population, according to polls taken at the time, believed that she had been chosen by God. As news of the king's death was broadcast on the grey morning of 6 February 1952, men stopped their cars, got out, took their hats off and bowed their heads reverently in the street. Theatres and cinemas closed that night and the radio stopped playing its usual programmes, taking comedy shows – and the daily wireless soap opera *Mrs Dale's Diary* – off the air for several days as a mark of respect. After the government and opposition had paid their tributes, parliament was adjourned for a fortnight. Since the BBC was the sole provider of broadcast news, on the day of the king's death more than half the population listened to the evening bulletin and 46 per cent to the memorial service that followed. The radio listeners may not all have wanted it that way – BBC research afterwards found two-thirds were annoyed by the interruption to normal programming and fewer than 30 per cent in favour – but that is what they were given, without choice. When the Queen eventually dies, of course there will be special programming, news features and lengthy tributes, but it is hard to believe that everything will come to a stop in quite the same way.

In early 1952, the King had been seriously ill with cancer for many months; the previous autumn he had had his left lung removed in an operation at Buckingham Palace. But for all most people knew he had recovered from his illness, whatever it was; even he himself had not been told by his doctors that he had cancer, so when he died in his sleep at Sandringham in the early hours of that morning, after spending the previous day out on the estate shooting rabbits, it was a considerable shock to many of the public. Even the prime minister, Winston Churchill, sitting up in bed at Number 10 Downing Street, was surprised – and he knew just how ill the King had been. 'I found Mr Churchill in bed, papers scattered all over, a chewed cigar in his mouth and on the bedside table a green candle from which he was accustomed to relight it,' Sir Edward Ford, the king's assistant private secretary, who was sent round to tell him later told the historian Ben Pimlott. 'I said, "I've got bad news, Prime Minister, the King died last night, I know nothing else." He was shattered by it. There was a pause and then he said, "Bad news? The worst." Then he added: "I do not know the new Queen. She is but a child."' The quaint patina of time hovers over the scene: the image of an elderly prime minister, brought up in the Victorian era, himself in his late seventies – twenty years older than the dead king – receiving the news while doing his morning paperwork in bed and bursting into tears as it all sank in, is impossible to imagine today.

In this more intrusive age, we will surely have comment and speculation, media doctors emoting, perhaps for days, and then rumours of the Queen's death spreading via Twitter and on social media, before being confirmed by television and announced around the world far in advance of a modern Sir Edward summoning a taxi. Perhaps even more astonishing, the following year, in the month following the Queen's coronation, Churchill, still prime minister at the age of seventy-eight, had a stroke which temporarily incapacitated him and remained unknown to the public thanks to media complicity. 'Overtiredness caused by...a lack of respite from his arduous duties' was blamed, but it did not stop him remaining in office and he continued as prime minister for a further two years. In 1936, George V's passing had been accelerated by his doctor with a large dose of morphine in the early hours of the morning so that his death could be announced in *The Times*, rather than the less seemly London evening papers. Now, that will not be an option either.

Attitudes to the monarchy in the Britain of 1953 – the Queen's coronation year – were rather similar, if more naively expressed, than those today. It was a time of the Mass Observation organisation's regular questioning of respondents about the events of the day and the public's comments bear a recognisably lugubrious air to them. 'I've nothing against the Queen,' said one, 'But I am just absolutely sick of seeing her face on everything from tinned peas upwards.' And John Summerson, the architectural historian, just before the big day, said: 'We shall not be sorry to see the end of decorated London, this litter of strung bits, bearable only as the days mount to *the* moment, intolerable hereafter.' Many though aired the same sentiments their successors voiced two generations later: 'Very good thing for the country, bringing foreigners to spend money here,' said one middle-aged woman and, more simply: 'It's wonderful; makes you feel proud of London...a tonic,' from some East Enders.

On council house estates both Tory and Labour supporters decorated their houses – the former perhaps a little more enthusiastically – and there were street parties, carnival processions and village shows despite the rain. When questioned further, a slight majority of members of the London working class said they would have preferred a king to a queen, but most were indifferent. Among the loyalists who camped out along the processional route, the wet weather on the day produced a sense that the Almighty was in some sense displeased: 'I can't understand how we can have had such weather when they are such a good family. They are so good and kind, it seems wicked to have had it all spoil like this,' said one in the crowd, while another took it as divine retribution for the display of military power in the procession – which must have been a distinctly fringe opinion even then.

After more than sixty years, the coronation seems astonishingly remote, its technicolour newsreel footage and black-and-white television pictures accompanied by reverent commentary of a timbre that has long been out of fashion. During the past seven decades, Britain has not just lost its empire but much of its heavy manufacturing industry. There were 700,000 coal miners in the early 1950s, but there are virtually none today. In 1952 Britain had nearly half the international car export market and its textile mills were still going strong, recruiting over the next few years a willing workforce of immigrants from the Indian sub-continent and the Far East. The woollen mills of Yorkshire and the cotton mills of Lancashire would soon close, however, unable to compete on price with cheaper manufacturers in the very countries from which they were now drawing their workforces. New, cheaper, artificial materials such as nylon and Terylene, made from polyester resin, were now coming in – 'very interesting, clammy isn't it?' said the Duke of Edinburgh, exhibiting his famous tact while touring the ICI stand at the British Industries Fair shortly before the coronation.

In 1952, there was national service, recruiting all able-bodied young men into the armed forces for two years and swelling the army itself to 700,000 men. It was fighting in Korea as part of an international United Nations force against a Chinese-backed Communist invasion from the north, and in neo-colonial insurgencies against Communist guerrillas in Malaya and Borneo, and in Kenya against the nationalist Mau Mau movement. In these minor wars some of the recruits would die in places and against causes they knew scarcely anything about. Sixty years on, the armed services are professionals and volunteers; now the figure for the army's strength is nearer 200,000. When the Royal Navy held its coronation review off Portsmouth in 1952 there were two hundred ships of the line sailing past; at the review fifty years later there were five and now there would be even fewer. But wars in far-off places are still being fought, with the added danger that home-grown terrorism can also cause fear and occasional atrocities on the streets of Britain.

In 1952 church attendance and Christian religious belief were widespread, if in gentle decline. Seventy per cent said they believed in the divinity of Christ in the early 1950s, less than 40 per cent said they did so in 2010; back then four million went to church regularly, now fewer than a million do. Even Catholicism then remained an alien creed, still being viewed with centuries-old suspicion, its adherents regarded as outside the mainstream of British life and isolated from it. News of a Catholic being appointed to an official, or senior, position in a major institution, such as the government or the BBC, was rare indeed – the source of headlines and a cause for celebration only in Catholic churches. The idea that the United States could elect a Catholic president for the first time in 1960 was regarded as remarkable. Other religions were also marginalised: in the early 1950s there were only half a dozen mosques in the entire country.

At the time of the Queen's coronation, non-Anglicans were not invited to the service, or to watch in person her oath to maintain the Protestant reformed religion and preserve inviolate the doctrine, worship, discipline and government of the Church of England – an oath she has kept even as the church has slid in popularity and influence, and its communicant numbers have dwindled. Then it was unthinkable to criticise, still less mock, the Queen: those such as John Grigg and Malcolm Muggeridge who dared to do so in the later 1950s risked being assaulted in the street. Nor was it socially acceptable to criticise august personages such as the archbishop of Canterbury; now it is almost obligatory to do so. When Grigg, already by then Baron Altrincham, complained in a magazine article in 1957 that the Queen's court was too upper class and British, advocating instead a more 'classless' court and suggesting that her style of speaking was 'a pain in the neck', he found himself in trouble. He wrote: 'Like her mother, she appears to be unable to string even a few sentences together without a written text... The personality conveyed by the utterances which are put into her mouth is that of a priggish schoolgirl, captain of the hockey team, a prefect and a recent candidate for confirmation,' for which he was slapped in the face by a member of the League of Empire Loyalists called Philip Kinghorn Burbidge on behalf of decent Britons everywhere. One can only hope that Mr Burbidge was no longer alive by the time *Spitting Image* was aired thirty years later, though Grigg lived long enough to see it.

In an age of deference, public figures were not supposed to be ridiculed or even robustly questioned and when they were it caused a sort of numbed shock at best and outrage at worst. 'I say! That's supposed to be the prime minister,' exclaimed one astonished young Conservative as the penny dropped when he attended an early performance of *Beyond the Fringe* in May 1961. His outrage came as he and his girlfriend watched Peter Cook's lampoon of Harold Macmillan, according to the writer Michael Frayn who was sitting behind him. The Lord Chamberlain censored plays to make sure that nothing salacious, obscene or licentious, or language that might cause a blush, slipped past – an irksome duty for the senior member of the royal household that was only discarded in 1968. Aristocratic young women were presented at court in their white ballgowns during the season each summer, but were only invited to the palace to curtsey to the sovereign if their mothers or other female relatives had once done so too in their day. The debutante season proceeded with Queen Charlotte's Ball, where the teenagers were expected to deploy their curtseying skills before a large cake. These rituals were on the wane – the last presentation of debutantes at court took place in 1958, for by then they were regarded as arcane, the Duke of Edinburgh thought it 'bloody daft', or, more superciliously, in Princess Margaret's lofty words: 'Every tart in London was getting in.' But abolition came not at the Queen's behest but as a sort of spring-cleaning exercise led by officials at court.

Other social practices were also becoming dated: divorce required a court hearing and divorcees were barred not only from the royal enclosure at Ascot, but also from polite middle-class society. This was especially if adultery had been involved, for the breakdown of a marriage still carried a stigma: witness the anguish in David Lean's 1945 film *Brief Encounter*, where rectitude and conformity poignantly trump passion. Until the late 1960s, homosexuality was a crime, punishable with imprisonment. The code breaker Alan Turing was arrested in Manchester on the evening after King George VI's death, his sexual orientation held to be more important than the burglary he had just reported to the police; the charge led to the effective end of his career. Turing was only one victim however – about a thousand men a year went to prison for homosexual acts in this period, often as victims of police agents-provocateurs. Sometimes they found themselves convicted – as Lord Montagu of Beaulieu was in 1953 – on scant or perjured evidence. 'Male vice', as it was termed, was an easy crime for home secretaries like Sir David Maxwell-Fyfe to crusade against and for police to prosecute.

This was a period when murderers were hanged and disruptive prisoners could be birched. Princess Elizabeth's first official act at the age of seventeen, when she stood in for her father who was on a trip to North Africa in 1943, was to counter-sign a death warrant. By the early 1950s public concern about capital punishment was rising in the wake of a number of controversial cases: Timothy Evans was hanged in 1950 for the murder of his baby daughter while lodging in the house of John Christie, who was subsequently found to be a mass murderer and was hanged a month after the Queen's coronation; the nineteen-year-old learning-disabled Derek Bentley had been hanged six months earlier in January 1953 for the murder of a policeman committed by his accomplice during a burglary, when Bentley was already in police custody; and, perhaps most disturbing of all, the execution of twenty-eight-year-old Ruth Ellis in 1955 – the last woman to be hanged – for shooting her unfaithful and violent lover dead. Punishment could be savage, ruthless and corrupt.

The population was still overwhelmingly white; Britain was an homogeneous society. It has been estimated that, in a population of about 50 million only 50,000 people were from an ethnic minority: roughly a tenth of one per cent.[3] The majority still viewed black people with surprise and hostility, and often treated them with discrimination in housing and jobs. Councils would still try to buy up properties so that they would not be occupied by black tenants and landlords placed signs in their windows saying: 'No Irish, no blacks', or invented reasons not to let rooms to them. The 'n' word was still in common parlance, as was the only slightly gentler, patronising term 'darkies', and as late as 1964 the Tories won a by-election in the West Midlands town of Smethwick, helped by using the slogan: 'If you want a nigger for a neighbour, vote Labour.' When West Indian immigrants danced and sang jubilantly at Lord's after their test team had beaten England there for the first time in 1950 – a relief of pent-up tension surely caused by the experience of prejudice – there was bemusement by white English cricket commentators who had not seen such scenes before. When two decades later the sons of Indian and Pakistani immigrant textile workers formed their own teams and cricket leagues in Yorkshire, they were ignored for many years by the county club, riled and disconcerted by the second and third generation's assertiveness – attitudes that seem to hail from long ago and far away today, despite the best efforts of the English Defence League.

After the 1951 general election, there were seventeen women MPs: fewer than 3 per cent of the total: six Conservatives and eleven Labour;

---

3   Now, in a population of 64 million, the approximate figure is 12 per cent. Though in much of the country the population is still overwhelmingly white, in cities such as London the immigrant population is much higher. The nature of immigration has also changed, from the Afro-Caribbean, Indian and Pakistani waves of the later 1950s to 1970s, to Eastern European and sub-Saharan African migration in more recent years.

now there are 191 – 29 per cent, which is something of an improvement though not yet near parity. Women faced overt discrimination in the workplace – lower wages and job opportunities and many fewer career choices then than for men, leaving them a choice between nursing, teaching and secretarial work for the brighter girls, factory drudgery and housework for the rest, and for those who got married. As most had no domestic help, a woman on the throne was scarcely a role model. The old universities were no longer closed to women, but they were ghettoised in distant, segregated colleges – women had only been admitted to full membership and degrees at Cambridge in 1948 (Oxford had admitted them in 1920) – and even in professions such as journalism they were regarded as exotic oddities, usually suitable only to write about 'women's issues'. Those aspiring to act might hope for starlet status with J. Arthur Rank.

Few members of the public ever saw the inside of one of the royal palaces and no one seriously thought of opening them to the paying public as Windsor Castle and Buckingham Palace are now, at least for part of the year. That was something only publicity seekers such as the Duke of Bedford at Woburn Abbey and the Marquess of Bath at Longleat did in the 1950s – both the inheritors of large death duties as well as historic estates with enormous upkeep costs. Elsewhere many aristocrats were throwing in the towel and surrendering their families' ancient seats, to the National Trust, or to desolation and demolition. They had to – the days before the First World War when the aristocracy could rival the royal family for opulence in their estates and lifestyles, the *Downton Abbey* generation, had all but gone, undermined by taxes that royalty still did not have to pay. Nowadays, of course, the super-rich are back and their wealth does not come from the land but from hedge funds and industry, banking and overseas investment – and the Queen staggers in on the Sunday Times Rich List some way behind Internet games entrepreneurs, newspaper owners and scrap-metal dealers.

In the 1950s, when a member of the royal family wished to marry, a European prince or princess was still the first to be considered. The young Queen had already married an impoverished, Greek-born, Royal Navy officer. When he came to stay with his future in-laws the valets sneered at the holes in his socks and shoes, and the battered state of his suitcase as they laid out his clothes. But at least he was a member of a royal family, albeit from the Danish house of Schleswig-Holstein-Sonderburg-Glücksburg, originally deposed from the throne of Greece when he was a baby. An ordinary officer, or rating from a non-aristocratic background would not have done for the heiress to the throne. Meanwhile, Princess Margaret, the Queen's younger sister, was also now eligible for matrimony, but her ambition to marry one of her father's former equerries, a group-captain in the Royal Air Force and a war hero, with whom she was in love, was bound to be frustrated as Peter Townsend was not only a commoner, but a divorced man. Her elder sister, who had to give approval to the marriage under the archaic Royal Marriages Act of 1772 since Margaret was under the age of twenty-five, would force her to choose between marrying him and surrendering her royal title and, even more importantly, her allowance. When a few years later she did indeed marry a commoner, the old Etonian, Cambridge rowing blue, society photographer Antony Armstrong-Jones, it was a sign that the ice was beginning to crack, but the match was still publicly regarded as greatly, wonderfully, daring.

By the 1950s, such manoeuvrings were no longer taking place privately: a media stung by the abdication crisis in 1936, when the British press had kept a vow of silence while Edward VIII was canoodling with his mistress Wallis Simpson, was less concerned about discretion than before. The idea, once propounded by Sir Alan

(Tommy) Lascelles, the private secretary to George VI, to the King's official biographer Harold Nicolson, that the royal life should be regarded as 'the subject of a myth and will have to be mythological', omitting 'things and incidents which were discreditable' because his first duty as an historian must always be to the monarchy, was fast dying out. The proposed Townsend/Margaret marriage was the first occasion that the monarchy had faced such intrusive interest into its marital affairs for a long time. The *Daily Mirror*, the biggest-selling newspaper at the time, ran a readers' poll which found 97 per cent in favour of the princess marrying, while *The Times*, voice of the establishment, urged her to 'choose the path of duty and conscience...in harmonious concert with her beloved sister'. But it would not be the last. An intrusive and ever-widening media, from newspapers, to television, to satellite broadcasting, to the World Wide Web, to social online chat, to Twitter would be its lot.

In a changed world, royal powers remain much as they were – powers of advice and warning, and the right to consultation by prime ministers. MPs and judges still swear to be faithful and bear true allegiance to the Queen, barristers and solicitors entering courts still incline their heads to the royal coat of arms behind the judge's head in recognition of the Queen's justice. She signs assent to all legislation, her signature is appended to the appointment of bishops and armed services officers, prime ministers attend her when they take office and formally resign to her at the palace when they leave. Ministers and privy councillors still bend the knee. The Labour minister Tony Benn expostulated in his diary in 1966: 'We went up to the Queen one after another, kneeling and picking up her hand and kissing it and then bowing...I left the palace boiling with indignation and feeling that this was an attempt to impose tribal magic and personal loyalty on people whose real duty was only to their electors.' As postmaster general, Benn did not ever succeed in his ambition to have the Queen's head removed from postage stamps and it is fair to say that very few others before or since have objected to the flummery. Ministers should be cautious of meddling with the monarch's prerogative: they are aware that she is immensely more popular than any elected politician.

The Queen stands ready to advise (or pass on her private secretary's advice) to governments in times of constitutional crisis: a hung parliament or, as might have occurred, a Scottish referendum vote for independence in September 2014. The long history of conflict over royal authority, which has been at the heart of much of the nation's story at least from medieval times, through the Wars of the Roses, the Reformation, the Civil Wars, the Glorious Revolution, the Hanoverian succession, Queen Victoria's maids of the bedchamber, the constitutional crisis of 1911 and the abdication crisis of 1936, is seemingly settled – at least for now. What has replaced open conflict and argument has been a delicate balancing act and one that could easily be unsettled by a monarch with too decided opinions, too capricious a will or too little sensitivity to public opinion. The royals have lost absolute power, but have so far saved its constitutional vestiges and trappings and, in doing so, have saved their skins.

Perhaps nothing better illustrates the gap between the Britain of 1953 and today than the presents Birmingham Corporation offered all the children in its schools to celebrate the coronation. They could have a Bible; a celebratory book, *Elizabeth Our Queen*, by the esteemed BBC commentator Richard Dimbleby; a spoon and fork; two commemorative mugs; a tin of chocolate; a propelling pencil; a penknife; or a dish bearing a portrait of the Queen. By the time of the next coronation, Birmingham will probably not have the spare resources, to offer such a display of civic largesse – and a penknife would certainly fall foul of health and safety considerations.

Chapter 3

'Do you come here often?'

(Time-hallowed royal cliché conversation opener)

A bright, blustery spring weekday morning in Margate and a small crowd has gathered on the pavement opposite the modern monolith that is the Turner Contemporary art gallery, built on the site of the boarding house where in the nineteenth-century the painter J.M.W. Turner used to visit the landlady, his mistress, Sophia Booth. From the outside the gallery looks like a mail-order warehouse, but inside all is whiteness, with huge windows looking straight out on to the Channel whose seascape so inspired the artist. And today there is a special visitor: the Duchess of Cambridge, Kate Middleton as was, patron of the National Portrait Gallery and holder of a degree in art history, is coming to see the gallery's exhibition of artists' self-portraits.

The wind is keen and the crowd is small at first, an hour before the duchess's arrival. As it is a working day it consists of pensioners, young mothers with small children in buggies, the unemployed and, inevitably, since no public occasion seems complete without them these days, a gaggle of French teenagers. The sole flag seller, a middle-aged chap called Rupert in a macintosh with a sheaf of plastic Union Jacks under his arm is already cheesed off: 'Bloody hell, I've seen more life in a cemetery. I'd have thought she'd get more than this – the Queen 'ud have got more of a crowd. I've only sold thirty quids' worth.' The young men from the local newspaper handing out free flags and baby-grows (it is seven weeks before the birth of the second royal baby) are having a little more success. There are a few small flags with 'We love you Kate' being waved and some nearby residents of a block of flats have hung a banner saying: 'Can we have a royal wave please?' over the front of their balcony, but it is all very low key.

This is what the royals do these days, crossing the country, working to a grid that establishes who needs to go where, when and to see what. Have they done enough schools? What about hospices? Who has been to Suffolk recently? The palace staff know when each area was last visited, where the invitations are coming in from – some lord lieutenants, the Queen's representative in each county, are more assiduous and proactive than others in forwarding suggestions, some need to be nudged and others gently restrained – and accordingly visits are arranged. This is not an entirely new system: George V nearly a century ago used to keep a record of royal engagements and embarrassed the family at Christmas by reading out which of them had been most active. But it is much more systematic now and a department at Buckingham Palace matches personnel to possibilities – hence the duchess coming to see the art today.

The self-portraits exhibition is a good one that will tour the country. Its exhibits include Sir Anthony van Dyck's last, brilliant self-portrait from the year of his death in 1641, through Joseph Wright of Derby, Constable and, yes, Turner, to a naked Tracey Emin and a somewhat too-realistic mannequin of a drowned man, complete with apparently wet clothes and drenched hair, sprawled on the gallery floor, modelled in silicone by an artist called Jeremy Millar. The duchess merely stared and blanched slightly at Millar's model. But this was not what the crowd of locals – most of whom had probably never visited the gallery – were waiting to see. They wanted her. By now numbers had swelled, the bored French kids had wandered off to be replaced by slightly younger Spanish ones and there was a smattering of the elderly and disabled on mobility scooters all waiting for the royal touch – and a small gaggle of toddlers from a nursery school, dressed in party princess finery and homemade paper crowns, sitting obediently on a bench and tucking into their sandwiches. The press photographers, armed with their stepladders to get a loftier view, were standing around bemoaning their fate and comparing expenses, as is the habit of photographers the world over. One veteran royal photographer, remembering the more rapturous 1980s' days of Princess Diana, eyed the crowd with a jaundiced look: 'I don't think Kate mania's ever going to take off. Back in the eighties, there'd have been a crowd of thousands all along the front...'

But he spoke too soon. A few minutes later there was a gasp and shouts of 'Kate! Kate!' and the duchess had appeared. 'Look! There she is,' cried the woman standing next to me with a small infant in her arms. 'A real, live princess!' Well, not quite. Instead of making towards her Range Rover, the duchess crossed towards the crowd. There would be a walkabout after all. She was nodding and smiling and saying nice, inconsequential things – 'very sensible, having gloves on today' to a small child – and working her way down the line, accepting flowers, being offered teddy bears. And then she was gone and the convoy of cars drove off to the next engagement. The crowd, however, was left chattering and laughing excitedly: five minutes was worth the three-hour wait in the cold. 'It's different though, innit? Something unusual for Margate. Not every day...' said a voice nearby; 'Fantastic – I knew she'd come over – I shook her hand,' a young girl told her friend. 'It's a nice day so we thought we'd come but we didn't expect to see her as close as we did,' an elderly woman was telling a local radio reporter, 'I'm shaking, I am.' And a man's voice: 'That's it. Can we go to the pub now?'

Just another royal visit and a crowd happy to have seen a celebrity. She has impressed them on a personal level and it is nice that she has been to their town, but she probably does not obsess them and their lives will be back to normal the next day. Do they *love* her like the local newspaper's tatty little flags suggest? No, not really – and only one shop in the vicinity had put the slogan in its window – but it was a cheery little occasion. A small cementing of royalty in a few more hearts, this time in one of the most deprived and rundown seaside resorts in the south-east corner of England. Tomorrow would be another day, another photo opportunity: this time at Ealing Studios to meet the cast and crew of the television drama *Downton Abbey*, a visit predicated on her husband's presidency of the British Academy of Film and Television Arts but most likely to be noticed for the pictures it garnered of the couple with the stars of the show. The day after that there was a full line-up of the royal family at St Paul's Cathedral for the Afghanistan war commemoration service, men in uniform, women in black. Different events, different costumes, different emotions; this is all part of the modern round.

Monarchs who wish to survive have to be seen by their people – 'seen to be believed', in the Queen's words. If they are not seen, the monarchy is weakened and its purpose is lost – this is as true now as it was in medieval times. Partly, public appearances have always been to prove that they are still alive: William the Conqueror famously raising his helmet during the course of the Battle of Hastings – an incident depicted in the Bayeux Tapestry – to show his faltering Norman troops that he had not been killed. Later kings, too, had to demonstrate their power in an age when the overwhelming majority of their subjects would have had little idea who they were or what they looked like. Coronations were expected to take place in the sight of the people, though the first one really to do so, before more than a few hundred, was the Queen's televised ceremony in Westminster Abbey in 1953. Medieval kings, never sure of their security, or sometimes of their legitimacy, and often under threat from usurpers and upstarts, did show themselves: their weddings were public ceremonies and so were royal Christenings to demonstrate the royal succession. The King's presence demonstrated legitimacy and strength – the size of the retinue intended to overawe potential rivals and demonstrate authority, the magnificence of the array to signify wealth and power. Keeping on the move was a way of avoiding plots, securing loyalty and disarming and depleting the reserves of potential rivals and critics. It also had another ulterior purpose: of avoiding the diseases and foetid air that accumulated and stifled the atmosphere in royal palaces lacking internal drains and sanitary facilities. It also saved on household repairs and renovation. After the monarch was gone from the palace, servants could move in to clear out the ordure, wipe the floors and walls, and lay new rushes on the floors.

Queen Elizabeth I, one of the most energetic of royal tourists during her forty-five-year reign, made annual peregrinations each summer around either the south of England, East Anglia or the Midlands counties, descending on the houses of local magnates with hundreds of servants. The Queen's baggage train was said to be three hundred carts long and its stately progress across the rutted tracks of the country – it was hard to do more than 10 miles a day with such a retinue – meant that she never got to the north or West Country. Those she chose to stay with were expected to house, entertain and, if they wanted preferment, feed her and her followers. It had the added advantage of saving her money. Meanwhile, the towns on her route were also expected to splash out, often with the presentation of a silver, or silver-gilt, cup stuffed with money and garnished with much flattery. When she arrived in Coventry, the corporation put a thousand pounds in gold in its cup, whereupon the Queen had the nerve to tell them: 'It was a good gift. I have but few such gifts.' Ah, said the mayor oleaginously, 'If it please your grace, there is a great deal more in it...the hearts of all your loving subjects.'

Her hosts hoped for special favours, in which they were sometimes disappointed, but invariably found themselves severely out of pocket, if not bankrupted following her stay. A four-day royal sojourn with Sir Nicholas Bacon cost him £577 in 1577, four days at Lord Burghley's house in Hertfordshire in 1591 cost more than £1,000 and three days with Lord Egerton in 1602 was double that. When the Queen moved on from Kenilworth Castle after 19 days in 1575, her host and favourite, Robert Dudley, the Earl of Leicester, sent after her and begged her to stay longer but was probably rather relieved when she rode on. He had had all the clocks stopped to indicate that time stood still while she was present.

The Queen clearly had the knack of communicating vividly with her subjects in public. On her progresses and at formal events in London she seems to have been highly accessible, stopping to talk to people lining her route, almost as if she was engaged in a modern walkabout, except that they approached her as she was riding on horseback or being carried in a litter, rather than she approaching them. 'All her faculties were in motion,' wrote a clearly captivated observer at the time of her coronation. 'Every motion seemed a well-guided action: her eyes were set upon one, her ear listened to another, her judgement ran upon a third, to a fourth she addressed her speech; her spirit seemed to be everywhere and yet so entire in itself as it seemed to be nowhere else. Some she pitied, some she commended, some she thanked, at others she pleasantly and wittily jested, contemning no person, neglecting no office and distributing her smiles, looks and graces so artificially that thereupon the people again redoubled the testimony of their joys and afterwards, raising everything to the highest strain, filled the ears of all men with immoderate extolling their prince.' The fact that she was succeeding her gloomy, persecuting, Papist sister Mary, riding through her Protestant capital probably did no harm either. The Spanish ambassador watched the Queen's procession in1568 and reported back to Mary's former husband, the devoutly Catholic Philip II in Spain: 'She was received everywhere with great acclamations and signs of joy, as is customary in this country; whereat she was extremely pleased and told me so, giving me to understand how beloved she was by her subjects and how highly she esteemed this, together with the fact that they were peaceful and contented, whilst her neighbours on all sides are in such trouble. She attributed it all to God's miraculous goodness. She ordered her carriage sometimes to be taken where the crowd seemed thickest and stood up and thanked the people.' If the ambassador's report shows her implicitly conveying a political message, which he dutifully relayed to his master, an account of her visit to Norfolk indicates just what an astute politician she was: 'I have laid up in my breast such good will as I shall never forget Norwich,' she cried, shaking her riding crop and with tears in her eyes. 'Farewell Norwich!'

These tours were not just holidays or political exercises. They also demonstrated the religious and quasi-mystical nature of the monarch to her subjects. Elizabeth I was human – as she showed in chatting to even menial spectators – but she was also, in her and their eyes, divinely appointed, ruling by right, and was guardian of her people – an image underlined in the masques, displays, sermons and addresses laid on during her progresses, which expressly linked her to the classical virtues and classical heroines. As a demonstration of the monarch's sanctity and divine approval, the King or Queen might touch, and thereby hope magically to cure, those afflicted with scrofula – known as the 'King's evil' – the swollen neck nodes and protuberances that indicated the presence of tuberculosis. Sometimes monarchs also blessed cramp rings, which were supposed to cure epilepsy. Instead of antibiotics their solution was to press the ring or a coin into the hand of the sufferer as a kind of touch piece to ward off the infection. Some monarchs were more assiduous in doing this than others – the fourteenth- and fifteenth-century kings did not exercise their therapeutic touches much, but Henry VII, who possibly had a usurper's conscience, restored the practice and it was then revived again, though largely in private, by the devout Mary. It was also customary for monarchs to distribute coins and wash the feet of the poor on Maundy Thursday, in imitation of Christ before the Last Supper, and those such as Mary who were especially religious would also on that day crawl on their knees in their chapels to the adoration of the cross. Characteristically, Elizabeth made more of a public show of touching sufferers and also washing feet, though she dispensed with handing out the cramp rings and displays of public crawling. The ultra-sensitive and hypochondriac James I had to be persuaded to carry on touching the scrofulous who presented their sores to him and it was a practice that only died out following the reign of Queen Anne in 1714. By then the practice of the monarch distributing money to the poor had also died out. The Queen's Hanoverian successor George I was far too fastidious to continue the tradition of the King's evil, though on the grounds that it was too Catholic and superstitious, rather than dangerous, ineffective, demeaning or time-consuming. George also dropped any idea of washing the smelly feet of his subjects, giving archbishops of Canterbury an excuse to do so, too – it was not until a more sanitary age, in 2004, that Archbishop Rowan Williams revived the practice. The Queen does not perform the ritual although her attendants at the Royal Maundy carry towels as though she might.

Although Londoners and those on the routes of the royal progresses might see the monarch from time to time, paintings and engravings could be used to depict their image and reinforce messages about their power and sanctity. Most painting and sculpture in England before the seventeenth century was portraiture: monuments on tombs and church walls illustrating the lineage, qualities and likenesses of local worthies, aristocrats and merchants. Increasingly, in the Tudor age, the monarchs, too, commissioned portraits of themselves and these were copied, or also commissioned, by courtiers, noblemen, the gentry, city guilds and Oxbridge colleges. Even now, portraits of Henry VIII and Elizabeth I loom out of the wood panelling of the great halls and grand chambers of castles and country houses across the nation, as they have done for the past four hundred years and more. Many were by journeyman local painters, but increasingly the Tudors wanted works of accomplishment and distinction by rather more talented Continental artists such as Holbein, Zuccaro, Gheeraerts, and later van Dyck and Rubens. Queen Elizabeth's privy council ordered that no portrait of her would be allowed until its painter's work had first been assessed as up to standard by the Queen herself once 'some special person that shall be by her allowed shall have first finished a portraiture thereof' at which point others might 'at their pleasures follow the said (pattern) or first portraiture'. So, from the 1570s, a stream of royal portraits was produced, all based on a few authorised patterns, such as the Darnley portrait or the ermine portrait, showing the Queen with a small white, weasel-like creature – indicating purity – leaning against her left arm. Those who produced less flattering, or possibly more truthful, portraits found their work consigned to obscurity.

A royal tradition had, however, been established – flattering portrayals of strong, authoritative monarchs. Thus, the apotheosis of James I ascending to heaven in clouds of glory on the ceiling of the Banqueting House in Whitehall, painted by Rubens in 1635, floating above the room from which his son Charles I would step outside to his execution fourteen years later. Charles I himself, one of the greatest of royal art collectors, commissioned from van Dyck an imposing portrait of himself, mounted on an enormous horse, attended by his adoring and obsequious riding master Monsieur de Sainte Antoine. The large painting, 12ft long by nearly 9ft wide, was apparently intended to be hung at the end of the King's Gallery in St James's Palace to impress and overawe visitors. It shows Charles, who at the age of thirty-three in life was a diminutive 5ft 4in tall, as a commanding, triumphant, resolute figure instead, clad in armour, in full control of a beast that would have been much larger, taller and stronger than he was. Anyone who saw the portrait before catching sight of the King must have been surprised by his sudden diminution unless they fully understood the iconography involved. As it is, in the picture the King's legs are long and strong – no sign, obviously, of the weak ankles that had plagued him since childhood – and his jaw is firmly set. The King's shyness, his stammer and hesitant manner could not, of course, be depicted. The painting's effect is achieved by placing the spectator's viewpoint from below so that the king looms powerfully overhead: a colossus bursting through a triumphal arch. Van Dyck, newly arrived in England from Flanders, knighted, appointed principal painter in ordinary to the King and Queen, given a substantial pension and set up in a house in Blackfriars, surely earned his position with this painting alone and he proceeded to paint several more versions to underline the message. After the royal defeat in the Civil War and the King's execution in 1649, the painting was sold by the parliamentarians for £150, but it was reclaimed after the restoration of Charles II in 1660 and intriguingly thereafter came to be seen by Royalists not as a portrayal of power or hubris, but of martyrdom and sacrifice. Van Dyck also painted an altogether more vulnerable-looking and humane Charles: the famous triple portrait now in the Royal Collection, but it was also a painting with an iconographic purpose, sent to the Italian sculptor Bernini in Rome to enable him to make a bust of the King.

Seen more widely was the engraving of the King in the frontispiece of the *Eikon Basilike*, the Royal Portrait, a book emphasising his religious devotion and justifying his conduct, published just after his death, which ran to thirty-nine editions in its first year. The picture shows the King kneeling devoutly, with his eye on an eternal, heavenly crown.

William of Orange and the first Hanoverians cared more for their European estates than England, but George III, the first truly English king for three-quarters of a century, seems to have been a monarch who was popular for his lack of pretentiousness. News of his plain tastes and affable manner spread across the country, though he himself did not: during his sixty-year reign he never went abroad, not even to Hanover, and never travelled west of Plymouth or north of Worcester – so did not see Scotland, Wales or Ireland, and he went into London as rarely as possible too. Nor did he particularly choose to mingle with ordinary people. Though he held public levees twice a week, only those wearing court dress were permitted to attend. In this regard, eighteenth-century English protocol was stiffer than that of contemporary French monarchs who at least allowed the lower orders to inspect Versailles – though much good it did the Bourbons. On such occasions, the King generally tried to have a word, if not necessarily a conversation, with everyone present – and if he missed anyone out it was regarded as a deliberate snub and sign of royal displeasure.

Probably George III, a creature of habit and formality, did not give much thought to meeting ordinary people, but he seems to have quite enjoyed his brief, anonymous occasional encounters with peasants and labourers – all the more so because they did not recognise him and had no idea who he was. Thus a chance encounter with a country farmer near Cheltenham, who after chatting for a quarter of an hour about livestock and land prices, asked him whether he had ever seen the King and, on being told yes, replied: 'Our neighbours say he's a good sort of man but dresses very plain.' To which the King answered: 'Aye, as plain as you see me now.' Or, the pig-herding boy encountered in Windsor Great Park (who might at least have been expected to see the King in the distance from time to time) who told him that the land belonged to 'Georgy – he be king and lives at the castle but he does no good for me,' whose opinion was confounded when the King subsequently found him a job on one of his farms. There are plenty of such stories, some of which may have been apocryphal but were circulated with relish to show what a good, condescending sort of chap the King was: a man who could be engaged in conversation despite his lofty status. Those lucky enough to meet him formally, too, at a levee or a rout, found he chatted with them, asked questions, listened to their replies and, if they met him again on another occasion, remembered who they were. The King, naturally, was expected to start any conversation. He would ask them where they lived, who their neighbours were and what the harvest was like, lines of conversation not unlike those deployed by his successor today. Even his much-mocked, barked vocal tic at the end of sentences: 'What? What?' seems to have been an attempt to elicit a response. Then, as now among people meeting royalty, those introduced to him could be tongue-tied. The novelist Fanny Burney was instructed by her friend Mary Delany not to answer in monosyllables when addressed by the King or his wife, Charlotte: 'The Queen often complains ... of the difficulty with which she can get any conversation, as she not only always has to start the subjects, but commonly entirely to support them . . . she says there is nothing she so much loves as conversation and nothing she finds so hard to get.' It did not help – she was initially struck dumb in the royal presence, too, though she soon grew chattier and subsequently spent five years at the royal court. In general though, no wonder the King found the pig boy a refreshing change.

On the occasions when the King and his entourage did venture forth, to take to the waters at Cheltenham or stay by the sea at Weymouth, they were greeted enthusiastically in the towns they passed through on the way. Such visits were, after all, special occasions, with bands playing the national anthem and other patriotic tunes, ox roasting – bread and meat provided free by the local landowners – and a day off work for the peasantry. Burney was told by an elderly woman living near the Dorset resort in 1791: 'There was such a holiday then as the like was not in all England . . . not so much because he was a king but because they said he was a worthy gentleman and that the like of him was never known in this nation before.' Perhaps that is why there was general rejoicing at his recovery from his first bout of madness in 1789 and why he seems to have been rather admired – because he was diligent, honest and afflicted, not like his errant children, and furthermore because, as The Times said, his attributes were of a sort that anyone diligent enough could attain. Lord Bulkeley wrote in 1809: 'His popularity is very great for the mass of the people look up to his good moral character and to his age and to a comparison with his sons.' At the time of the fiftieth anniversary of his accession, in October the following year, even in the midst of the Napoleonic wars, there were the first royal jubilee celebrations. No previous monarch since the Middle Ages had reigned for so long and in many places there were village feasts, prayers and church services, and bands playing the

national anthem and 'Rule Britannia' – 'all was harmony, gentleness
and joy' it was said of the commemoration in Highgate, still then a
hamlet outside London. 'The number of people in the street...was
immense and the illuminations remarkably beautiful,' wrote George
Rose, one of the King's confidantes in his journal. An ode of the time
caught the mood and the hubris of a country congratulating itself:

> *From Thames to Ganges' common shores rejoice,*
> *A People, happy, great and free,*
> *That People with one common voice,*
> *From Thames to Ganges' common shores rejoice,*
> *In Universal Jubilee.*

By then, unfortunately, the King was on the verge of his final breakdown,
which occurred on the anniversary itself, and from which he never
recovered even though he lived for a further ten years. George's jubilee,
although he was not really there to see it, was the first instance of what
might be called an official national celebration. Coronations were held
in the sight of the people, but it was a very restricted vision, entirely
limited to invited members of the aristocracy, and other family events
such as marriages and funerals took place in private.

The jubilee celebrations contrasted somewhat with public attitudes
to George III's son and successor, the Prince Regent, who eventually
became George IV only when his father finally died – blind, deaf and
mad – in 1820. No royal prince has been so ruthlessly mocked and
ridiculed in print and cartoons for so long, and it was entirely his own
fault. It started from the time of his father's first illness in the late 1780s
and the prince's rather too public attempt to be declared regent,
through his highly partisan support for his cronies among the Foxite
Whigs. There was also his virtually public liaison with the Catholic Mrs

Fitzherbert and then a succession of other mistresses, and meanwhile a disastrous marriage to the malodorous Caroline of Brunswick. Through his extravagance and absurd posturing, many of the public knew more about him and his appearance than any previous monarch, because they could see what he looked like in the cheap caricatures hanging up in the shops and wayside inns. The prince did not hide himself away: he could be seen out riding and latterly, after he had grown too fat to mount a horse, driving a phaeton carriage through Hyde Park; he attended the theatre, he went to Bath and down to Brighton so many people were well aware of his appearance. For those who did not see him in the all-too-solid flesh, the cartoonists of the day, given licence, were not afraid to depict him in the most lurid terms, as a licentious wastrel leering at women in his youth, as a pot-bellied debauchee surrounded by an overflowing chamberpot and unpaid bills as Prince of Wales in 1792, and later as a fat, gout-ridden, over-made-up old pantaloon – in one case ridden like a bicycle by his fat mistress, in another like a spouting whale – as he reached the throne. In the face of such vivid, demotic imagery the elegant portraits of the prince by Sir Thomas Lawrence were bound to look wan and meretricious.

The likes of James Gillray, Isaac Cruikshank and his son George, and William Heath were particularly severe, which is no doubt why the prince's private secretary was regularly sent out into Piccadilly and Pall Mall to buy up the most egregious cartoons as they appeared in the print shops. Incidentally, that is why such a large number of examples survive, since they were kept in the royal archives rather than destroyed, until being sold off to the US Library of Congress to raise funds for George V's stamp-collecting hobby in 1921. If the cartoonists did not desist, there were attempts to buy them off – George Cruikshank was paid £100 'for a pledge not to caricature His Majesty in any immoral situation' in the 1820s – but that scarcely stopped them. Nor did it modify the prince's behaviour. The newspapers also piled in with a startling virulence which made some wonder for the future of the monarchy, particularly after what had happened across the Channel in the French Revolution. In March 1812, the *Examiner* published a poem by Charles Lamb:

> *Not a fatter fish than he*
> *Flounders round the polar sea*
> *See his blubbers – at his gills*
> *What a world of drink he swills . . .*
> *. . . about his presence keep*
> *All the monsters of the deep.*

The Tory loyalist *Morning Post* was then paid to publish a hyperbolic defence of the prince, who had also recently been hissed at a St Patrick's Day dinner. He was, the paper declared, 'the glory of the people' and 'an Adonis of loveliness'. That only caused Leigh Hunt, the *Examiner*'s editor, and his brother John, the paper's publisher, to resume the attack: 'That this Adonis of loveliness was a corpulent gentleman of fifty! In short that this delightful, blissful, wise, pleasurable, honourable, virtuous, true and immortal Prince (was) a violator of his word, a libertine over head and ears in debt and disgrace, a despiser of domestic ties, the companion of gamblers and demi-reps [prostitutes], a man who has just closed half a century without one single claim on the gratitude of this country or the respect of posterity.' The Hunts were sued for libel by the prince, fined £500 each and imprisoned, relatively comfortably, for two years. That merely made them martyrs to free speech: celebrity prisoners, allowed their own rooms, books and furniture, to be visited in jail by celebrities such as Lord Byron and greeted on release with a celebratory poem by John Keats.

When the Prince Regent finally became king in 1820 at the age of fifty-seven, his public behaviour had scarcely improved. The coronation ceremony itself was lavish but chaotic, remembered now for the successful but demeaning attempts by boxers acting as security staff to prevent his estranged wife Caroline from getting in either to the abbey or to the banquet afterwards in Westminster Hall. Despite all this happening in the distance, George IV was seen with some disgust to be ogling his mistress Lady Conyngham at his coronation: 'The King behaved very indecently, he was continually nodding and winking... and sighing and making eyes at her,' wrote Mrs Harriet Arbuthnot, the Tory diarist and friend of the Duke of Wellington. 'At one time in the Abbey he took a diamond brooch from his breast and, looking at her, kissed it, on which she took off her glove and kissed the ring she had on! Anybody who could have seen this disgusting figure, with a wig the curls of which hung down his back and quite bending beneath the weight of his robes and his 60 years would have been quite sick.' It was perhaps just as well that he could only be seen by a few hundred spectators in the abbey and none of those were from the working classes. So afraid of the hostile London mob was George IV that when his carriage was forced to take a diversion on the way back to Carlton House after the banquet in Westminster Hall, George Keppel recalled: 'The King was horribly nervous and kept constantly calling to the officers of the escort to keep well up to the carriage windows.'

The King made two important public outings to his realm, to Dublin in 1821, after his chaotic coronation, and then to Edinburgh in 1822, both further than his father and the previous Hanoverian kings had ever ventured in the course of more than a century. In Dublin it was said that the King scarcely drew a sober breath during his entire visit and his sole mark on the country was when the city's port, Dunleary, was renamed Kingstown in his honour (it was subsequently changed to an Irish spelling, Dun Laoghaire, after independence ninety-nine years later). Nevertheless, there he was greeted by ecstatic crowds; allegedly it was said because the Irish knew so little about him. The Scottish trip in August 1822 created something of a precedent for future royal tours – and for the establishment of the Scottish tartan myth. It was not really a display of regal power and authority so much as an outing in order to be seen as a benign and popular figure by the populace; indeed, it became known satirically as 'the King's jaunt'. The visit in the late summer of that year was undertaken as a propaganda effort to head off a possible rebellion by Scottish workers – as had taken place briefly but violently in 1820 – and to restore the King's public image, which had been battered by the long, drawn-out and highly public wrangles with his former wife. It was also intended by its main organiser Sir Walter Scott to create a pageant that would restore Scots' proud sense of themselves and their history and culture, and bind them into allegiance with the monarchy down south. Actually, it constructed a mythic, idealised past which has helped Scots to identify romantically with their own country ever since, binding lowlanders as much as those from the Highlands into a unified, tartan sense of themselves.

At a time when the lairds and clan chiefs were energetically evicting their tenants from their estates in order to replace them with more profitable sheep flocks, Scott helped to orchestrate a plaid panorama, full of supposed customs and traditions, including a sort of ersatz Highland dress and invented tartan patterns. Previously, the kilt had been despised as the mark of unkempt and savage peasants from the barbarous northern mountains – it had even been banned for a period following Bonnie Prince Charlie's clan uprising in the 1740s – but for the jaunt, it became the costume of gentlemen. Scott insisted that the peers and gentlemen of the country should wear kilts to the grand ball held for the King at Edinburgh and it suddenly became fashionable.

Scott even wrote a guidebook for the visit, outlining what he expected gentlemen to wear and offering advice on etiquette. The author saw it as a 'gathering of the Gael...cocking of bonnets and waving of plaids' and encouraged the lairds to bring a handful of their retainers with them to pay formal homage: 'Do come and bring half a dozen or half a score of clansmen,' Scott wrote to one chieftain. 'So as to look like an island chief as you are. Highlanders are what he will best like to see.' Landowners and clan chiefs had themselves painted in full Highland costume and heroic poses by Scottish artists such as Raeburn and Wilkie – and the King followed suit. George had been persuaded by Scott that he had distant Scottish roots, making him the legitimate as well as de facto king of Scotland, and he kitted himself out at vast expense with scarlet, Royal Stuart-patterned kilts in both silk and velvet, a goatskin sporran with a gold spring clasp, a Glengarry cap, a plumed bonnet studded with diamonds, pearls, rubies and emeralds, tartan stockings, dirk, claymore sword, gold-encrusted powder horn and pistols before the visit. He was thrilled to be toasted by the assembled lairds as 'the chief of chiefs'. The imposing martial effect was somewhat undermined by his enormous bulk, kept in check by whalebone corsets, the flesh-coloured taffeta tights he wore to hide his mottled and swollen legs, by the fact that his gout meant he could hardly walk and by the spectacle of him being hoisted on to a horse to review the troops. He was genial and gracious, however, and even appeared on the battlements of Edinburgh Castle for a quarter of an hour in pouring rain to wave his hat at the cheering crowd gathered at a safe distance far below, murmuring to himself: 'Good God! What a fine sight...and the people are as beautiful and as extraordinary as the scene. Rain? I feel no rain. Never mind, I must cheer the people.' They themselves were cheered and flattered by the royal attention, as one correspondent wrote to Sir Walter Scott afterwards: 'A continuous line of pale faces, with expectations wound up to actual pain and a sort of bewildered smile on their first glimpse of that being called a king – Britain's king – Scotland's king – their own king! The moment came, the first in their lives, when they could compare the actual thing called Majesty, with all they had from childhood dreamed and fancied of it!' This was more or less precisely the effect Scott had hoped to achieve. George IV, the first monarch to visit Scotland in 190 years, was thrilled by the success of his jaunt, especially by the unusual experience of being cheered by the crowds. In the words of the *Observer* he had won 'the affection of an unattached and ordinary people . . . not in the smoke of London where he has ever been insulted and reviled.'

The Irish and Scottish jaunts were the first state visits of a sort that would be recognisable today. In particular, Sir Walter Scott had not only concocted a new, ancient image of Scotland and bound it into the rest of the United Kingdom, he had also devised many of the features of future royal tours: the orchestration of pageantry, reviews and military parades, balls and receptions for the great and good and informal public appearances, waving to the crowd, by the monarch. The fact that this particular monarch was by now a ludicrous figure, did not seem to matter. The press loyally reported that the costume 'displayed his manly and graceful figure to great advantage'. When someone suggested that the King's knee-length kilt was rather on the short side for modesty, especially when he sat down, Lady Hamilton-Dalrymple genially replied: 'Since he is among us for so short a time, the more we see of him the better.' Scotland would subsequently experience even more of royalty almost from then onwards. Queen Victoria and Prince Albert were entranced by the Highlands and built Balmoral Castle for themselves to facilitate their visits in the depths of Aberdeenshire in the 1850s – a summer retreat for the royal family ever since, where the menfolk continue to sport their kilts.

George IV was becoming quite a spectacle during the course of his reign, as he himself well knew. As his weight ballooned and his health declined he retreated increasingly to Windsor Castle and was rarely seen in public during the latter half of his reign, though he and his architect John Nash left their name-checked vision of London from Regent's Park down to the Mall via Regent Street. George IV did not visit his former pleasure dome at Brighton at all after 1827, nor did he venture into London during the last year of his life. The apogee of criticism came with famous savagery in *The Times* following George's death at Windsor Castle in June 1830: 'What eye has wept for him? What heart has heaved one throb of unmercenary sorrow? If George IV ever had a friend – a devoted friend – in any rank of life, we protest that the name of him or her has not yet reached us. An inveterate voluptuary, especially if he be an artificial person, is of all known beings the most selfish.' George IV had stretched the bonds of loyalty: the unspoken contract with the people, bringing the monarchy into disrepute with his behaviour and sense of entitlement. And everyone in the political and politically aware classes knew it and knew what they thought of him. In such circumstances a public royal commemoration was bound to be a distinctly underwhelming affair. The crowds in London, it was said, had 'more the appearance of rejoicing than of mourning' and Lord Howick wrote that there was 'no sign of sorrow to be seen...It looked much more as if some good news had arrived than anything else.' Dozens of pickpockets arrived in Windsor and lifted watches and money from sightseers who had turned up to see if any celebrities were attending. The funeral itself, hurried through in St George's Chapel at nine o'clock in the evening, was largely undignified. The congregation crowded in, jostling for the best seats, and then chatted noisily among themselves. 'We never saw so motley, so rude, so ill-managed a body of persons,' *The Times's* correspondent reported (though his view may have been tainted by the paper's editorial). When William IV turned up for the funeral he waved to friends, chatted through the service and then left early. True to form, the old king was buried with a locket containing a portrait of Mrs Fitzherbert, his first love, hanging around his neck. At least the undertakers were not drunk, as they had been at the funeral of George's daughter and heir, the Princess Charlotte who died in childbirth in 1817.

William IV, George's younger brother, became the oldest king so far to ascend the British throne, at the age of sixty-four. He had spent almost all his career in the Navy and until the death of the Duke of York, the second brother in 1827, had never expected to become King. William had formerly lived impecuniously – and in deep debt – for twenty years with the celebrated Irish actress Mrs Jordan, who had born him ten children and subsidised the household with her work, but latterly, when a degree of respectability and additional income was required he had abandoned her to marry a minor German princess, Adelaide, who was thirty years his junior. Unlike his brother, he seemed to be a genial, garrulous old cove, with a naval penchant for salty language and unsuitable jokes. Shortly after succeeding to the throne, he decided to do what George would never have dared to try, by going for a stroll on his own in the middle of London. It was what he had been able to do all his life as a private citizen and he saw no reason to stop. He was surprised therefore to be mobbed once he was recognised in Pall Mall. This took the monarch's duty to show himself to the people to an unexpected level. As the diarist Charles Greville noted: 'When he might very well have sat himself quietly down and rested, he must needs put on his plain cloathes [sic] and start on a ramble about the streets, all alone too. In Pall Mall he met Watson Taylor and took his arm and went up St. James's Street. There he was soon followed by a mob making an uproar and when he got near White's [club], a whore came up and kissed him. Belfast who saw this from White's and Clinton thought it time to interfere and came out to attend upon him. The mob increased and always holding W. Taylor's arm and flanked by Clinton and Belfast, who got shoved and kicked about to their inexplicable wrath, he got back to the palace amid shouting, bawling and applause...'

William only reluctantly agreed to have a ceremonial coronation and the money spent on the occasion was less than a fifth of that expended on his brother's behalf ten years earlier (the £238,000 spent on George IV's coronation was only exceeded more than a century later for that of George VI in 1937; William IV's coronation cost just over £42,000). Among the other changes to royal protocols, the new King opened the terraces at Windsor Castle and the nearby great park to public access and reduced the fleet of royal yachts. All this, his lack of pomposity and his visceral dislike of foreigners, particularly the French, tended to endear him to the populace.

When William IV himself died in June 1837 there was also a private funeral at Windsor and, if not quite as undignified as George's had been, it was a perfunctory affair. The service, wrote Greville, was intolerably long and tedious 'and miserably read by the Dean of Windsor'. But royal funerals would never be so unseemly ever again. Nor would they be in private, nor as perfunctorily organised. Through the course of Victoria's long reign, there were two lasting changes to royal ceremonial: the milestones of royal family life became public events and they grew to be better organised and more decorously handled.

Queen Victoria also became used to crowds, although she did not like them much: understandably, they frightened her. As a child long before she became queen she had been taken on lengthy family holidays in Britain and undertaken what the old King derisively called 'royal progresses' around the country: up to the north and the West Country and, for a summer, to the spa at Tunbridge Wells. These outings were self-consciously organised by Victoria's mother, the Duchess of Kent, if not – quite – to supplant or undermine the King at least to promote her daughter as heir apparent and herself as potential regent should William IV die before the princess reached her eighteenth birthday. Not surprisingly, the nakedness of the duchess's ambition, and that of her secretary Sir John Conroy, infuriated the King, who publicly insulted her as an incompetent, but also managed to live for a month past Victoria's birthday and so effectively thwarted her plan. Nevertheless, because of the jaunts, Victoria had probably seen more of the country than any of the preceding Hanoverians by the time she came to the throne: the first woman in 130 years and the first teenage monarch in nearly three centuries.

Once she married Prince Albert, too, he systematically undertook her education in the nature of the society she ruled. The royal couple embarked upon lengthy regional tours on a regular basis, travelling by train. They visited towns and cities across the country, opened civic buildings and parks, saw farms and factories, ventured into a prison on the Isle of Wight and went down a tin mine in Cornwall ('the miners seemed so pleased and are intelligent good people', she wrote in her journal). The highlight was perhaps in 1851, when the Queen opened the Great Exhibition – the brainchild of her husband – in Hyde Park. She enjoyed it so much that she went again and again. But, across the country, everywhere the Queen and her Consort visited, they were feted by civic dignitaries and greeted by cheering crowds and ceremonial arches. There was much local rivalry to outdo the neighbours. When the royal couple went on a tour of Lancashire in 1851, Manchester Corporation spent as much as £150,000 on entertainment and boasted that for every pound Liverpool had spent the week before, they would spend ten. The ceremonial arch they erected in St Anne's Square was

60ft high and illuminated with four thousand oil lamps. Eighty thousand local Sunday school children were rounded up to sing the national anthem to Victoria and Albert in Peel Park. Such displays were not entirely disinterested and many a mayor was knighted after a successful visit. But they were certainly occasions both to show off the royal visitors to the public and to demonstrate civic pride and local decorum, as the *Birmingham Post* told its readers in advance of the Queen's visit to open Aston Park in June 1858: 'The most democratic town in England must also be the most orderly in its loyalty.'

But there were downsides to all this. Victoria was shot at in her carriage at least seven times during the course of her reign, the first time by a deranged young man named Edward Oxford in 1840, the last forty-two years later by another unbalanced assassin outside Windsor railway station (the man, Roderick McLean, was scragged by passing Eton schoolboys). All these attempts, some more half-hearted than others, had the effect of increasing her personal popularity. People praised her sang-froid, though mostly her preternatural calm was because she had not realised what was going on: 'It is worth being shot at,' she wrote in a letter, 'To see how much one is loved.' But even when the crowds were benign there was always a danger of being overwhelmed. When she and Albert stayed at the Brighton Pavilion in 1841 and ventured out on to the nearby Chain Pier they were mobbed by tourists and errand boys, with people poking their faces right under her bonnet to see what she looked like. Not surprisingly, they did not stay at the Pavilion again and sold it off, building themselves a private Italian palazzo at Osborne on the Isle of Wight instead. For the Queen, the arrival of the railways was a godsend: they meant speedier, safer, cleaner and more punctual journeys, and privacy from the crowds. In 1842, after her first excursion from Windsor to London, she wrote that the trip had been 'free from the dust and crowd and heat and I am quite charmed with it'.

After Albert's death in 1861, although the Queen travelled abroad occasionally on holiday to see relatives, and paid regular and prolonged visits to Osborne and Balmoral, she avoided public events, declining even to attend the State Opening of Parliament. In the early 1870s, her seclusion helped to create a burst of republicanism, which, though temporary, alarmed her son and eventual successor the Prince of Wales, later Edward VII. Personal communication between them being strained, he wrote to her in the early 1870s: 'If you sometimes even came to London from Windsor – say for luncheon – and then drove for an hour in the Park and then returned to Windsor, the people would be overjoyed – beyond measure. It is all very well for Alix and me to drive in the Park – it does not have the same effect as when you do it; and I say thank God that is the case. We live in radical times and the more the people see the sovereign, the better it is for the people and the country.' Or, as Lord Salisbury, her later prime minister, wrote in the *Saturday Review*: 'Seclusion is one of the few luxuries in which Royal Personages may not indulge . . . loyalty needs a life of almost unintermitted publicity to sustain it.' Lord Halifax told the Queen's private secretary Henry Ponsonby in 1871: 'The mass of the people expect a king or queen to look and play the part. They want to see a crown and sceptre and all that sort of thing. They want the gilding for their money.' That the republican tide suddenly receded a few months later when the Prince of Wales fell seriously ill with typhoid fever and nearly died was merely fortuitous. The course of his illness and subsequent recovery were obsessively covered in the newspapers and the story of his struggle back to health provoked a wave of sympathy for the royal family and a celebratory service at St Paul's Cathedral.

Royal events could no longer just be privately organised. When the Queen's oldest daughter Vicky, the Princess Royal, wed the Prussian

Crown Prince Friedrich Wilhelm in 1858 and then five years later the Prince of Wales, the future Edward VII, married the Danish princess Alexandra, there were protests in the press and from local authorities that insufficient attention was being paid to the public's interest in the occasions and these criticisms forced changes. The conservative *Daily Telegraph* bemoaned the 'growing system of reserving the exclusive enjoyment of State ceremonials and spectacles for particular classes', while the radical *Reynold's News* argued pointedly that the public expense of the ceremony might be worth it so long as Londoners were given a sight of the married couple. When Alexandra arrived from Denmark in March 1863 the original plan was for her to proceed quietly to Windsor for the wedding, but following protests from the City of London (rather than the public) that was changed and she was given a public procession from the Bricklayers' Arms station (near modern London Bridge) to Paddington, via Trafalgar Square and Hyde Park. The crowds straining to see her were so large – a stand for ten thousand people was even erected near St Paul's Cathedral – that her carriage could barely squeeze through the throng.[4]

By the 1840s, newspapers and magazines had the technical means to publish line drawings of the young Queen and her consort. They were also the first members of the royal family to be photographed – Albert's first photograph was taken in 1842 and Victoria's followed soon afterwards. These were daguerreotype pictures, not copyable and accordingly just for private display. But from the late 1850s onwards improved technology meant that reproduction of photographs was possible and from then on the royal family's image became much more familiar to the public – the first publicly made available being a photograph of the Queen and Prince Consort at Osborne House on

---

4   The crush of the crowd was so great that seven people were squashed to death.

the Isle of Wight in 1857, surrounded by their nine children. Prince Albert was fascinated by the possibilities of photography and by the modernity and technological advance it demonstrated, and the Queen followed his passion. The first royal event to be commemorated in this way was the marriage of the Prince of Wales and Alexandra, and photographs of the happy couple's engagement portrait: the prince sitting stolidly (and slightly superciliously) in a chair, his bride standing behind him with her arms decorously touching his shoulders, gained wide circulation. The demure portrait, made in London by the official royal Belgian photographer from Ghémar Frères in October 1862, is not a million miles away in style from the formal engagement photograph of Prince Charles and Lady Diana Spencer 120 years later. It sold more than two million copies, though there were adverse comments about royalty allowing themselves to be depicted as if they were ordinary people – and also that Alexandra's light touch on the prince's shoulders showed disgraceful sexual intimacy. The *London Review* could not believe that the couple would ever have allowed such a thing: 'Pretty is it not? Sentimental, sweet and lover-like? Very – only not quite probable or in the best taste. That a young lady may have stood in that attitude of tender watching at the chair of her future husband is likely enough – but she would never think of being photographed at so confiding a moment... Can Paterfamilias possibly believe that the Prince and Princess allowed themselves to be shown after this fashion to the general gaze?' It thought the photograph must have been faked, or at the very least that the photographer was pandering to public prurience. Almost as bad was the fact that the couple were not dressed in robes of state, but just like ordinary couples. If they dressed the same as their subjects, how could you tell their majesty? That, of course, was largely the point: the photographs showed, and were meant to show, members of an idealised Victorian family: a sanitised public display of a private institution. It was one that could be held up as an exemplar of respectability and what would now be called family values and, as such, was not a bit like the rackety earlier Hanoverians with their mistresses, bastard children and illegitimate pleasures. This was a recognisable family that could be looked up to and emulated by ordinary people. The fact that the Prince of Wales was already sexually experienced and would go on through his married life having affairs and liaisons with a string of mistresses so that the pictures did not indeed reveal all was something that passed the commentators by.

Another observer called Andrew Wynter, writing in a paper called *Once a Week,* argued that Ghémar must have taken advantage of the couple's affability 'to pose them in a manner which, to say the least of it, jars on the good taste of the fastidious beholder'. It seems that criticism of the paparazzi started early, though how the critics could have assumed that the formal portrait could have been obtained by subterfuge and published illicitly defies belief. The criticisms were echoed when mourning photographs of the Queen herself, dressed all in black and gazing soulfully at a bust of her beloved Albert were also published in 1863. This too was regarded as an intrusion into private grief, as if the pictures had been snatched by a passing cameraman, but there is no indication that the Queen herself objected. In fact they probably served her purpose in illustrating the depth of her distress to the general public – and graphically demonstrating why she was too devastated to return to her official duties.

In fact, there was no way to hold back the tide of photographic representations, at a time when millions of the Queen's subjects across the world were having their photographs taken, too. There is no evidence that the Queen tried to prevent the spread of her image either and over the course of her reign – and despite her long seclusion – she became one of the most photographed personalities of the nineteenth

century, with 428 official portraits registered for commercial sale at
Stationers' Hall between 1862 and her death in 1901. (By comparison,
Mr Gladstone had 366 portraits, though Victoria's son had 655 official
photographs and his wife Princess Alexandra 676 – so pictures of royalty
were popular, frequent and evidently lucrative.) The photographs made
the Queen graphically accessible, yet also still remote and untouchable.
The Queen's image became very familiar on cartes-de-visite and
advertisements for everything from cocoa to toilet soap – no excuse for
her subjects in Britain and across the empire that she never visited not
knowing what she looked like. There she was, as commonplace and
almost as vivid as if she was present in real life, available in shops and
homes from Cardiff to Calcutta. There is even some evidence that, as
she grew stouter in later life, her formal portraits were touched up to
make her appear slightly slimmer and younger than she really was. The
photographs taken by Alexander Bassano in 1882 bear the marks of
manipulation by retouchers. The Queen's waist was pared down by
several inches and her bust was made more curvaceous, her double chin
was excised, her hair thickened and her wrinkles removed. As the
historian John Plunkett observed: 'A moderate proportion of Victoria's
face . . . disappeared under the gentle touch of the retoucher's pencil.
Her forehead and an area of cheek [were] thoroughly smoothed. The
rest of her cheek [had] a suspiciously stippled effect that suggests some
delicate and skilful work . . . the final picture shows a Queen who looks
more youthful than her sixty-two years.' When Bassano got to a full-
length portrait, he obviously made Victoria, who was less than 5ft tall,
stand on a box largely disguised under the folds of her train in order to
appear grander and more statuesque.

Eventually, gradually and grumbling, the queen did re-emerge into
public life and, rather to her surprise, found that it was true: people did
want to see her in the flesh and cheering crowds generally gathered

when she was known to be coming. In 1887 she had to be talked into celebrating fifty years on the throne. It would just be hustle and bustle, she said. The government, too, was reluctant to spend any public money on the occasion. Victoria initially refused an invitation from Birmingham to celebrate her jubilee by opening the city's new law courts and when she did go, reluctantly, there was disappointment and a complaint from Joseph Chamberlain, the city's former radical mayor, now its MP, that she had not put on a proper show by bringing the Household Cavalry with her. The country's 'most democratic town' of thirty years earlier now wanted some pomp and circumstance. The public had not got its money's worth – she should have brought splendour. When the anniversary itself came to pass that summer, the Queen refused all entreaties that she should wear her crown, but did unbend sufficiently to wear a bonnet trimmed with diamonds for the occasion. The crowned heads and princes of Europe gathered to celebrate their matriarch. In faraway India there were firework displays and professions of devotion. Closer to home there were massed choirs, a service at Westminster Abbey, garden parties and receptions and a Naval review off Spithead. But there was also jeering from a section of the crowd when Victoria ventured into the East End to open the People's Palace, a working men's college. It was 'a horrid noise, quite new to the Queen's ears, "booing" she believes it is called,' she wrote to the prime minister Lord Salisbury. Ah, he replied, it was socialists and the worst Irish. Much more in keeping with the time was a nationwide collection raising money to train nurses and to pay for yet another statue of her Albert.

Ten years on and the old queen's diamond jubilee was celebrated even more lavishly, almost with surprise and wonder that she had lived so long. It became a grand imperial celebration, more lavish and bombastic than the golden jubilee, with troops from across the empire and colonial leaders in attendance – Joseph Chamberlain, by now Conservative colonial secretary, was responsible for that idea. European royal rivalries were too mutually antagonistic to be accommodated on this occasion, but as many as a million people came from all over the world to watch the spectacle. Bunting, electric lights and triumphal arches decked the streets of London and choirs along the route from Buckingham Palace to St Paul's sang the national anthem as the Queen's carriage passed. Victoria even sent a message to her subjects across the empire by pressing a button to dispatch an electric telegraph: 'From my heart I thank my beloved people. May God bless them!' The parade was a triumphalist display of British power just before horsepower became obsolete: rank upon rank of cavalry, breastplates and helmets gleaming in the sun, plumes wafting in the breeze and marching troops from all corners of the empire. We can see them still because the zenith of Britain's imperial might was even filmed by the newly invented movie cameras, operated by companies in fierce rivalry with one another. It was the first filmed media event and snatches of the film survive. There, Queen Victoria herself, a small black blob in an open carriage sheltered from the sun by a white parasol, can just be seen. 'Very wonderful but a little hazy and too rapid,' she rightly thought when she watched the pictures afterwards. The crowds were enthusiastic – no booing – although the Queen was by now too immobile to get out of the landau and ascend the flight of steps into St Paul's Cathedral for the thanksgiving service, instead the service came to her and was performed outside. She was extremely moved by the whole experience: 'No one ever, I believe, has met with such an ovation as was given to me, passing through those six miles of streets... the crowds were quite indescribable and their enthusiasm truly marvellous and deeply touching. The cheering was quite deafening and every face seemed to be filled with real joy.' She wept quietly in the carriage.

Although a show was good, the monarch did not actually have to *do* anything: being there was enough.

In a way that Victoria probably never realised, or imperfectly understood, the popularity of the monarchy increased with the decline of its real power: its symbolic importance in inverse proportion to its actual authority. William IV was the last monarch to dismiss a government – he did it three times in seven years, twice dissolved parliament and publicly interfered with a vote in the House of Lords, a real exercise of regal power – and, although Victoria sought to influence ministerial decisions and early in her reign attempted to frustrate the formation of a Conservative administration, she largely failed and her executive power was strictly limited. As the journalist Walter Bagehot realised in the 1860s, the monarch's strength and popularity lay in being above politics, which enabled her to become a ceremonial symbol of national unity, to be wheeled out at times of celebration.

That symbolism, too, was enhanced by something new in royal ceremonial: it was organised, rehearsed and perfected. Far from the ramshackle and disorganised ceremonies of earlier eras, the royal jubilees with their military parades, martial music and precise timings introduced a new discipline and prestige into royal events. They were glittering public spectacles, fortunately held in midsummer sunshine and the religious rituals that accompanied them were also impressive.

Lord Esher, who orchestrated the diamond jubilee unashamedly described such events as vulgar, though, as an old Etonian, he probably meant the word in the classical sense of being of the people, rather than pejoratively – though they *were* vulgar as well. There were no more inaudible incantations or muttered and confused readings from the presiding clergy, no more execrable singing from the choir, no more slipshod ritual as there had been at earlier coronations, most notably

Victoria's own. Despite the fact that hers was the third coronation in eighteen years, in June 1838 the presiding bishops had not bothered to rehearse properly, so were ignorant and confused about the order of service. The elderly archbishop of Canterbury, William Howley, caused the young queen excruciating pain when he rammed the ruby-encrusted coronation ring on the wrong finger – to get it off later she had to soak her hand in ice-cold water. Howley later tried to give her the orb of state when she was already holding it: 'He (as usual) was *so* confused and puzzled and knew nothing and went away,' she wrote in her journal. 'Pray tell me what I am to do,' she whispered to the sub-dean, 'for they don't know.' The bishop of Bath and Wells turned over two pages at once, did not notice and so ended the service prematurely, then had to call her back to finish it off properly. When the young queen progressed to St Edward's Chapel to take off her ceremonial robes, she found the altar there already covered with sandwiches and bottles of wine for the refreshments afterwards – to which the prime minister, Lord Melbourne, weighed down and exhausted by carrying the heavy sword of state, helped himself ravenously.

Such chaos, which previously had been regarded as quite unexceptionable and only to be expected, would not do in future. This was partly due to a change in Anglican practices including the increasing use of High Church vestments such as copes, stoles, mitres and crosiers – no longer as great a source of evangelical, Low Church outrage and offence as they previously had been – which gave a touch of flamboyance and theatricality and a more ritualistic aspect to services. The established church was at the heart of much of this ceremonial – as it has remained ever since – giving a point and an inner core of seriousness and weight to the proceedings, which served the incidental purpose not only of revering divine authority but also bestowing it by proxy on the monarch as well. It usefully dignifies the ceremonial and separates it from being no more than a partisan political rally. God might be the ultimate spiritual power, but He certainly seems to sanction earthly royal authority, too.

Alongside this came important renovations at Westminster Abbey: the organ was restored and electric lighting brightened the ancient Gothic interior from the 1890s. The abbey choir, no longer ancient retainers but boys with treble voices, were now dressed in red cassocks and given proper training. This display was part of a revival of interest in church music by the high Victorian generation of composers. Stanford, Stainer, Bridge, Sullivan, Parry (despite his own private religious scepticism) and later Elgar all composed for services and national occasions, and imposed new disciplines on cathedral choirs and organists. The National Anthem, which had not been sung at Queen Victoria's coronation or indeed at other royal events in earlier years, received new settings in the last years of her reign and much of what is now thought of as the traditional mood music of ceremonial occasions dates from that period, too: 'Jerusalem', 'Pomp and Circumstance No. 1 (Land of Hope and Glory)', 'Coronation March', 'I was Glad' – joined the anthems of Purcell and Handel from two centuries earlier, and where would a formal royal event now be without them? Increasingly, too, everything had to be done to the minute, precisely timed. In 1937, for the coronation of George VI, the Duke of Norfolk, who as Earl Marshal was responsible for organising the ceremony, told a colleague that he would pay him a pound for every minute that the crowning itself was delayed. He had to hand over just £5. That new precision did not eliminate all mistakes of course. The octogenarian Archbishop William Temple at Edward VII's coronation in 1902 was so blind he could hardly read the order of service, placed the crown on the King's head the wrong way round and had to be helped up by the King when he kneeled down. Thirty-five years later,

George VI, already tense because of his stammer, found he could not read the coronation oath held up for him by Archbishop Lang because the primate's thumb was covering it, then when the King tried to rise to approach the throne he could not move because a bishop was standing on his robe: 'I had to tell him to get off it pretty sharply as I nearly fell down.'

Perhaps it is lucky that such incidents have not subsequently been incorporated as part of royal events' age-old customs. Even when things went wrong, sometimes they could be turned to advantage and used as part of a new, invented tradition. This occurred most famously after there was a hitch during the arrival of the coffin containing the body of Queen Victoria in the royal train at Windsor following her death in January 1901. It was a bitterly cold day, the funeral party had been waiting outside the town's railway station for a long time and when the half-ton coffin was loaded on to a gun carriage to be carried up the steep hill to the castle, part of the harness traces snapped, causing two of the horses to rear and buck and the coffin to slide dangerously towards the edge. The team had to be unharnessed before the Queen's body fell off completely and slid into the road and down the hill, so a hundred naval ratings, part of the honour guard from HMS *Excellent*, were ordered forward to haul the whole thing instead. Following that accident, sailors have dragged the gun carriage bearing the sovereign's body ever since.

Other traditions have also been invented, as if hallowed by time. The annual State Opening of Parliament, with the Queen in full regalia, including crown, travelling from the palace to the House of Lords in the state coach, waiting on the throne for the summoning of the House of Commons and then trying not to sound bored as she reads out the government of the day's future legislative programme, originates in its present ceremonial form with Edward VII. Queen

Victoria had opened parliament in the early years of her reign, though without much pomp and circumstance or dressing up. Since governments did not tend to offer great rafts of policies at the time, the speeches then were brief and usually perfunctory surveys of what had happened in the year gone by, rather than the one to come. Victoria refused to do it ever again after the death of Prince Albert, so it was left to her son to revive and amplify the occasion when he became King forty years later. The attendance at the Royal Maundy service was another ancient tradition revived by George V in the 1930s. Similarly, the annual Garter ceremony at Windsor Castle, during which holders of the Order parade in their ceremonial robes for a service in St George's Chapel, is held on the Monday of Ascot week to combine convenience with pleasure and looks suitably time-hallowed and ritualistic. But although the Order itself may be medieval, the procession only dates back to 1948.

The tradition of the monarch lying in state in Westminster Hall after death was also an innovation after Edward VII died in 1910 – an experiment, said the courtier Lord Esher, 'which proved extremely popular'. A quarter of a million people filed past the King's coffin to pay their respects and that, too, has been followed since for the deaths of George V, George VI, the elder George's widow Queen Mary in 1953 and, after her death in 2002, for the Queen Mother. Two commoners have also been so honoured: the practice started with Mr Gladstone in 1898[5] followed by Winston Churchill in 1965. In the Queen Mother's case, more than 200,000 people filed through the hall and past the catafalque during the three days' lying in state.

---

5 Victoria, who could not stand Gladstone, at that time her longest-serving prime minister, did not attend his state funeral, but two future kings: her son Bertie and his son George were pallbearers.

That was the internal ritual of ceremonies. Outside, too, there was a new imperial way – literally so, since the approach to Buckingham Palace became more grandiose as the Mall was widened. This was in conscious emulation of the grand ceremonial boulevards in other capitals such as Paris, Berlin and Washington DC, to show off and display the monarchy in all its pomp and authority. The Mall, replacing what was originally an area for playing a croquet-like game using mallets, called pall mall, which had become by the eighteenth and nineteenth centuries a narrow promenade through the park, was turned into a broad, straight highway stretching all the way from Trafalgar Square to the palace. It ran from the Admiralty Arch, built between 1905 and 1911, to the Victoria Memorial, the huge triumphal statuary in front of Buckingham Palace, also dedicated in 1911 by the old Queen's grandsons, George V and the Kaiser. The whole effect was set off by the resurfacing of the east front of Buckingham Palace to replace the dull, soot and smoke-scoured early Victorian facade built seventy years earlier. What emerged was the imposing but bland grey-faced structure that has been the public frontage of the building ever since, including the famous balcony from which generations of the royal family have waved to the crowd beyond the gates. All these changes, from the arch to the palace, were largely the work of the now all but forgotten Edwardian architect Sir Aston Webb, designer of public schools and grand, dull, monumental projects. He did not personally sculpt the marble statue of Victoria, many times life size, which peers grimly up the Mall – that and the accompanying retinue of assorted winged angels, cherubs, semi-naked reclining warriors and growling lions was the work of Sir Thomas Brock – but Webb orchestrated the surrounding piazza and its colonial pillars and gateways. When the ladies of the court protested that the central island around Queen Victoria's statue would allow people to get too close,

Lord Esher informed them that that was the whole idea. All this has seemed so much a part of the official furniture for so long that it is hard to remember that it actually dates back only a hundred years. The huge flags that line the Mall on ceremonial occasions and the pinkish tarmac on the road – to give the illusion of a red carpet stretching down to the palace – are even more recent additions. The whole triumphal ensemble, except for a statue or two, was finished just in time for the First World War.

When George V took part in the next jubilee parade in 1935, after he had been on the throne for twenty-five years, he too was astonished by his popularity: 'I'd no idea they felt like that about me,' he is said to have muttered with tears in his eyes on returning from a visit to the East End, which was evidently better behaved than for his grandmother's visit half a century earlier, 'I'm beginning to think they must like me for myself.' Indeed, gruff old King George, stiff and rectitudinous almost to a paralysing degree, was consciously seen – and promoted in the press – as a real father to the nation. As Kingsley Martin, editor of the *New Statesman*, wrote at the time of the jubilee: 'People constantly reiterated that he was "a father to us all" . . . he had become a universal father figure.' When the King died the following winter a ditty circulating in the streets ran:

> *Greatest sorrow England ever had*
> *When death took away our dear Dad*
> *A king was he from head to sole*
> *Loved by his people one and all.*

'The British public has had a fit of grief which surpasses all ever known,' wrote Virginia Woolf to her nephew in the authentic *de haut en bas* tones of the Bloomsbury set. 'It is a curious survival of barbarism, emotionalism, heraldry, ecclesiasticism, sheer sentimentality, snobbery and some feeling for the very commonplace man who was so like ourselves.' The old King would probably have been happy to be thought commonplace. Woolf might well have said the same thing following the similar wave of sentimentality that followed the death of Diana sixty years later.

However, as much as the Queen is admired, it is impossible to think of a similar song being sung today – though similar sentiments to Woolf's will doubtless fill the letters pages of the *Guardian* when she dies. Actually George was the antithesis of either fatherly – his relations with his own children were brusque – or populist. In newsreels he can be seen relatively genially riding on a miniature steam train, dressed in a grey suit and bowler hat, at the Empire Exhibition at Wembley in 1924 – although a small boy, lifted in the carriage to sit opposite him promptly clambers out in terror as fast as his legs can carry him. With the advent of the Box Brownie and more portable press cameras, then movie newsreels, royal pictures became more informal just as everyone else's did. The Prince of Wales could be seen in a swimming costume and his younger brother George, dressed in shorts, open-necked shirt and pullover, was filmed engaging in sing-songs at a youth camp, complete with all the gestures for 'Under the Spreading Chestnut Tree'.

But George V never wanted to be thought 'an advertising sort of fellow' courting popularity. It was a more innocent and deferential age, where the King could be wildly cheered when he toured a Yorkshire coal mine following a pit disaster and, after being serenaded by a miners' choir, could exclaim without irony or apparent condescension that he felt himself among 'true friends'. But he actually often looked grim at public events – 'We sailors never smile on duty' – and was obsessed with protocol and precedence. When his son, the Prince of Wales, suggested that something he had done was good propaganda, he was told in no uncertain terms: 'I do things because they are my duty, not as propaganda.' The fatherly reputation came not from his geniality – fathers probably were generally less benign and playful with their children then – but from the public's appreciation of that sense of duty and from their knowledge of his dull and mundane habits and commonplace middle-brow enthusiasms, such as for stamp collecting and his penchant only for salubrious light operettas. There was nothing highfalutin there.[6] As his eldest son, the future Edward VIII, said, he 'disapproved of Soviet Russia, painted fingernails, women who smoked in public, cocktails, frivolous hats, American jazz and the growing habit of going away at weekends' – almost everything in fact that the prince most enjoyed. And actually he was wrong: the King rather enjoyed the Original Dixieland Jazz Band, which toured England to great acclaim in 1918 and gave several performances at the palace.

George was nevertheless the personification of middle-class rectitude and was resolutely and adamantly British in outlook – no Germanic airs and graces like his grandmother for him, especially once the First World War broke out and the family name was changed from Saxe-Coburg-Gotha to plain-brown Windsor. Told that H.G. Wells had deplored the spectacle of Britain struggling under 'an alien and uninspiring court', George replied in spritely fashion: 'I may be uninspiring, but I'll be damned if I'm an alien.' Most people seemed to prefer it that way. The Labour thinker Harold Laski, a republican, wrote rather approvingly after the King's death: 'He was identified with the spirit of hard work and personal sacrifice that had won the war; he established a friendly and considerate relationship with the first Labour

---

6 Advised by the prime minister's office to send a celebratory telegram to 'Old Hardy' on the novelist's seventieth birthday, the King complied – and Mr Hardy, the maker of his fishing rods, was surprised to receive congratulations from the palace.

government; his family life epitomised middle-class virtues and avoided overt ostentation; he, the Queen and the princes were identified with a concern, albeit superficial, for the problems of social and industrial welfare. The monarchy, to put it bluntly, has been sold to the democracy as the symbol of itself; and so nearly universal has been the chorus of eulogy which has accompanied the process of sale that the rare voices of dissent have hardly been heard.'

He added, wonderingly: 'It is not without significance that the official daily newspaper of the Trades Union Congress devotes more space, of news and pictures, to the royal family than does any of its rivals.' Nearly eighty years on, republican sympathisers remain equally perplexed and perpetually disappointed by the apparent enthusiasm of people for royalty, patronisingly putting it down to the gullibility of a public seduced by the tabloid press and their wicked plutocratic owners. The Queen has followed her gruff old grandfather's example – 'Grandpa England' – in dutiful seriousness successfully throughout her reign.

Charisma by now, however, would only carry a monarch so far. Edward VIII was the most charismatic king of the twentieth century. He was handsome, dashing and apparently concerned for the welfare of his people, yet they largely turned against him within days during the abdication crisis in December 1936, as if they had been betrayed. As Prince of Wales he had been the most travelled and feted heir to the throne ever: there had been world tours to Canada, Australia and New Zealand, then the US and South Africa, East Africa and South America, all in the 1920s. He had served as a junior officer in the First World War, though not as he had hoped on the front line; had been made patron of numerous hospitals, ex-servicemen's associations and charities; he had met a wider range of people from all walks of life than his predecessors; and he had had an energetic social life in the nightclubs of London and the country houses of the rich and aristocratic. He took an interest in social policy and welfare, and in housing improvements on the Duchy of Cornwall estates. But if he thought these were a useful preparation for ruling, he was soon disabused by his father and court advisers such as Sir Frederick 'Fritz' Ponsonby, the keeper of the privy purse – treasurer – to the royal household, who bluntly advised him he was too accessible. Royalty had to keep its distance. His father told him that although the First World War had changed social attitudes and made it possible for the prince to mix freely, that did not mean that he could behave like other people. Unfortunately, the prince thought not only that he could, but that his special position gave him particular privileges to act just as he liked.

He had cultivated a public image at odds with his character, which was privately wilful, selfish and self-indulgent. His politics were dangerously murky too: like some ex-servicemen he was attracted to Oswald Mosley's British Union of Fascists: a private allegiance which would have become disastrous if he had still been King in 1939. Insofar as they knew this, the press kept quiet about it in favour of boosting the image of him as a glamorous, attractive and modern King for modern times. Even down to earth: the press were struck when he took tea in a miner's cottage and, seeing the man unaffectedly pouring the liquid into the saucer – the old way of drinking tea – and supping from that, Edward did the same. Similarly when as King, shortly before the abdication crisis, he toured the South Wales coalfields, and visited the derelict Dowlais iron and steelworks, his empathy was noticeable. The unemployed workers there stood and sang him a Welsh hymn and the King, clearly moved, told an official: 'Something must be done to find them work.' It was a bogus image. This was a monarch who at the same time was buying his mistress thousands of pounds worth of jewellery while sacking royal retainers as a cost-saving measure: in the words of MP Victor Cazalet: 'Sympathising with the miners and so on while on the other hand wanting everything that a rich, idle bachelor desires in material pleasures – lavishing jewels on his mistress while getting rid of his father's servants.' Within a fortnight of his tour of South Wales his dedication to getting something done for his destitute subjects was so committed that he had abdicated just in order to be with the woman he loved, the twice-married American-born divorcee Wallis Simpson. There were those at the time who suggested his remarks at Dowlais had precipitated the government's determination to get rid of him, but the truth was much more simple and had nothing to do with his concern for the unemployed. It was true that ministers and courtiers had been already alarmed by his private behaviour, by his louche friends and mistresses, his laziness and contempt for his responsibilities before he ever met Wallis Simpson, but his obstinacy over his relationship with her crystallised their sense that abdication was the only option and they manoeuvred him in the same direction.

The discretion shown by the British press in keeping their readerships in the dark over the affair, at the behest of the press barons Lords Beaverbrook and Kemsley – though plenty of people in London society knew all about it – actually played to the King's disadvantage because it gave no time for public opinion to form in his favour or for Edward to rally support for him to both marry and remain King. The news of his relationship with Mrs Simpson and her recent divorce leaked out publicly in Britain on 2 December 1936 and eight days later he was gone.[7] The National Archives at Kew bulge with letters from the public

---

7 The Hearst Press's *New York Journal* had run the story under the deathless headline: 'King Will Wed Wally' on 26 October 1936, but it was not reported in Britain until 2 December, six weeks later, after the Bishop of Bradford, the appropriately named Dr Blunt, had unknowingly blundered into the affair with a speech to his diocesan conference calling on the King to do his duty as a Christian leader. Blunt had no idea what Edward was up to with Wallis Simpson – he thought he was urging the King more generally towards an appropriate Christian lifestyle – but his innocent remarks finally gave newspapers the excuse they had been looking for to run the story. A few days later Edward abdicated.

to the government, written at this time but only finally released seventy years later, and they are largely hostile towards the King and especially to Simpson, variously described by indignant correspondents as an octopus, fake, legalised prostitute and 'a woman climber from a boarding house in Baltimore'. There was no need for the government to disseminate the knowledge garnered by undercover police surveillance that Wallis was also having an affair with a used Ford car salesman called Guy Trundle at the same time. The public simply felt that while the King might, just, have married an American, he really could not marry a serial divorcee. As Prime Minister Stanley Baldwin who handled the crisis, murmured, she was a godsend: she could not have been more unsuitable. Furthermore, he was abandoning his people, forsaking duty for pleasure and when he and Wallis later went on a trip to meet Hitler, the reaction was cold in Britain and even frostier in the US. He could not see that he was being used by the Nazis for propaganda purposes and made a poor fist of remaining neutral in his discussion with Hitler, though he did claim that his Nazi salute to the Führer was merely a wave. The so-called 'King's party' in Britain, Churchill among them, were mainly malcontents and rebels and they soon melted away. The Labour politician Herbert Morrison wrote in a party magazine: 'The choice before ex-kings is either to fade out of the public eye or to be a nuisance. It is a hard choice, perhaps, for one of his temperament, but the Duke will be wise to fade.' So he did, but not willingly. The trauma of the abdication is seared into the family's soul: the ultimate betrayal of royal duty, even if fortuitously it turned out to be for the best. 'The "A" word is something that you never mention in the Queen's presence,' a courtier told me. 'It would be like saying "fuck" in church.'

None felt Edward's abandonment more than his brother, George VI, thrust unwillingly on to the throne, fearing the institution might crumble under the shock and strain of it all and furious with his older brother for putting him through it. 'How do you think I like taking on a rocking throne and trying to make it steady again?' he complained plaintively to the now Duke of Windsor. It was a task not made easier because he was widely considered by senior politicians, churchmen and courtiers as being not up to the job, even retarded because of his speech impediment – a sort of nitwit, in the words of Lloyd George. Perhaps if one of his younger brothers, the dukes of Gloucester and Kent, had been regarded as being more suitable, the succession might have passed to them instead; but neither were: Henry, the third son, was a shy and stiff soldier and George[8], the youngest, was reputed to have a louche private life that included affairs with both women and men.

So the second son succeeded – the second king of three who was the second son, not the original heir – an unprepossessing prospect at a time of increasing international tension. 'He was uninteresting and unintellectual but doubtless well-meaning,' wrote the diarist Chips Channon, who knew him, after George VI's death. 'He improved with the years. His natural shyness and inferiority complex towards his elder brother made him on the defensive. He had no wit, no learning, no humour except of a rather schoolboy brand. He was nervous, ill at ease, though slightly better after some champagne, and had few interests other than shooting. He had few friends and was almost entirely dependent on the Queen, whom he worshipped.'

In other words, perfect monarchy material. Unprepossessing as he was, the new King possessed one of the key virtues in a monarch. As *The Times* pointed out on the morning of his coronation in May 1937, successful kingship depended 'not upon intellectual brilliance or superlative talent of any kind but upon the moral qualities of steadiness, staying power and self-sacrifice'. And George had those.

---

8   George VI was known as Albert to his family; George was only his fourth Christian name.

As is well known, he had his own difficulties communicating with his subjects on a personal level – though his stammer was quite sympathetically understood by the public at the time – but he adopted his father's approach to kingship rather than that of his brother: dutiful, low-key, solemn and definitely, absolutely, not frivolous. Even a little dull too: 'There must be no more high hat business,' he told an aide. 'The sort of thing that my father and those of his day regarded as essential as the correct attitude – the feeling that certain things could not be done.'

He might join in boy scout community singing, but his advisers scarcely expected him to be able to go out among the public and converse with them. Yet that is what he had to do during the war, which broke out three years after his accession. The King and his wife, Queen Elizabeth, had to be seen by their subjects, just as much and for almost the same purpose as William the Conqueror at the Battle of Hastings nine hundred years earlier. They needed to turn up to inspect the wrecked homes of citizens in the cities in the Blitz, to tour factories and hospitals, and to meet and empathise with those whose lives had been damaged by the bombing. And they did so, very effectively. George VI found it easier to talk to ordinary people than to many of his generals and the Queen was a public relations star, as she would be for the next sixty years – and, as she famously said, once Buckingham Palace had been bombed she felt she could look the East Enders in the face. Whereas the King was painfully shy and occasionally prickly, impatient and always conscious of protocol, his Queen developed the theatrical knack of appearing down to earth and charming, adapting her approach adroitly to whoever she was talking to and smiling benignly throughout. Even though the royal family had a serviceable and relatively safe castle to go home to in Windsor each evening, they instituted economy measures to show that they shared at least some of the deprivations of more ordinary people: no central heating, only one light bulb per room and a ring painted at the 5in mark in baths to limit the amount of water used – and this was made publicly known too. George VI's almost painful integrity; the obvious effort he made to rise to a role he had never expected to have to fulfil conveyed itself to the public. His biographer, Sarah Bradford observed that *Time* magazine in 1941 had noted two of the most popular songs of the day were: 'The King is Still in London' and 'The Day I met His Majesty the King' with its refrain:

> *He just smiled at me as if he'd known me all his life,*
> *The day I met His Majesty the King,*
> *He talked and we spoke*
> *Just like two ordinary folk . . .*

This was precisely, of course, the sort of message that the King wished to convey: ordinary, yet not. He even received a gold medal from the Trades Union Congress for his hard work for the war effort.

His daughter has been at the popularity game herself, dating right back to the late 1940s and specifically a royal visit to South Africa in 1947, which was intended at least partially to cool her growing friendship with the penniless Philip Mountbatten. In those days a trip could be relatively leisurely, even if crowded in its schedule and arduous in its travel itinerary; the royal family was away for four months. A later Commonwealth trip would keep the young Queen and her by-then spouse away from home (and their two young children) from November 1953 until May 1954: sailing in those days on HMS *Gothic*, from Bermuda, through the Panama Canal, to Fiji and Tonga, then New Zealand and Australia. It was a royal progress *and* a stately duty: the young Queen was confronted by Australian veterans with tears in their eyes exclaiming: 'This is what I fought for!' She often had to give six speeches a day. These days, a trip to Australia can be over in a week, though it is still a strenuous routine for a monarch a quarter of a century past retirement age – and, for those who claim it's not much in the way of work, they perhaps have not seen many royal visits: the requirement of being permanently nice, and smiling, observant and questioning, is a strain. On that first royal visit Down Under nearly sixty years ago, the young Queen told a helper: 'It's awful. I've got the kind of face that if I am not smiling I look cross. But I am not cross. If you try to smile for two hours continuously it gives you a nervous tic. But the moment I stop smiling, somebody will see me and say: "Doesn't she look cross?"'

Now there is an annual routine. The Queen and Duke, formerly making two overseas trips a year are now down to one, short one, usually in the summer. Their year follows a regular pattern: Christmas to early February at Sandringham, spring and summer at Buckingham Palace, visits around Britain, late summer and into autumn at Balmoral, then later until mid-December in London: still more than two hundred visits a year, though many engagements are contracted out to other members of the family firm. In the jubilee year of 2012, the royal couple paid visits to every part of the British Isles, while younger members were sent abroad: Charles and Camilla to Australia, where every trip these days is a sounding-out exercise to test the monarchy's ongoing popularity; William and Kate as far as the south Pacific; and Harry to Jamaica, to check his stamina and ability to carry out grown-up visits on his own. If there is no sense of duty, soon there will be no monarchy either.

If anything, the crowds who turn out abroad are much more enthusiastic than those at home, especially on a cold day in Margate, even in the more republican-minded of the 'realms', as the palace calls those overseas countries that still have the Queen as head of state. In part it is the novelty, in part it is the showbusinessy glamour and hype of the occasion, but there is unquestionably excitement too. When William and Kate visited Canada and the US on their first overseas tour after their marriage in July 2011, it was estimated that about five per cent of the entire Canadian population, as many as 1.5 million people, turned out to see them. On Canada Day in Ottawa, the crowds stretched as far as the eye could see: a sea of people dressed in the red and white of the national colours, most with no hope of even catching a glimpse of the duchess's scarlet maple-leaf fascinator bobbing in the distance. Even if the numbers meant that 95 per cent of Canadians did not crane for a view, they were not organising counter demonstrations either; except in French-speaking, separatist Quebec – and even there the protesters were heavily outnumbered. Nor is it just ordinary folk who show up for the circus. When the royal couple arrived in Los Angeles a few days later to attend a celebrity dinner to promote the British film industry, normally blasé stars who might easily have chosen to spend the hot evening by their swimming pools went along to meet them instead: Barbra Streisand, Tom Hanks, Quentin Tarantino, James Gandolfini, Jennifer Lopez and her mother...a little sprinkling of stardust for both sides. Perhaps they could not resist the red carpet laid in the street outside.

Back home, the daily routine remains the same on high days and holidays: the sound of bagpipes played by a piper on the terrace below as the Queen wakes; the BBC Radio 4 news; a breakfast of tea and toast and a quick scan of the *Racing Post* and *Daily Telegraph*; and then meetings with her private secretary; documents in official boxes to be read and answered – this may take several hours; then maybe an investiture or an official lunch; a visit; a meeting with ambassadors or more discussions with officials, or perhaps with her official dresser

Angela Kelly, who is responsible for looking after her clothes, jewellery and insignia. In the evening there may be a dinner. On most Wednesday evenings at 6.30 p.m. there will be a private meeting with the prime minister. Here she can express her opinions frankly, advise the head of her government and discuss the events of the week. No notes are taken, no one else is present and nothing should be ever disclosed – and will not be, at least by her. One or two of her prime ministers have dropped hints – and David Cameron had to apologise when he disclosed near an open microphone that Her Majesty had 'purred' to hear the result of the Scottish referendum in September 2014. This is a round that has been going on for sixty years and will not stop until she does.

Elizabeth II is very much her father's daughter: shy and sometimes unsmiling in public but much warmer and more informal in private. Her reign has seen a decisive evolution in royal protocol, interacting with the populace directly in royal walkabouts, now practised with varying degrees of enthusiasm and success by all members of the family firm. The etymology is incongruous and ironic since it derives from the Australian aboriginal practice of wandering off into the bush, sometimes without notice and for prolonged periods, occasionally as a rite of passage and periodically to take leave from employers without seeking permission. Almost nothing could be further from the highly controlled and intensely organised practice of members of the royal family on official visits, breaking off for a few minutes to go over and speak to members of the watching crowd. The practice, which began in the 1970s at about the time of the Queen's silver jubilee, would have shocked her predecessors and probably the Queen, too, in the earlier days of her reign, but has proved so immensely popular that it is now a permanent feature of royal tours and visits. It has two purposes: to show off the royal personage as a walking, talking approachable human being, sort of just like us, and to encourage the creation of crowds of well wishers. If the sovereign, or a prince or princess, is coming to town and you think the only glimpse you might have is of a distant hand waving fleetingly through the window of a passing limousine – the experience of many spectators during the Queen's early years on the throne – you may not bother to go; but if there is a chance, however distant, that they could stop and speak to you, then it might be worth the wait of several hours. For the royal person, too, a walkabout is a direct affirmation of their popularity and public endorsement. Not everyone in the royal family gets to make them, only the sure-fire hits who the public might want to stand behind crush barriers waiting to see: the Queen and the Duke of Edinburgh, less frequently Prince Charles and his duchess, Camilla, and, most of all Prince William and his duchess, Kate, who are the stars. Charles is not at his best in crowds: he is too self-conscious and wry (he used to get peevish too at the amount of attention his former wife, Princess Diana, drew on walkabouts). You wouldn't get much of a crowd for Prince Edward or Prince Andrew these days – both give the impression that their welcome may be uncertain – or, sadly, for Princess Anne, who can share her father's saltiness.

Inevitably, such apparently spontaneous events have to be tightly controlled. There cannot be Queen Victoria's experience of being jostled and peered at in the face, or William IV's of being hugged by a prostitute. Equally, the threat of terrorism or assassination means that – unlike Franz Ferdinand's ill-fated visit to Sarajevo in 1914 whose itinerary was helpfully published in the press beforehand – the possibility of walkabouts cannot be advertised in advance (except to the media under strict confidentiality). Despite the initial trepidation of both royals and security officers, there have been very few troublesome incidents, still less any violence, on walkabouts – no mean feat considering that the practice has coincided with a worldwide increase in terrorism, some of it focused on Britain. The occasions are carefully assessed in advance: when the Queen visited Ireland for the first time in 2011, access even to see her in the distance was strictly controlled in Dublin – the barriers went up all over town – but three days later, with the popularity of the visit assured, a 'spontaneous' walkabout was allowed in the centre of Cork, outside the English Market and she was greeted ecstatically.

The conversations on such occasions are inevitably stilted and brief, though the Duke of Edinburgh occasionally gets into trouble for trying to enliven them, or alleviate his boredom, by making interesting or provocative comments to stir a reaction. He probably thinks of it as breaking the ice, but if so he occasionally falls through it. At worst it is usually an elderly man's ill-judged attempt at banter, perhaps the sort of remark that would have been unexceptional seventy years ago. Mostly it is casual facetiousness: 'Dontopedalogy – the science of opening your mouth and putting your foot in it, a science which I have practised for a good many years,' as he says. The remarks range from rude and aggressive to tasteless, and he never feels the need to apologise for any of them. He has had more than sixty years to get used to the open-mouthed, awestruck responses of those he meets – his beady, looming presence and menacing grin is somehow intimidating rather than reassuring – so a feisty reply, when it occasionally happens, is pleasing to him. He would probably be offended if someone told him he was being rude or impertinent. But the world – that is the media – is very seldom interested in what is said to him, unless it is particularly striking or the response is made by someone famous. It is the Duke's remarks that can get him into trouble. The so-called gaffes irritate him, sometimes because they are made up or distorted, mostly because they are endlessly recycled by the press (and here) years, sometimes decades, later. The famous comment to a British student studying in Beijing: 'If you stay here much longer you will go home with slitty eyes,' dates from 1986; the question to an Oban driving instructor: 'How do you keep the natives off the booze long enough to pass the test?' derives from 1995. The remark about loose wiring at a factory: 'It looks as if it was put in by an Indian,' apparently arises from a momentary memory lapse, a sort of spoonerism: 'I meant to say cowboy. I just got my cowboys and Indians mixed up,' and that dates from 1999. The Duke insists he never told a group of deaf children standing next to a steel band in Cardiff: 'Deaf? If you stand near there, no wonder you're deaf,' because, after all, he knows all about deafness: his mother was hard of hearing and he has been a long-standing patron of the Royal National Institute for Deaf People.

The gaffes arise essentially after the event: there are few indications that those he makes them to are usually upset. Sometimes they are simply baffled, at other times surprised into silence. The protocol on such visits is that the media are not allowed close enough to overhear what is said (or sufficiently close to hear through lofting microphone booms overhead), but are then allowed to descend immediately afterwards to ask the crowd what they heard. The correspondents then foregather afterwards to compare notes and share the best quotes between themselves: this so that no one misses anything vital. This process is largely done to gain a flavour and some colour from people's reactions to speaking to royalty – to give immediacy and a variety of responses to what W.S. Gilbert would have called otherwise a bald and unconvincing narrative – and almost invariably the remarks are utterly banal. Sometimes, however, there is a spark that may begin to smoulder or, better, blow up into flames. The 'slitty eyed' remark was actually picked up by Alan Hamilton, *The Times* correspondent and shared with the colleagues: numbers give strength and veracity. The Duke was infuriated that the remark was reported – especially by the fact that it was overheard by *The Times* – and that it has had such a prolonged shelf life, but he has never denied or retracted it. On the Queen and Duke's visit to Ireland in 2011, the Duke listening to a very convoluted answer remarked: 'That sounds very Irish,' and this led to a conflab among the attendant press as to whether this constituted a gaffe, in the line of a vaguely racist remark about Irish people's volubility. The consensus of opinion on that occasion was that it did not. It is rare sport, this gaffe-hunting.

This is the royal round these days. Royal princes no longer touch the sick to ward off scrofula and do not – if they can avoid it – allow the multitude to watch them get dressed (perhaps unless they are Prince Harry). But they do press the flesh on walkabouts, visit the sick as they open hospitals and cheer for Britain when asked to do so. William and Kate's appearance at the Hollywood banquet at the end of their North American trip in July 2011 may not have produced tangible results, or ones that could not otherwise have been obtained – how many of those young British actors got a bit-part in a movie on the strength of bumping into a mogul at the Belasco? But they may have helped and the funds raised might just have assisted BAFTA's proselytising work on the west coast of California. If sometimes these public appearances seem like a never-ending political campaign – even longer and more draining than a US presidential election – that is because they are: an eternal quest for popularity and survival in a modern world awash with sentimentality and obsessed with celebrity. A search for relevance and usefulness, powered by a sense of duty, yes: but also a symbol and a need to be seen, to be on display in case people lose interest and drift away. Their lives may not depend on it, like those of their medieval predecessors, but the survival of the institution is what keeps them on the road.

Chapter 4

'Our great problem is democracy'

(2nd Viscount Esher)

D uring the first weekend of September 2014 there was alarming news at the breakfast table in Balmoral: for the first time in the lengthy, two-year-long referendum campaign in Scotland, just a fortnight before the vote, an opinion poll in the *Sunday Times* indicated that the 'Yes' side were marginally ahead. Previously, the 'No' campaigners supporting the union with England, Wales and Northern Ireland, led by the Labour former chancellor of the exchequer Alastair Darling, had been comforted and lulled into complacency by polls showing they were well in line for a comfortable majority. They had relied too much on a negative message, focusing on fears about what might happen economically if Scotland opted for independence and unanswered queries about the currency the new nation would use and whether it would be allowed to stay in the European Union without having to apply to join. Now the outcome was too close to call – Yes was two points ahead – and there was a possibility that the Queen would lose part of her realm. Since one of the chief concerns of any monarch is that they should hand on their country intact to their successor, this was a pretty fundamental concern, even though Alex Salmond, the Scottish Nationalist leader, anxious not to deter a single potential voter, had promised that the Queen would still be head of state, or at least Queen of Scots. Now the opinion poll was not just worrying for the Queen but deeply embarrassing for her prime minister, David Cameron, who happened to be staying with his wife Samantha at Balmoral that weekend.[9]

The Queen murmured cryptically over the breakfast table that she supposed Cameron would have a busy week and indeed he flew into panic mode back in Downing Street to energise the sagging No campaign, with more than a little belated help from the former prime minister Gordon Brown, whose impassioned warnings about the consequences of independence appear finally to have hit home with voters. In the meantime, the Queen herself was enlisted in the cause. She could not intervene directly, of course, even though it could be assumed what she thought, but there were urgent talks that week between the cabinet secretary Sir Jeremy Heywood and her private secretary Sir Christopher Geidt about what she might say that could be helpful in registering her concern. This was both highly unusual and sensitive territory for the monarch.

On her one previous intervention in a devolution debate in 1977 – the last time politically that the issue had arisen at Westminster – it was generally judged that she had teetered too close to the edge of making her own views known. Then, in a speech to both houses of parliament, she had said: 'I cannot forget that I was crowned Queen of the United

---

9 All prime ministers are invited to pay an annual weekend visit to Balmoral in late August or early September while the Queen is in residence. Sometimes they find it a bit of an ordeal, as Tony and Cherie Blair apparently did – all those valets and flunkies, not something they were used to then at all, nor semi-compulsory visits to the local Highland Games at Braemar. It did not, however, stop the Blairs from conceiving their youngest son Leo during their visit in 1999, as they rather tastelessly boasted later.

Kingdom of Great Britain and Northern Ireland. Perhaps this jubilee is a time to remind ourselves of the benefits which union has conferred at home and in our international dealings, on the inhabitants of all parts of the United Kingdom.' She got away with it then – the Callaghan government, which was fighting Scottish and Welsh separatism, had insisted the speech was not written by them and was only an expression of the Queen's personal opinion, but clearly such a statement could not be contemplated in 2014 ten days before the referendum. The Queen did, however, want something to get out. Any intervention might backfire, the royal family being regarded as an expensive and unnecessary English import by many committed nationalists, whatever Salmond might say, so it had to be carefully devised.

The solution was adroit and cunningly achieved. As usual, on the Sunday before the vote, 14 September, the royal party attended Crathie Church, the nearest kirk to Balmoral, and paused to speak to the small group of well-wishers on the way out. Also, as usual, reporters were kept on the very edge of earshot but went up afterwards to talk to the members of the group to whom the Queen had spoken. They were rewarded with an interesting apercu. She had been asked about the referendum and had replied: 'Well, I hope people will think very carefully about the future.' The terms were more demotic than the 1977 speech, they did not breach propriety or amount to an intervention – but they smuggled out into plain public view exactly what the Queen thought. They were also sufficient to lead coverage of the referendum the following day, which was not at all to the palace's displeasure: indeed they pointed journalists to the remarks. It is even conceivable that they were fed to the journalists by a junior female member of the palace staff insinuated into the crowd, as the Queen's words were recited precisely and verbatim, which is unusual to say the least since members of the public who have just met the Queen often struggle to remember even vaguely, let alone precisely, what she has said to them only a few moments earlier. One of the local reporters, Jim Lawson, told the *Guardian* later that the young woman had refused to give her name because, 'It's my job'. It is not entirely unknown for people not to wish to be quoted in such circumstances but it is unusual since they normally want their friends and relatives to know that they have met royalty. As a Whitehall source told the *Guardian* later: 'She knew exactly what she was doing. There are two possible responses on the referendum: one, you buy into this as a fantastic festival of democracy; or two, you suggest this is a decision filled with foreboding. So, by saying I hope people will think carefully, you imply the second. If they'd said: "What do you think of the referendum, Ma'am?" and she'd said: "Oh, it's lovely" that would have been very different. Without her taking a side, it cast just the right element of doubt over the nature of the decision.'

Such interventions cannot come too often, however subtle, but the potential division of the country was one occasion when it could be done. It certainly showed the Queen and her adviser using fast footwork and sharp reflexes, born of years of experience. No wonder Cameron – an altogether less adroit operator – was caught out telling the mayor of New York that the Queen had purred down the line when he telephoned her to tell her the outcome of the referendum the following week. Royalty Inc. is a much more subtle operator than that and its shrewdness derives from long experience. Cameron had to apologise for divulging even tangentially and inadvertently[10] a private conversation with the Sovereign.

---

10 Cameron was overheard by a television sound recordist speaking in triumphalist mode to the mayor of New York. The prime minister should have known better but could not help boasting.

Until 1914 most Europeans lived under monarchical governments, many of them autocratic, some absolutist. The First World War swept some of them away: Germany, Austria–Hungary, Russia and Turkey's sultanate. More were toppled subsequently: Bulgaria, Yugoslavia, Italy and Greece. Portugal's monarchy had already been overthrown in 1910 as France's had been initially in the French Revolution. Often it ended badly for the monarch: Umberto of Italy, assassinated by an anarchist in 1900; King Alexander and Queen Draga of Serbia, shot, disembowelled, hacked to pieces and tossed out of a window during a coup in 1903; Carlos of Portugal, assassinated in 1908; George I of Greece, shot in the back by an anarchist in 1913; the Tsar and all his family murdered by Bolshevik troops after the Russian Revolution in 1918; Alexander I of Yugoslavia shot during a state visit to France in 1934 (an assassination caught at close range by a newsreel cameraman). Luckier were those who merely escaped into exile, disinherited and despised, bound for obscurity but usually comfortably off.

Now just ten European monarchies remain: the Scandinavian royal houses of Denmark, Sweden and Norway; the Low Countries, Holland, Belgium and the Grand Duchy of Luxembourg; Spain (that rarity, a restored monarchy), the tiddlers Liechtenstein and Monaco; and Britain. All have learned survival skills, involving democracy. Mostly they survive because they represent something that their country respects: a sense of identification with their populations, a unifying cohesion and obedience to national values. They do not get above themselves, lead extravagant lifestyles or interfere in politics – or, if they do, their thrones rock. They marry commoners, or go out to work before they ascend the throne. They get their own shopping and live unostentatiously, emerging in uniform to take salutes only on national days. They even retire or abdicate when they have had enough. They can be symbols of national unity – sometimes, as in the case of the

Belgian royal family, the only institutions that the whole state accepts – and they know that they are there not because of some divine mystical compact, but at the pleasure of their populations.

Britain's monarchical history is rather longer than most of the rest (though Denmark's royal line dates back at least a thousand years to the days of Harald Bluetooth and Gorm the Old, who died in 958). The long struggle to define and usually curb or control the powers of the monarchy in the British Isles is at the heart of our history. Emerging from the regional tribal chieftains of the Dark Ages came kings who sought to regulate their territories more systematically, framing laws and regulations, co-opting local warlords. Then came the Normans and Plantagenets, who had to assert themselves against the powerful territorial nobles and bishops who controlled large parts of the kingdom, and at the same time to elicit money from them if they could to fight their wars. If the money ran out and campaigns were lost – as they were by John in the early thirteenth century – the King would find it hard to govern and the barons would rein him in and force concessions, as with the Magna Carta in 1215. The great charter was indeed intended to curtail the monarch's powers, requiring him to rule according to law and to make himself accountable under it. It was quickly repudiated by the King (and denounced by Pope Innocent III) but all subsequently have paid lip service to it. The document was in no sense a proto-democratic instrument but it was a limitation on royal arbitrary powers against the King's subjects – and has been cited as such ever since. The nobles demanded more equitable judicial processes, at least for themselves, and increasingly wanted to be consulted, particularly over the taxation they would have to find to pay for the monarch's foreign adventures. Kings needed advisers and civil servants to write their letters, count the money, run the courts and assess the dangers to their masters' throne. By the time of the Tudors a more central administration

– of sorts – was emerging at both national and local levels, and a settled succession. First Wolsey, then Cromwell, then Burghley, and later his son Robert Cecil, guided the monarch's government as administrators, courtiers and plotters: men who accumulated great power by providing largely self-effacing management of royal debts and policies, keeping an eye on potential rivals and traitors and guiding the Tudors through the pitfalls of domestic and international diplomacy.

Then the Stuarts' attempts to assert their divine right to rule appropriately, as they saw fit, culminated in disaster for a would-be absolutist dynasty. If alternative forms of government were still almost inconceivable, despite Oliver Cromwell's brief interregnum, parliament was ready to flex its muscles both in selecting the monarch and the religion of the country, and then in defining the King's powers and controlling the purse strings. Parliament not only altered the royal succession – so much for it being ordained by God – but also in the Bill of Rights of 1689, following the Glorious Revolution, restricted the powers of the monarch against parliamentarians and their rights. The beneficiaries of the revolution, William of Orange and his wife Mary, daughter of the deposed James II, became rulers through the will of parliament. The King was given a substantially larger grant than his predecessors but his powers were curbed. There was no more question of absolute regal rights. The bill established that kings could not interfere with elections, or with the courts and judiciary, and that they could only rule through parliament. They could not raise taxes for themselves without approval – were indeed to be dependent on parliament for funds – and the bill also laid down that Catholics could not succeed to the throne: a separate act also laid down that the sovereign had to swear to maintain the Protestant religion. Parliament had to be summoned at least every three years, and freedom of speech and debate were guaranteed.

The King could not maintain a standing army in peacetime without parliamentary consent.

Ministers, said George II in 1744, were the real kings of the country. The early Hanoverians needed parliamentary managers now to maintain the government of the country and keep them in funds, and strikingly the men they were forced to choose as ministers were not who they would have chosen for themselves, but men who could control the Commons. As the Hanoverians did not trust the Tories, who had been loyal to the Stuarts, they were obliged to call upon members of the Whig factions, the very party that had engineered the limitation of royal power in the Bill of Rights. Both George I and George II distrusted Robert Walpole, the Norfolk squire who became their chief minister, but he could manage the business of government and secure majorities in the Commons by manipulating patronage – every man had his price – to secure the king's finances and push through royal policies. He and his longest-lasting successors such as Pelham, North and the Pitts, father and son, recognised the growing importance of the House of Commons and chose to remain as MPs (though the elder Pitt eventually accepted a peerage). Walpole moved easily between Commons and Court, manipulating both and representing the King's interest in parliament and the Commons to the King as 'the minister for the House of Commons in the Closet'. When George II did not trust him, Walpole ruthlessly worked his influence on the King's wife, Queen Caroline, having spotted – unlike his rivals – that it was she who wielded more political sway with her husband than his mistress Henrietta Howard: Walpole had, as he said ungallantly, 'the right sow by the ear'. The 'Robinocracy', as it was called, lasted twenty-one years.

By the end of the eighteenth century, although a king might appoint or dismiss a government, he had to choose a prime minister who could command parliamentary support and approval. Both George II and his successor George III had to tolerate governments in which William Pitt the Elder served, though they detested him – 'the blackest of hearts' – for opposing the spending of British money to defend their Hanoverian estates. They needed to do so because Pitt's oratory dominated the Commons and they had to do so even when he attacked them, or even occasionally his own colleagues, because he was indispensible. Pitt's pugnacity and success in the Seven Years' War against France, also made him popular in the country – he claimed that 'the voice of the people' had brought him to office, a remarkable claim for someone who had represented the rotten borough of Old Sarum – but that too made him hard to ignore.

When the young King admitted: 'I will never make my inclinations alone nor even my own opinions the sole rule of my conduct in public measures. I will at all times consult my ministers and place in them as entire a confidence as the nature of this government can be supposed to require of me,' he possibly did so through gritted teeth, but it was no more than the truth. George III did undermine administrations and sack ministers, but when Lord North resigned at the end of the American War of Independence the King could not prevent him from going, because the administration had lost the support of the Commons. The King's long descent into madness further undermined the monarchy's political power.

A succession of kings ceded power and authority to prime ministers and they did so in return for pay. In 1760 George III reached a financial settlement which was to hold for 250 years: surrendering the hereditary revenues of crown-owned lands and receiving a (smaller) grant back from the government instead. The Hanoverians might veto legislation and summon or dismiss ministers, but it was not something monarchs could do lightly or, by the mid-nineteenth century, do at all. They could not, publicly at least, contradict their governments or countermand them and they had to grant a dissolution if requested in order that their government might secure a parliamentary majority. These parliamentary reforms and the gradual extension of the franchise meant they had to accept who the electorate bestowed on them, whatever their own political beliefs (and these were scarcely hidden and mainly Tory). The growth and strengthening of party organisation in the mid-nineteenth century also empowered governments and made it harder for the sovereign to peel off loyalists or create a loyalist corps of MPs as a king's party. So Queen Victoria had to accept the detested Mr Gladstone four times over a period of nearly thirty years; he held office for a fifth of her reign – and George V had to send for the not-so-dangerous socialists of the first Labour government in 1924. Britain was, in the provocative words of the nineteenth-century journalist Walter Bagehot, 'a secret republic'. Victoria would have been shocked by such a thought, had she ever read Bagehot, but she could not exercise power independently of her ministers and their parliamentary majorities.

Victoria had been the last monarch to try to choose a prime minister, or rather to retain one: Lord Melbourne in 1839, during the so-called Bedchamber Crisis, when the incoming Tory leader Robert Peel sought the dismissal of the Queen's more obviously Whig-supporting ladies-in-waiting. The teenage Queen had her way that time, but two years later had to accept Peel, who at that time she instinctively disliked, after he won a general election. The elderly Melbourne entranced the young Queen with a mixture of flattery, guile and grandfatherly advice, but, under Prince Albert's guidance, she came to accept and then admire Peel as 'the only person fitted to govern the country' in the 1840s. Nevertheless, much as she might regret it, in 1846 she could not prevent Peel's resignation after a parliamentary defeat and thereafter she had to accept the parliamentary leader who could command a Commons majority, as have all subsequent monarchs. It is known that Edward VII did not much care for Henry Campbell-Bannerman, the Glasgow industrialist who came in following the Liberal landslide of 1906 and that he resented Asquith's pressure to appoint Liberal peers to swamp the House of Lords, as later did George V, in order to get reforms through the Tory-dominated second chamber. George V, deeply conservative, found that he could cope quite well with Labour ministers and George VI managed to get on with Clement Attlee after the Second World War, though he found himself at a disadvantage in not being able to discuss partridge shooting with him.

There is no doubt that Victoria and her successors were conservative – with a big 'C' as well as a small one – by temperament as well as inclination. Their office and the nature of the institution instinctively requires it, and that means accepting the status quo established by election results. Just occasionally, there have been glimpses of partisanship in action, most notably when George VI and Queen Elizabeth invited Neville Chamberlain to appear on the balcony at Buckingham Palace in front of cheering crowds when the prime minister supposedly returned bearing 'peace with honour' following the Munich Agreement in 1938. Both King and Queen (and much of the country) were supporters of appeasement; but they should not have done it.

There is some private wiggle-room, occasionally, in confidential suggestions about ministerial appointments. It is thought that George VI probably influenced Attlee to choose Ernest Bevin rather than the temperamental and impulsive Hugh Dalton as his foreign secretary after the war. In so far as he had to mingle with socialists, the King rather liked the salty, down-to-earth Bevin[11] and enjoyed his company

---

11   Asked by the King where he gained his political astuteness, the former Bristol milkman is said to have replied: 'I plucked it from the 'edgerows of hexperience.'

and he was certainly correct in his judgement of character over the waspish Dalton. He seems to have got on quite well with Attlee, too, though their meetings – two shy, reticent men together – must have been excruciating.

But that is as far as it has gone – the King did not dictate the prime minister's choice of ministers. There is occasional and entertaining guess work, but any revelations about Queen Elizabeth II's relations with her governments may have to wait for decades to be revealed. Despite Peter Morgan's play *The Audience*, about the Queen's weekly meetings with some of her prime ministers, very little has emerged – it is more a parlour game of suppositions and gossip. Only some suggestions seem likely: that her earlier prime ministers patronised the young queen and that her later ones have been somewhat mothered by someone who has much more experience on the world's stage than they have. The constitutional historian Peter Hennessy said: 'She has been in receipt of every intelligence briefing paper and significant cabinet document since 1952. Everything has passed across her desk. It's absolutely breathtaking – she is a walking repository of modern British history. I think all her male prime ministers have fallen a bit in love with her.'

The young Queen was clearly in awe of her first prime minister, Churchill, who regarded himself as an almost grandfatherly figure towards her, and she certainly did not challenge or question his determination to stay in office even into his eighties and after he had been largely incapacitated by ill health. Later she was patronised and manipulated by Harold Macmillan, but she was probably relieved when he determined his successor should be Alec Douglas Home, a Scottish landowner with whom she could talk countryside pursuits. She was flattered by Harold Wilson and treated with avuncular courtliness by Jim Callaghan – though it was he who admitted that when he had asked her for advice he was told sharply: 'That's for you to decide. That is what you are paid for.' It must certainly be true to say that Margaret Thatcher never asked her advice, for had she done so, the Queen might well have urged her against the social divisiveness of some of her policies. 'Are you *sure*?' she may have said to a prime minister who never publicly expressed doubt. With Tony Blair there seems to have been a degree of mutual incomprehension, though he helped her considerably with – inevitably – presentational advice during the Diana crisis. David Cameron, a distant kinsman, has surely been more callow and inexperienced than any of his predecessors. This though is all quite speculative: no word of criticism, of like or dislike, has ever seeped out from under the Queen's door. If she has not offered them advice, what she has done is listen to the angst and enjoy the political gossip.

The weekly meeting, on Wednesday evenings, has been the one chance that a prime minister has to mull over the events of the week in complete confidence with the head of state. It usually lasts about an hour to an hour and a half, no one else is present and no notes are taken. The audience is essentially a chat, but that does not mean that no business is conducted. Harold Wilson, Labour prime minister in the 1960s and 1970s, said that the Queen was the only person who did not leak information and who was not after his job. While she meets the head of government upstairs, downstairs in the private secretary's office, officials meet and mirror the conversation between themselves. One said: 'That is how you get to know your opposite number, the prime minister's private secretary from Downing Street. You know them and become friends. You go to see them in Whitehall and they come and stay at Balmoral when the prime minister goes there too. We are probably discussing the same things as they are talking about upstairs.'

Bagehot astutely recognised – and more cogently expressed than anyone before or since – in his book on the English Constitution, published in 1867, that the monarch had ceded real power for ceremonial and dynastic power and that this gave the king, or in his case queen, a real and lasting authority. Their best advantage was to have security of tenure. The point was not to have an elected figurehead like a president, who could be changed, but a symbolic, dynastic figure, placed at the head of society and above politics, who would be regarded with a sort of awe: a stable, apparently unchanging and unchallenged sovereign, seemingly powerful but actually powerless. It was the great constitutional secret: 'The secrecy is...essential to the utility of English royalty as it now is. Above all things our royalty is to be reverenced and if you begin to poke about it you cannot reverence it. When there is a select committee on the Queen the charm of royalty will be gone. Its mystery is its life. We must not let in daylight upon magic.' What the monarch did have was three rights – to be consulted by ministers, to encourage them and to warn: 'A king of great sense and sagacity would want no others.'

The institution's continuing influence would persist only if it did not get involved in partisanship and did not throw its weight around: its occupations should be grave, formal, important, but never exciting: 'Nothing to stir eager blood, awaken high imagination, work off wild thoughts...' The Queen had no veto: 'She must sign her own death warrant if the two Houses unanimously send it up to her.' For this purpose, it was best not to have an imaginative or dynamic head of state: 'A constitutional sovereign must in the common course of government be a man of but common ability...Theory and experience both teach that the education of a prince can be but a poor education and that a royal family will generally have less ability than other families,' just like the 'retired widow and unemployed youth' who at that moment occupied the throne and the succession. Best would be to have a young and inexperienced prince with a capacity for diligence – a situation, though Bagehot did not know it, that would take another seventy years to come to pass – or at least one who was idle and so would do little harm. He added: 'It is easy to imagine, upon a constitutional throne, an active and meddling fool who always acts when he should not, who never acts when he should, who warns his ministers against their judicious measures, who encourages them in their injudicious measures... such a king would be the tool of others; that favourites should guide him; that mistresses should corrupt him; that the atmosphere of a bad Court should be used to degrade free government.' So far at least the House of Windsor appears mostly to have taken those strictures to heart.

The paradox is that the monarch is nominally in charge and everything is done in her name: it is Her Majesty's government, Her Majesty's ministers, Her Majesty's armed forces, Her Majesty's laws and law courts; she signs all legislation into law, she calls parliament and prorogues it before an election, her prime minister offers his resignation to her and a new prime minister is summoned to take office, but she has no power to change any of it. The royal prerogative whereby she supposedly has powers to act alone is never exercised except on the advice of ministers with the consent of parliament. She is a cipher and if she were not – if she suddenly decided to dismiss the government or refused to sign a bill of which she disapproved, or even to influence legislation going through its discussion stages – she would be gone. Any show of open partisanship would be disastrous: it would destroy the magical illusion that the monarch is the 'dear dad' – or in the current case 'grandmum' – of the whole country. We can guess how we think the Queen might vote (if she had a vote, which she doesn't). But we can't be sure and there lies the power of and difference from a presidency. A president whose views were known – because he or she had had to stand for election – would almost automatically alienate half the population. A politician – and it would almost certainly be a politician, or at least a candidate acting politically – would need a platform and would have a past track record and an agenda. It would maybe shape his or her performance in government prior to standing. But they would not suddenly become neutral. And they would look ridiculous as a ceremonial figure. The pomp and circumstance that people like so much would be diminished.

The sacred mystery of royal power is that there is now none, or very little. What they have is influence, but only in so far as they go along with the elected government – they could not openly oppose it. The constitutional settlement is easily understood in Britain (if only semi-consciously by most people) but often not so abroad. When the Labour government's civil partnerships legislation was passed, allowing gay couples to go through a conjugal civil union, I received furious emails from the United States – where at the time gay marriage and the appointment of an openly gay man, the Revd Gene Robinson, to a bishopric were hotly contested – demanding to know why the Queen had allowed such pernicious legislation to pass. Wasn't she head of the Church of England? How could she endorse such an ungodly, heretical measure? The answer was quite simple: she had no choice. The same emails often asked why Rowan Williams, the then archbishop of Canterbury, did not insist on getting himself carted off to the Tower of London by opposing the unchristian, wicked law more forcefully. But that was another story.

Chapter 5

'An entire effacement of self'

(Lord Stamfordham, private secretary to George V)

*I*f the monarchy's constitutional position has evolved to leave them the trappings of power but not the substance, that does not mean that they have been inactive on their own behalf. A number of pragmatic decisions, some selfish, have acted to preserve their position. During the First World War, the title of the royal house – their very surname – was changed from Saxe-Coburg-Gotha, inherited from Prince Albert, to the much more English-sounding Windsor in the summer of 1917. This came as the war approached its third anniversary and anti-German feeling in Britain was running high – nor did it help that the country was currently being bombed by Gotha bombers and being starved of food by a naval blockade. No one could claim that the King was not whole-heartedly behind the war effort, but there were rumblings of criticism, even from the prime minister Lloyd George, who had started to talk facetiously about his little German friend, the King. Hitherto, George V, who made the decision, had remained rather impervious to the sort of populist belligerence that had already cost the German-born First Lord of the Admiralty Louis of Battenberg and the German-educated Lord Chancellor Haldane their jobs. He had also opposed the removal of the Kaiser and his family's Knights of the Garter banners from St George's Chapel in Windsor and the stripping of their honorary appointments on the grounds that it was a mean and ungentlemanly gesture. He eventually agreed to do so only under pressure from his mother, admitting that 'otherwise the people would have stormed the Chapel.' The change in surname was not accomplished without some thought and anguish. The King wondered about using one of the family's alternative Germanic titles – would Guelph or Wettin perhaps be less contentious? Or should they revive an old royal monicker such as Plantagenet, Tudor, Stuart, York or Lancaster? But George eventually settled for his private secretary Lord Stamfordham's suggestion of Windsor as an alternative – and the decision was warmly greeted in the press. It at least had the merit of being thoroughly and recognisably English: 'A Good Riddance' said *Punch* to the old title under a cartoon showing the King sweeping away assorted Germanic regalia with a yard broom. The Kaiser commented sardonically when he heard about the name change that he was looking forward to seeing a performance of *The Merry Wives of Saxe-Coburg-Gotha*. The Bavarian count Albrecht von Monteglas, demonstrating the style that cost many a nobleman his status, was rather more scathing: 'The true royal tradition died on that day in 1917 when, for a mere war, King George V changed his name.'

More pragmatic still, not to say venal, was George V's refusal during the same period, the summer of 1917, to help rescue his cousin the Tsar, Nicholas II, after he had been forced to abdicate during the Russian Revolution. The British wartime government was blamed for many years for the fact that the Tsar and his family were kept out of Britain, but were left being held prisoner in Russia, and were eventually captured by the Bolsheviks and shot in the summer of 1918. The true story took many decades to come out – finally in Kenneth Rose's biography of the King published in the 1980s – but essentially the correspondence shows that while initially Lloyd George and his government had been willing to give the Russian royal family asylum, they were persuaded not to do so by the King himself, through his private secretary Stamfordham. It was a pretty cynical game. Initially after the February revolution, when a moderate provisional government had taken over in Petrograd, George had sent cousin Nicky a sympathetic telegram: 'My thoughts are constantly with you and I shall always remain your true and devoted friend, as you know I have been in the past.' Anxious to get the Tsar and his family out of Russia, the foreign minister Pavel Milyukov wrote urgently to London asking if Britain would take them. He received an encouraging reply via the British ambassador, with the only proviso that the Russian family must have the means to support themselves financially. But then the King stepped in. A week after the offer, Stamfordham wrote to the foreign secretary Arthur Balfour that George V had had second thoughts: 'His Majesty cannot help doubting not only on account of the dangers of the voyage, but on general grounds of expediency, whether it is advisable that the Imperial Family should take up their residence in this country.'

The King appears to have taken fright at the possible effect on public opinion of giving refuge to a foreign autocrat and especially to his unpopular German wife Alexandra ('not only a Boche by birth but in sentiment'), even if she was one of Queen Victoria's granddaughters. Stamfordham wrote again: 'From the first the King has thought the presence of the Imperial Family (especially of the Empress) will raise all sorts of difficulties and I feel sure that you appreciate how awkward it will be for our Royal Family . . . the subject has become more or less public property and . . . people are either assuming that it has been initiated by the king, or deprecating the very unfair position in which His Majesty will be placed if the arrangement is carried out.' And again the same day: 'He must beg me to represent to the Prime Minister that from all he hears and reads in the press, the residence in this country of the ex-Emperor and Empress would be strongly resented by the public and would undoubtedly compromise the position of the King and Queen.' In fairness to George V he possibly did not imagine the carnage that the Bolsheviks would later wreak on the entire Russian royal family. The government was left making half-hearted suggestions that the Romanovs might move to France, Spain or Denmark at someone else's expense, but within weeks the provisional government had been overthrown by the Bolsheviks and the chance was lost. When a year later the family was assassinated, George V wrote in his diary: 'It is too horrible and shows what fiends these Bolshevists are. For poor Alicky, perhaps it was best so. But those poor innocent children!' Neither he, nor his advisers, it seems, felt a twinge of conscience and he attended a memorial service for the family at London's Russian Orthodox church. Stamfordham blamed the Kaiser for not making the Tsar's safety a condition of the peace treaty the Russians had signed at Brest-Litovsk and was unconcerned to see the government rather than the King accused of moral cowardice. Maybe the Tsar could not have been rescued, probably allowing him into Britain would have been unpopular. But clearly what primarily motivated George V was fear for the safety of his own throne. Interestingly, when Rose submitted his text to the palace sixty years later, the Queen did not share her advisers' doubts about the suitability of the story for publication and noted that it should go ahead.

Stamfordham was one of a series of private secretaries since the late nineteenth century who have shaped a vital office, which is that of the monarch's closest adviser.[12] The private secretary is independent of party politics, appointed by the monarch, not the government or the civil service, and their role is to safeguard both the constitutional position of the sovereign and the institution itself – the latter ultimately being more important than the person, as was shown during the abdication crisis in 1936. They have to keep the monarch informed of what is going on from day to day. Their job, seeing the monarch each morning; liaising with the government of the day – and informally with the opposition; keeping ministers, especially the prime minister, in touch with the view from the palace; dealing with correspondence; organising the office; writing speeches; arranging the diary; and most importantly advising on what to do, is crucial. Only rarely does this backstairs influence emerge, as with the referendum intervention. And it is lonely. As Harold Laski wrote in 1942:

> *He is the confidant of all ministers, but he must never leave the impression that he is anybody's man. He must intrude without ever seeming to intrude... Receiving a thousand secrets he must discriminate between what may emerge and what shall remain obscure... It is a life passed amid circumstances in which the most trifling incident may lead to major disaster... The royal secretary walks on a tight-rope below which he is never unaware that an abyss is yawning... A bad Private*

---

12 The private secretary is only one of the monarch's officials, of course. There is also the lord chamberlain who organises the ceremonials and the palace, the lord steward, in charge of the household, even the master of the horse – all posts still held by peers – and that is before you get to the gentlemen-at-arms, the ladies of the bedchamber and the mistress of the robes, a post which has been held by the Duchess of Grafton, who is now ninety-five, since 1967. These latter posts are largely ceremonial, but others require at least occasional work: the master of the Queen's music, poet laureate, astronomer royal, pipe to the sovereign, bargemaster, keeper of the jewel house and warden of swans. In Scotland there are even more quaint posts: the master carver, the historiographer royal, and the painter and limner (interestingly, Dame Elizabeth Blackadder, since 2001). The post of armour bearer and squire of Her Majesty's body, however, appears to be in abeyance.

Secretary, who was rash or indiscreet or untrustworthy might easily make the system of constitutional monarchy unworkable.

On top of all this, the private secretary is also the monarch's secretary and adviser for each of the Commonwealth countries where he or she is head of state.

One former private secretary said to me:

Most of us have done eight or nine years in recent times – it is not good to go on longer: it is a very stressful job, especially now with the tyranny of emails. The private secretary and his deputy see the Queen every morning when she is in London and you would be working into the evening most days, dealing with correspondence and working on speeches. You get to know the realms where she is head of state: you would go on recces for royal visits, stay with the governor general, and then accompany the Queen on the tours themselves, meeting the prime ministers, so you build up a network of what's going on that way. You are also sworn of the Privy Council[13], so you can make up the numbers if a decision has to be reached in a hurry: I think that happened when the Falklands War broke out over a weekend.

Nowadays the Palace uses head-hunters, but they did not do that in my day. You have to remember, yours is the key advisory job from day to day and crises can bubble up very suddenly as they did following Diana's death for instance. You can never tell: when the decision was made to pay tax in 1992, for instance, although the ground had been prepared and there had been discussions, the Queen just said yes. But the flag

---

13 The Privy Council is the formal group of senior figures, mainly politicians, but also archbishops and other appointees, who advise the sovereign formally. There are about six hundred, though only three are required to make up a quorum.

issue, about flying the flag at half-mast on Buckingham Palace after Diana's death – that was unexpectedly difficult. The Press went absolutely berserk. You just can't tell. When things need to change – that can be frightfully awkward, ceremonial things – that sort. We've cut back on quite a lot of that: not so many hangers-on in the procession at the State Opening of Parliament – that sort of thing.

The Queen's very punctilious, you know, and she's the expert because she had been doing it for so long, so she notices when things go wrong. There are no shortcuts – you have to be on top of everything and know your brief. She won't criticise directly but she'll look at you and the worst she'll say is: 'Are you sure?' That is when you have got to know. But generally, she's a very considerate employer: if she rings you up at home on a Sunday, or makes you late, she always apologises. But I think it is always best to work with someone who has high standards, don't you?

The role of private secretary first emerged as a post independent of government in the early nineteenth century, to help the ailing George III and was regarded with suspicion by ministers because they had to go through the secretary to get to the King and he was unaccountable to them. Prince Albert acted effectively as private secretary to Victoria and it was only after his death that the job became formalised.

They have tended to be naturally self-effacing, diplomatic figures, almost invariably with a public school and military background, though a smattering – increasing in number in recent years – have also been to Oxbridge. By and large they have not separated the court from what has been characterised as a certain 'tweediness' of both dress and outlook: maybe not tweedy in the sense of dressing for the country, except at Balmoral and Sandringham, but perhaps in attitudes, outlook and priorities, distant and insulated from the world beyond the palace walls. A monarch who relied merely on their private secretary to keep abreast of opinion in the country would find themselves distinctly out of touch. The similarities of class and personality are perhaps not surprising given that they have been largely from backgrounds with which the royals have felt most comfortable, but also most have needed private means to supplement the relatively low pay until recently – the royals never having been notably generous payers to their servants.

In these circumstances, too, there has been something of a dynastic element: a brace of Ponsonbys serving successive monarchs for sixty-five years; Michael Adeane, whose mother was the daughter of Lord Stamfordham, becoming in turn private secretary to the Queen and then his son Edward serving Prince Charles; and Robert Fellowes, brother-in-law to Princess Diana also acting as the Queen's private secretary in his time. There is an air of family retainers here. Only relatively recently has administrative competence or political and strategic vision been deemed the primary qualification; earlier private secretaries sometimes found difficulty sorting out the important from the trivial. Thus, Sir Clive Wigram wondering at the height of the First World War whether female munitions workers should be required to remove their gloves when being introduced to the Queen during a factory visit, or worrying what colour would be most suitable for the crown printed at the top of royal writing paper.

The private secretaries have been largely unknown to the public, but their close personal relationship with the sovereign has made their guidance of critical importance in moments of crisis. Naturally, they are supposed to be politically neutral. Perhaps surprisingly, however, several of the early private secretaries in Queen Victoria and Edward VII's time held different political views to their employers, which may in itself have been an advantage in steering the monarch away from rash decisions. In particular, Sir Henry Ponsonby, Queen Victoria's private secretary from 1870 almost until his death in 1895 – the man who first shaped the office, having previously been Prince Albert's secretary – was a Liberal who frequently saved the increasingly reactionary queen from herself. Even more strikingly, Ponsonby's wife Mary was a feminist and an intellectual (one of the founders of Girton College, Cambridge) and Victoria, who could not abide cleverness and advanced views especially in women, was still pleased to have him easing the daily routine of business.

He toned down her more offensive and rancorous missives to Prime Minister Gladstone – and made sure that the cabinet was not aware of them – and also smoothed the fractious and often rancorous relationships between the Queen and her children. Apparently his sense of humour and discreet irreverence was a help here. Almost as importantly, if frustratingly for historians, he also deftly prevented the Queen from publishing her effusive memoir of her Highland ghillie John Brown following his death in 1883 and made sure that Brown's letters to her were also burned: their very existence if known would have caused a public scandal.[14] He also tried to head off the growing influence of the old lady's new favourite, the young Indian servant Hafiz Abdul Karim, known as the Munshi who arrived in 1887. Ponsonby's whole career involved what his successor Arthur Bigge – Lord Stamfordham from 1911 – described as 'an entire effacement of self' which extended to prolonged periods staying away from his family in the 'severe dreariness' of Balmoral, which he loathed.

The next two private secretaries, Sir Francis Knollys and Stamfordham were rivals, professionally, personally and – critically – politically at the time of the monarchy's first great constitutional crisis of the twentieth

---

14 Randall Davidson, the dean of Windsor and future archbishop of Caterbury, weighed in by telling her that the humbler classes would not be worthy enough to read it.

century, the Liberal Asquith government's attempt to prevent the Tory majority in the House of Lords from frustrating its reform programme in 1911. Knollys, a Liberal, had been Edward VII's private secretary from long before he became King, and supplanted Bigge, who had been Ponsonby's deputy and succeeded him as the Queen's private secretary until her death, whereupon Bigge became secretary to the heir to the throne, George. The constitutional crisis between the government and the Lords had begun when the Lords refused to pass Lloyd George's 'people's budget' in 1909 while Edward was still alive, but it was still bubbling along when George V became King in May 1910 and a general election only deepened the crisis when the Liberals lost their overall majority in the Commons. Asquith remained in power with the support of the Irish Nationalists, but to break the impasse with the other chamber he decided to threaten the obstructionist Tories in the Lords with a mass creation of Liberal peers, for which he needed the King's support. George was not being asked to create the peers – though a list of five hundred names was drawn up, including celebrities such as Thomas Hardy, Edward Elgar, J.M. Barrie and Robert Baden-Powell – but Asquith needed to make the threat credible by asking the King privately to promise that he would do so if the Tories continued their obstructionism after a further election. Bigge – a staunch Tory – advised the King that he should not make a political promise, but only act on the prime minister of the day's advice if there was no other option. This might well have drawn the monarch, who was still very inexperienced though of a conservative disposition, deep into the political crisis, publicly precipitating the downfall of the Liberal government and placing him in the potential position of asking the Tories to form a minority administration – which would have been seen as a highly partisan act. Had there then been a further general election – the third in eighteen months – the King's position would have been central to the campaign, and if the Liberals won George would have been publicly humiliated and deeply compromised. It was certainly, as Bigge, said: 'A bold, fearless and open line of action' and one fraught with risk for the King.

Knollys had made little secret of his support for the government – 'I am, as you know, a Liberal and whenever I have been in the House of Lords, I have invariably voted for the Government ever since they have been in office ... Of course, you will understand I am only stating my own *individual* views,' he had written to Margot Asquith, the prime minister's wife at the time of the 1909 budget, which had started the political crisis. He accordingly advised the opposite course, telling the King that he could constitutionally accept what Asquith's cabinet proposed. He even passed on to Asquith, highly irregularly, the details of a private conversation he had had with A.J. Balfour, the Conservative leader; a private secretary is not supposed to, under any circumstances, act as the agent of the prime minister or anyone other than the sovereign. What he did not tell the King though was that the Tories were indeed prepared to form a minority government if the Liberals resigned. This left George believing he had no option but to make the promise and, in the event, after Asquith made the swamping plan clear, the Lords finally backed down without the Liberal peers having to be chosen. But the manoeuvring left the King feeling misled and railroaded: 'I now see what a blunder I made then. I did it entirely on Knollys' advice,' he told the archbishop of Canterbury in 1913. Arguably, though, Knollys had saved George V from himself and preserved the monarchy's apparent political neutrality. Within a couple of years however, he had been forced to retire and Bigge – now Lord Stamfordham – a much more congenial figure to the King, had succeeded him.

Stamfordham was an unusual person to become private secretary in that he had originally come from outside court circles. The son of a Northumberland vicar, educated at Rossall, a minor Lancashire public school, he first came to the favourable attention of Queen Victoria when he was summoned as a young army officer to tell her about the death of his colleague, the Prince Imperial, descendant of Napoleon, then serving with the British army, who was killed by Zulus during the colonial war in southern Africa in 1879. Small, dapper and modest, Stamfordham did not leave royal service again until his death more than fifty years later, serving first as assistant private secretary to the Queen, then her last private secretary, then George's private secretary when he was Duke of York and finally private secretary again to him as King.

Stamfordham was diligently at the King's side throughout the First World War, during which he lost his only son who was killed in action, though he never quite regained the confidence of the Liberal government. Lloyd George in particular customarily made him wait on a wooden chair in the hall at 10 Downing Street when Stamfordham came to see him on royal business. Stamfordham did not seem to mind: 'We are all servants here,' he said, 'although some are more important than others.' He directed his punctiliousness to official business and important matters such as etiquette and the correctness of court dress. Nothing much escaped him: during the Battle of Loos in 1915, he rebuked Asquith for failing to consult the King about the appointment of the next dean of Ripon. But, as far as the King was concerned, his instincts for the monarchy's preservation were sound, as illustrated over the refusal to rescue the Tsar and his family. After the Russian Revolution, he advised George V: 'We must endeavour to induce the thinking working classes, Socialist and others, to regard the crown, not as a mere figure-head ... but as a living power for good, with receptive faculties welcoming information affecting the interests and social well-being of all classes,' – a rule the Windsors have followed ever since. It was Stamfordham, too, who urged the King not to send for Lord Curzon, the foreign secretary, to become prime minister in May 1923

when Andrew Bonar Law was dying from throat cancer and to appoint
the much less senior ministerial figure Stanley Baldwin instead. Curzon
was the most senior and experienced figure in the Tory government
and certainly thought he should be called upon, but was told instead
that it was no longer possible to appoint a prime minister who was
sitting in the House of Lords, not the Commons: an innovative and
democratic change in keeping with the post-war mood.[15]

Stamfordham welcomed the first Labour ministers to come to the
palace in 1924 at a time when the King was rather nervous of their
possible Bolshevist tendencies, which might be shockingly demonstrated
if they refused to wear court dress – the full fig with gold braid, cocked
hats, swords and knee britches – or morning suits and top hats.
Stamfordham smoothed the way, advising Ramsay MacDonald that if
he and his colleagues did not possess such outfits they might hire them
from 'Messrs Moss Bros, which is, I believe a well-known and
dependable firm.' And they did, much to the King's relief: Ramsay
MacDonald, who said 'a gold coat means nothing to me' nevertheless
wore one. Perhaps somewhat to his surprise, the King found he got
on rather well with many of the Labour figures: not the intellectuals
like the Webbs, but certainly the more working-class ministers –
J.H. 'Jimmy' Thomas, the former railwayman, was a particular chum
and the two enjoyed swapping earthy jokes.

Stamfordham died suddenly in 1931, still private secretary at

---

15 That was not the only reason Curzon was not chosen: his arrogant and supercilious manner
alienated voters and, more importantly, many of his colleagues consulted by Stamfordham.
It was a previous Tory leader, Arthur Balfour, who advised the King against him. 'Will dear
George be chosen?' a society lady guest asked Balfour after he returned from the palace to
the house party he had been attending in Norfolk. 'No,' he replied urbanely. 'Dear George
will not.' When the woman suggested Curzon would be terribly upset, Balfour murmured:
'I don't know. After all, even if he has lost the hope of glory, he still has the means of Grace.'
Grace was Curzon's rich American wife. The woman was quite right – dear George was
terribly upset at being passed over for a provincial middle-class ironmaster's son.

eighty-one, and the King wrote in his diary: 'I shall miss him terribly. His loss is irreparable.' He was succeeded by his deputy, Clive Wigram, who had been assistant secretary throughout the King's reign. Wigram was very different from Stamfordham: large, bouncy and sporty, though he shared his predecessor's military background in the Royal Artillery. 'He is always very genial, but it seems to take a good deal to make him understand things,' remarked Sir John Reith of the BBC. His heartiness and fondness for cricketing metaphors indicated a conservative turn of mind: on meeting a group of foreign ambassadors at Windsor Castle, he responded: 'On hearing them I thank God more and more that I am an Englishman.' He was, said his deputy Fritz Ponsonby (Henry's son), a man whose horizon was limited: 'He does not seem to be able to take a broad-minded view of the many perplexing questions that come here. He has the true British contempt for all foreigners, which is now rather out of date and his political views are those of the ordinary officer at Aldershot.'

Yet, Wigram did have some positive views about the future of the monarchy. To save it from Bolshevism in a period of industrial unrest, at a time when mention of the King was hissed at left-wing rallies and when the court was in danger of being strangled by its own stiffness and obsession with etiquette, as deputy private secretary he had advised that the royal family should get out more: go on overseas tours, visit factories, even appoint a press officer. This was not what some members of the court, who he called 'the palace troglodytes', wanted to hear. As he wrote to the archbishop of Canterbury in 1919, they 'shudder when any changes are proposed and consider any modification of the present court functions as lowering to the dignity and status of the sovereign. They are hard nuts to deal with, as from their long years of attendance they carry a good deal of influence. We are up against them, but the barriers have to be broken down if the Monarchy is to live.' He wanted the court to be open to more classes of the community and to drop some of the dress conventions:

> *People of all classes should have an opportunity of coming into Buckingham Palace and its gardens. I should like to see something started along the lines of White House receptions – school teachers, civil servants etc. should all have the entrée. I go as far as saying that trains and feathers at Court should be abolished. We have to look ahead and it is quite on the cards that the next government will be a Labour government. I feel that there is no place now for any duds...the organisation and inner workings of some of the departments are puerile and pre-Victorian.*

Such changes indeed proved much too revolutionary. Although the palace did, briefly, appoint a press officer, the experiment was abandoned in 1931 and not revived until the closing stages of the Second World War, a quarter of a century after Wigram's note was written. The requirement for women presented at court to trail trains from their shoulders and wear feathers in their hair was only abandoned in 1939.

Wigram's most decisive intervention was to urge acceptance of a national government in August 1931, the interwar point at which Labour's great betrayal took place. This was when Ramsay MacDonald led a rump of his Labour cabinet into coalition with the Conservatives and Liberals in order to introduce reductions in spending, specifically a ten per cent cut in unemployment benefit in an attempt to reduce a spiralling budget deficit. The cuts were demanded by American bankers before they would agree to giving the British government a loan to ease the financial crisis. The Labour government split on the issue and the prime minister told his colleagues that he was going to resign. But it was at that point of the crisis that the King insisted that MacDonald should remain prime minister as 'the only person who could carry the country through.'[16] That was rather a turnaround from his fears about a socialist prime minister six years earlier, but it was the King who stiffened MacDonald's resolve to remain prime minister when MacDonald was 'scared and unbalanced' – Wigram's words – about staying on. The King had certainly taken soundings from his personal financial adviser, Sir Edward Peacock, who was also a director of the Bank of England and partner at Barings Bank (and a senior Conservative) about how to resolve the crisis that day and Peacock was still lurking at the palace when MacDonald was summoned. But it was George V himself who urged, cajoled and flattered the prime minister into staying on and forming a unity government to carry out the cuts. The man who had gone to the palace scared, telling colleagues he was throwing in his hand, came out of the meeting 'with head erect and confidence restored'. It was also the King who initiated talks at the palace the following day between MacDonald and the other party leaders, Stanley Baldwin for the Conservatives and Herbert Samuel of the Liberals, which resulted in the formation of the new administration. The national government thus came about following the use of the royal prerogative, with the King summoning his preferred minister and brokering the discussions between the party leaders, which led to their cooperation. MacDonald was never forgiven by his party and if the King's role has now been largely forgotten, at the time Labour MPs accused him of interfering in political affairs. With the prime minister threatening to resign and the opposition parties unwilling to form a

---

16 The King's discussion with MacDonald had echoes of Queen Victoria's flattery of Sir Robert Peel eighty-six years earlier in December 1845 during the Irish famine crisis. Peel's administration subsequently forced through the abolition of the Corn Laws in the teeth of virulent opposition within his own party, but with the full support of the Queen and Prince Albert. Peel shared the Queen's view of his own abilities, perhaps rather more than MacDonald did of his own in 1931.

government on their own at a time of national economic crisis, however, it is difficult to see how the King could have stood back completely. Characteristically, Wigram referred to the crisis, weeks after he succeeded Stamfordham, as 'my first test match'.

Wigram was also responsible for the successful silver jubilee celebrations in 1935, which he saw as 'a dream – a miracle arranged by Providence', but which was, more prosaically, a working-out of his proposal that the monarch should be out among his people more. Six months later he was also by the royal bedside in Sandringham as the dying King – allegedly – uttered his last words: 'How goes the Empire?' Or, possibly, though less quotable at the time: 'Bugger Bognor.'

The private secretary stayed on for the first few months of Edward VIII's reign, but the two were never going to see eye to eye. Wigram already thought that the new King was irresponsible, bordering on insane – he probably knew that the old King had thought the same – and by the time of the abdication crisis he had retired to an agreeable grace-and-favour job as lieutenant-governor of Windsor Castle with an apartment in the Norman Tower. There he busied himself in converting the garden in the castle moat and developing a black dahlia.

Wigram's successor, in post at the time of the abdication crisis, was Sir Alexander Hardinge, a scion of the Kentish aristocratic family who owned Penshurst Place and whose father had been Viceroy of India, a man who was entirely unsympathetic to Edward VIII and had written a letter to the King urging that Wallis Simpson should leave the country immediately. He was unsurprisingly excluded thereafter from the decreasing circle of advisers to whom the King listened. Hardinge was perhaps the first to realise that the only alternative was for the King to abdicate if he would not give up Wallis. But it did not help him with Edward either that he had shown his letter to both Stanley Baldwin, the prime minister, and Geoffrey Dawson, the editor of *The Times*, before he gave it to the King. Hardinge seems to have rubbed Edward's successors, George VI and Queen Elizabeth, up the wrong way, too. Anthony Eden's secretary Oliver Harvey wrote: 'The Queen was determined to get him out.' If so, there may have been a reason. Harold Macmillan, who as the government's minister resident in North Africa met him during a visit by the King to the troops in June 1943, wrote: 'Alec Hardinge seems to me beyond the pale. He is idle, supercilious, without a spark of imagination or vitality.' He left the royal service shortly afterwards.

Instead of Hardinge, during the weeks of the abdication crisis, Edward relied entirely on an old Oxford friend, the barrister Walter Monckton, who became the mediator between Baldwin and the King. Monckton seems to have filled the role with discretion and tact, perhaps precisely because he came from outside traditional court circles or Edward's own personal entourage, and shuttled ceaselessly between Downing Street and Fort Belvedere, the King's residence during the crisis. He, too, pressed for Mrs Simpson to be sent abroad and, as a quid pro quo, urged the government to pass legislation to speed up her divorce settlement with her husband Ernest Simpson – which Baldwin declined to do. The possibility of a morganatic marriage was also briefly discussed – by which Edward might marry Wallis but she would not be queen – but that would never have worked either. She was simply unacceptable to the public, church and government in the climate of the time, not only in Britain but across the empire. Edward just could not see that his idea of the imperative of marrying her did not accord with the principle of royal duty believed in by his subjects. They expected a higher personal and constitutional standard from him.

Monckton was also engaged in the last-minute negotiations about Edward's pay-off settlement, as the departing King attempted to plead poverty in the hope of gaining a larger pension from his brother, hiding his savings of over a million pounds from Duchy of Cornwall revenues while pretending he had less than a tenth of that. The settlement was Edward's last sticking point before agreeing to abdicate, but the government declined to offer him a pension and he was forced to accept instead an annual grant personally paid by his brother George VI, of £21,000 – handsome in its day but only as much as he had been spending on jewels for Wallis that year as King – and it became a continuing cause of resentment on both sides afterwards. Since Edward had inherited rights to a portion of both Balmoral and Sandringham he even threatened to sue the new King and have him and his wife evicted as trespassers if they ever set foot in either house, but he was dissuaded from trying anything so foolish. Monckton failed to persuade George VI and more particularly his wife the Queen to give Wallis Simpson the title of Royal Highness and that too rankled with the ex-monarch, now Duke of Windsor, for the rest of his life. It seems to have annoyed his wife too: Monckton said: 'I told her that most people in England disliked her very much because the duke had married her and given up his throne, but that if she made him and kept him happy all his days, all that would change; but that if he were unhappy nothing would be too bad for her.' The evidence seems to be that the Duke remained infatuated with Wallis ever after, but that she grew impatient and tired of him and his spaniel-like devotion. She was trapped however: a further divorce from the man who had given up his kingdom for her would have been unthinkable and, much worse, certain social death. As for Edward, Monckton said afterwards, quoting from Psalm 58 in the *Book of Common Prayer*: 'One sometimes felt that the God in whom he believed was a God who dealt him trumps all the time and put no inhibitions on his desires . . . Once his mind was made up one felt he was like the deaf adder "that stoppeth her ears; which refuseth to hear the voice of the charmer".' He and Wallis spent long, empty lives, idly bickering and back-biting in Paris until the duke's death in 1972.

Monckton himself later became a Conservative MP and found himself made minister of defence shortly before the Suez crisis in 1956 – another poisoned chalice – then being moved by Anthony Eden to become paymaster general because of his opposition to the invasion. He later became president of the MCC but never attained the post he really coveted, lord chief justice, because he had been divorced himself.

Hardinge was succeeded by another career courtier, Sir Alan – 'Tommy' – Lascelles, a stiff, ascetic former soldier, who had once resigned as Edward's private secretary in 1929, making little secret of the fact that he could not stand the prince. Coaxed back into royal service a few years' later by Wigram on the assurance that George V had years to live, he soon found that he was serving the new King as Hardinge's deputy and was no more trusted than he was. Deeply conservative, instinctively reactionary, comfortable in a largely male and hidebound court, he later found himself in rivalry with George VI's wife, the Queen. Perhaps his most ludicrous intervention came in 1948 when Princess Elizabeth was pregnant with her first child. There had been a long tradition – it was no more than that – of home secretaries having to be present when a royal heir was born, as a sort of guarantor of the baby's legitimacy, something which had once seemed important. On this occasion, although he later denied it, Lascelles supported the King in telling the Attlee government that the Home Office's James Chuter Ede should attend the accouchement. This was only rescinded a few weeks before the birth of Prince Charles when the Canadian high commissioner pointed out that he and the other Commonwealth commissioners had a right to be present at the birth too, since the baby would one day be their monarch as well. This had apparently not occurred to anyone at court, including Lascelles. The prospect of the corridor outside the birthing chamber being congested with diplomats waiting to barge in to inspect the baby was too much and the practice was stopped. Lascelles later claimed he had long thought the practice out of date and ridiculous, but he had not challenged it and the risk of unseemly congestion in the labour room was a near thing

Lascelles stayed on during the early part of Queen Elizabeth II's reign and advised her against doing too much broadcasting, other than the Christmas message. It was also he who warned her that her younger sister Princess Margaret should not be allowed to marry Group Captain Peter Townsend, who had been divorced, (even though he had not been responsible for the marriage breakdown) and so beyond the pale. Divorcees were not allowed to be present at public events attended by the royal family, such as garden parties – as was pointed out at the time, they were allowed to kill the King's enemies but not permitted to join royal shooting parties to kill his pheasants. Lascelles, according to Townsend, told him brusquely that he must be mad or bad even to consider marrying the Queen's sister. After the relationship was brought to an end, Margaret always blamed Lascelles: 'I shall curse him to the grave.'

In hindsight, these decisions seem perverse: they perhaps should have appeared so at the time, too. The point was that they were wrong-headed and short-sighted and if Lascelles really was the man who stopped the public accouchements he should probably have realised also once she had come to the throne that there was a new, young queen for a new age, that the advice he offered was hidebound, and that the Edwardian certainties in which he had been brought up needed to change.

But change was not going to happen either with Lascelles' successor, Martin Adeane, who was private secretary throughout the formative years of the Queen's reign, from 1954 to 1972. A small, precise man,

Adeane was the grandson of Lord Stamfordham and, if not himself quite an hereditary courtier, was not a man to make other than the most cautious changes or offer anything other than deeply conservative advice. In the words of a prime ministerial private secretary of the period, he was 'civilised, intelligent and conveying the impression that you might at any moment commit an unpardonable solecism'. Like his grandfather he was diligent and old-fashioned – he declined to expand his private office to deal with the ever-increasing volume of business – and the speeches and public declarations he wrote for the Queen were ponderous and dull. He did not see the need nor obligation to challenge ministers or to proffer the Queen different advice from what they were telling her. Unlike his grandfather, however, he did not consult widely among Tory leaders when a similar leadership hiatus to the one in 1923 occurred in 1957 following the collapse of the prime minister Anthony Eden, and again in 1963 when Harold Macmillan fell ill.

During the Suez crisis of 1956, Adeane had supported the Eden government's intervention, in contradiction to the two assistant private secretaries. Following Eden's resignation a few months later, he did not suggest holding discussions to assess the real mood of the demoralised governing Conservative party and accordingly the decision as to who would be the Queen's new first minister was left to informal soundings undertaken solely within the party hierarchy – the so-called 'magic circle' – among the cabinet and other senior Tory figures by Lord Salisbury and Lord Chancellor Kilmuir. This was technically contrary to the royal prerogative by which the Queen – or actually her private secretary – should have had discussions and taken soundings about who should be appointed as her first minister. There was certainly nothing democratic or open about it either and the question of deciding between the two possible candidates – R.A. Butler and Harold Macmillan – was left to the grandees; the lisping Salisbury confining his question to 'Is it Wab or Hawold?' Rab, it seems, was the press's and possibly the country's favourite, but they had no say, nor did the Queen; the more dynamic Harold was the choice of senior Tories and accordingly Harold it was. Six years later, the process was repeated when Macmillan precipitately decided to stand down, citing his prostate cancer emergency, following the summer of the Profumo affair, and fixed the succession from his hospital bed, not for Butler, nor for his rumbustious and rather too ostentatiously keen rival Lord Hailsham, but for the little-known 14th Earl of Home – the last prime minister to be appointed from the House of Lords. The choice of Home, who renounced his peerage to become Sir Alec Douglas-Home was essentially Macmillan's and again Adeane did not ask for fuller checks on party opinion, nor was the Queen consulted. In fact, Macmillan manipulated his succession, offering the Queen heavily weighted advice when he had already resigned the premiership and so was technically no longer her prime adviser.

Only ministers were sounded out by the Tory whips with heavy emphasis placed on Home's candidacy, much to the annoyance of some Conservative MPs. They were only cursorily asked their opinions and the party in the country – which apparently was largely for Hailsham – was not asked at all. Macmillan's resignation was then choreographed: he sent his letter of resignation to the Queen, on receiving it she then visited him in hospital and asked his advice on who his successor should be. She then sent for Home after returning to the palace without asking whether he could form an administration or not. This was all constitutionally dubious and some senior Tories objected – having resigned, Macmillan should not have been trying to fix the succession, still less for the 14th Earl. The Queen was probably relieved: she knew and liked her fellow Scottish landowner (they talked dogs, guns and grouse moors together), but appointment through the closed magic circle of old Etonian senior Tories was not a modern way of doing things and would not happen again. As the frustrated rival Hailsham said: 'Never before in the history of the office of prime minister had advice as to his possible successor been tendered to his sovereign from a bed of sickness based on hearsay evidence prepared for him by others which he apparently had no possible means of verifying.' Enoch Powell, another of the disgruntled Tories, said Macmillan had it both ways: 'It was difficult for her in the circumstances to say; "You are not my Prime Minister and I don't want your advice."' Of course, the reason for the rush was that Macmillan was anxious to stop any bandwagon building for Butler who he did not want as a successor. The effect was to deprive the Queen of her constitutional prerogative of sending for her own chief minister for ever: in future it would all be done for her.

There was a sort of otherworldliness at the palace in those days and there was one more strange decision to which Adeane was a party. In April 1964, Sir Anthony Blunt, the art historian and surveyor of the Queen's paintings (a job in the Queen's own gift) admitted under MI5 interrogation that he had been a Soviet spy, in the network of Philby, Burgess and Maclean. As part of a deal to avoid alerting the Soviets, Blunt was offered immunity from prosecution and allowed to keep his honours and position as a royal adviser. Was the Queen told that he was a traitor? It seems possibly not, though she did not express surprise when Blunt was finally publicly exposed fifteen years later.

Adeane's successor, Sir Martin Charteris, came from the same sort of aristocratic, Eton-educated and army-service milieu as his predecessors, but was rather different from them. He was more outgoing and more relaxed, and it probably helped that his background was more aristocratic than that of his possible rival for the job, Philip Moore, who had had a civil service career. Instead of being given the job as of right by Buggins' turn, Charteris, who had been Adeane's deputy, had to fight for it by appealing to the Queen herself. His great advantage, it was said, was that he hugely admired the Queen, was almost in love with her, platonically of course, and so was her most ardent defender. Her speeches now started to contain jokes and it seems to have been Charteris who was behind the innovation of royal walkabouts at the time of the silver jubilee in 1977. Now the glacial stuffiness of the palace was beginning to crack, Charteris was certainly not afraid to speak his mind, including to journalists after his retirement – it was he who described Sarah Ferguson, Prince Andrew's estranged wife, as 'vulgar, vulgar, vulgar' when she started cavorting rather too ostentatiously with boyfriends at the time of her divorce. Moore succeeded Charteris in 1977: the first career civil servant (and a former public relations man) to be appointed to the role: more cautious and perhaps more stuffy than his predecessor. The historian Ben Pimlott reported a courtier saying he was very talkative and bored the Queen stiff, but this may have been a jaundiced view. Moore's background as the son of a civil servant, educated at Cheltenham and Brasenose College, Oxford, and a wartime prisoner of war after being shot down in his RAF bomber, was also somehow regarded by some courtiers as innovatory.

Moore's successor certainly was: William Heseltine is an Australian who had been a civil servant in Canberra and private secretary to the prime minister Robert Menzies there, before being recruited to the palace press office on the strength of his impressive performance on royal tours. Coming from outside court circles, he may well have been the most significant private secretary of the reign, in terms of changing the way the family firm operated. Heseltine was responsible for opening up the palace to be more media friendly and to engage with the press more, but even he was astonished by how far that went: further and faster than he had anticipated. The road from Heseltine's wish to be more open and helpful in answering newspapers' questions, to the undignified debacle in 1987 of the junior royals cavorting in mock medieval costumes in the silly television game show *It's a Royal Knockout*, was a stony one.

His successor Robert Fellowes was a reversion to more of an insider type and in the 1990s it happened that he had to deal with the great crises of the reign: the *annus horribilis* of 1992, when the war between Charles and Diana broke out in public and Windsor Castle was badly damaged by fire, then the royal divorces that followed and the death of Princess Diana five years later. The last was an event that was made all the more poignant because Fellowes is married to Diana's older sister, Jane. He is the son of the Queen's former Sandringham land agent and a cousin of Sarah Ferguson's father, Ronald. He was educated at Eton and had served in the Scots Guards, and then gone into banking before joining the private secretary's office in 1977. Fellowes has known the Queen since he was a small boy (actually, Princess Elizabeth had even held him in her arms when he was a baby) so he was steeped in the business of the royal family.

It was Fellowes who had to break the news to the Queen in 1992 following the Windsor Castle fire that the Major government had misjudged the mood of the nation when it promised to pay for the cost of repairing the damage and that, as a quid pro quo instead, the Queen would have to start paying income tax. Fellowes was apprehensive of raising the issue, but seeing the way the wind was blowing, the Queen caved in at once. Similarly, Fellowes had had to negotiate the minefield of Princess Diana's acrimonious and long, drawn-out separation and divorce from Prince Charles – including asking her whether she had colluded with Andrew Morton over the revelations in his 1992 book *Diana: Her True Story*. His sister-in-law lied to him. Apart from the abdication crisis this was the most devastating period in the monarchy's twentieth-century history – and a grievously affecting one for the private secretary whose personal and professional loyalties must have been strained. As Laski wrote nearly sixty years earlier: 'He must be at [the sovereign's] beck and call; even the claims of family affection must be sacrificed.' Fellowes was on holiday at the family home in Norfolk in August 1997 when Diana was killed in the Paris car accident. The assistant private secretary on duty with the royal family in Scotland that week was Robin Janvrin, Fellowes' deputy and successor (he is portrayed in the film *The Queen* by Roger Allam). It was Janvrin who took the initial call from the British ambassador in Paris, and to him and Fellowes that many of the arrangements for bringing Diana's body back from France and the funeral devolved. Unused to such an emotion-laden event, the private secretaries struggled to keep up, seeking help and reassurance from the new government in Downing Street, which had a surer grasp of spin and popular sentimentality. Liaison between Palace and Downing Street was never so pointed, or public.

Janvrin went on to replace Fellowes in 1999, and was himself succeeded in 2007 by the current private secretary Sir Christopher Geidt, a bullet-headed former soldier, intelligence officer and Foreign Office diplomat who helped to organise the Queen's diamond jubilee and crafted the subtle intervention in the referendum debate. He also kept a discreet eye on Prince William's progress as he started to undertake public engagements. It was Geidt who sat quietly at the back of the room, looking on beadily, as the Prince on his first tour to New Zealand in January 2010 opened the country's new supreme court building in Wellington. The private secretary had not been part of the royal party on the trip and no one had known he was going to be present. He was irked at being spotted when I approached him to ask whether he was reporting back to Buckingham Palace about how the Queen's grandson was doing. Not at all, he replied somewhat embarrassed, he just happened to be on holiday. Evidently, private secretaries like nothing better to do on holiday than spending their time off in the courts.

Geidt was on hand a few months later back in London following the inconclusive outcome of that May's general election. The Queen had experienced a hung parliament following the February 1974 election, but this time the permutations were new, with the Liberal Democrats holding the balance of power and entering into talks with both Labour and Conservatives about forming a coalition government. It is at times like this that the Queen comes closest to playing a political role. The outgoing prime minister, in this case Gordon Brown, remains in office until he either chooses to stand down (as he would do if the defeat was unambiguous) or if his party is subsequently defeated in parliament. If there had been deadlock and no deal after the prime minister resigned, the Queen and her private secretary would have had to have talks to ask another party leader to see if they could form a government capable of commanding the Commons instead. As it was, after five days of negotiations, Gordon Brown realised that the election result meant he had lost the confidence of the country and resigned, leaving the field to the Tories and Lib-Dems to form a five-year government. The Queen probably took it all in her stride: she had seen it before when Labour won fewer votes but more seats than the Tories in 1974 and Ted Heath failed to form a majority coalition with the Liberals, paving the way for Harold Wilson to return. That had all happened when David Cameron and Nick Clegg were seven, Ed Miliband was four and George Osborne two. By the time they had grown up and fought the 2015 General Election, it turned out that royal mediation was not required. The Conservatives, against polling expectations, won narrowly, but outright.

Chapter 6

'A sphere beyond politics'

(Rt Revd Richard Chartres, Bishop of London)

Sitting beneath a portrait of one of his eighteenth-century predecessors in a room in the Old Deanery, down a dark and narrow lane just round the corner from St Paul's Cathedral, the Rt Revd Richard Chartres, holder of the third-most-senior Episcopal position in the Church of England, was warming to his theme. 'Of course, the Queen is a very serious Christian. She talks more and more about God now. There is absolutely no doubt that she means what she says and she is deeply serious about her coronation oath about upholding the Protestant faith. She's quite Hanoverian really: she's not mystical. She says herself: "Not Low Church, not High Church, but short Church" – brisk sermons.'

He mused: 'They say you lose your shine after ten years in public office. Well, she's been going for eighty-seven in the public eye, hasn't she? And she hasn't lost hers. I was born as a subject of the King Emperor – for two months – and I hope to God I don't die as a citizen of a republic. I don't expect to: there is an enormous lake of sentiment towards the monarchy swashing around in Britain – and around the world. Television has been kind to the royal family and people appreciate there are very few office holders in the world as good at their jobs as she is. That's why they say two billion people watched the last royal wedding. Someone said that to Prince William on the day and he went pale and said: "Don't ever say that to me again." But it's true! I was in China with the Bible Society when Prince George was on his first foreign trip with his parents, in New Zealand, and pictures of him dominated the Chinese media. This baby prince already has a media presence across the world!'

Chartres continued: 'Our royal family offers a positive narrative in a world where people are disappointed and disillusioned, where they distrust many institutions and get their information from the digital revolution – there's a hunger there for a raft, for something to cling on to. In a naughty world where we find it difficult to craft a narrative of hope, there is the Queen as solid as she has always been.'

We were speaking a few days after the Remembrance Sunday commemorations at the Cenotaph, where Chartres, as usual, had led the prayers and the Queen, as ever, had led the nation's mourning and placed the first wreath. There had been intelligence service and police warnings in the media that the ceremony might come under attack from terrorists, that a suicide bombing was planned. There was heavier than normal security around Whitehall, and men had been arrested in London and the home counties on suspicion of plotting an explosion. And yet the number of veterans who turned up to parade past the monument was larger than ever. The line stretched as far as Trafalgar Square. On a fine, crisp, autumn morning the crowds watching were bigger, too. Bishop Chartres said: 'I've never known so many people present. At eleven o'clock, the silence was profound – not a sound anywhere. Then, at the end, when the Queen left, there was something I've never known before either: they burst into spontaneous applause. There's a reverence for her there, you know.'

Chartres knows whereof he speaks. He has been the closest prelate to the royals since his consecration as Bishop of London twenty years ago and has known Prince Charles since they were at Cambridge at the same time in the 1960s. Archbishops of Canterbury have come and gone, some more congenial than others. George Carey was somewhat resented in royal circles when he bustled about trying to offer advice about the Prince's failing marriage to Diana, particularly when he wrote about it in his memoirs later, and Rowan Williams was perhaps too intellectual and unworldly for them. But Chartres has been a constant: holding confirmation services, preaching sermons at their marriages and memorial services, as well as leading the prayers at the Cenotaph each November. His voice is sonorous and booming, his appearance dignified and commanding, beard self-consciously neatly trimmed like a Stuart-era divine ('I never read anything published after the seventeenth century,' which may be a joke) and his presence reassuring and serious: there will be nothing alarming on his watch. In private, however, he can be more witty and feline.

The church, particularly the Church of England, is intimately bound up with the monarchy and there is a paradox: although the English do not go to church much, they seem to appreciate the royal association with it. It does neither party any harm and may indeed enhance both. The Queen dignifies the church and the church bestows on her a sort of benign distance from politics, a neutrality floating above and beyond secular partisanship – which is odd, given the sectarian origins of the modern monarchy. When in the twentieth century other leaders went along with non-religious displays of power, most notoriously the Fascists, Nazis and Russian Communists – militaristic, belligerent and vainglorious – the British monarchy instead bumbled along with quasi-spiritual displays, emphasising a mystical power above themselves. Not only their coronations – which are themselves religious ceremonies involving anointing and solemn vows as well as prayers and oath taking – but many of their other public appearances have often involved a church service in the shape of weddings, funerals, thanksgivings, memorials and celebrations. Without the religious element, these would have lacked focus: where would the processions have gone? Religion's contribution adds dignity, other-worldliness and a sense of immemorial tradition and divine favour, even before you get to the question of belief.

This is a helpful distancing for both monarchs and politicians. Chartres said: 'The monarchy is detached from wheeler-dealing. It occupies a sphere beyond politics: a zone which seems to echo the fundamental values of society and provides a raft which floats above partisanship and around which we can argue, row and compromise.' The image of a raft again. Then he added: 'Compare and contrast: the American president is now the nearest thing to a Hanoverian monarch. The American polity is dysfunctional – they have no differentiated symbolic sphere from the political and in a time of great change its written constitution is a considerable weakness. On the other hand, the British constitution, being unwritten, can be changed very rapidly. Our monarch may not have political power but the monarchy has expanded into a symbolic role and religion is indispensible in that.'

The irony, of course, is that England has a state religion whereas the United States constitution explicitly forbids one. But it is precisely because it is a state-sanctioned church that the Church of England has to remain broad in its doctrines and practices. If it became narrow, as some conservative Bible-bashing evangelicals would like, it would rapidly lose its privileged status. Such folk probably would not mind that too much, for theirs is an essentially exclusionary religion, exiling those who do not share their version of Christianity, though they would quite like to keep hold of the Church of England's buildings and their own pensions. The status and property makes the church in the conservative evangelicals' own words, 'a convenient boat to fish from' – the allegiance is conditional not doctrinal. But if the Church of England started rejecting and anathematising those of whom it disapproves as the church's Calvinistic tendency would like – gay people in relationships, women in headship of organisations (a particular irony given the Queen's historic, inherited position as Supreme Governor of the Church of England and Defender of the Faith) – the Church of England's meaning as the established church would be gone. This is at the heart of its internecine rows. A certain flexibility and element of compromise are therefore required in the state church: in return for leading the nation at prayer, presiding at coronations, retaining a privileged position in the House of Lords and, less loftily but more importantly, maintaining a religious presence in every parish in the land, it cannot be seen to stray too far from a moderate theology. That its supreme governors have not always been paragons of virtue – Henry VIII, Charles II, George IV, William IV and Edward VII spring immediately to mind – is neither here nor there: monarchs hold the titles because of their office, not because of their personal morality or particular virtue. That is why the then archbishop of Canterbury, Rowan Williams, was able in good conscience to bless the marriage of Prince Charles and his former mistress, Camilla Parker-Bowles, though not to conduct it.

As Williams himself once said – admittedly before he became archbishop: 'We have a special relationship with the cultural life of our country and we must not fall out of step with this if we are not to become absurd and incredible.' Of course, the Church of England does occasionally become absurd and incredible – not least over gay clergy and women bishops during Williams' primacy – not to mention sanctimonious and hypocritical, but it has to remain as it sees itself, a broad church. That means broad enough to include evangelicals who do not particularly see themselves as members of an episcopal church because they have a pretty low view of bishops, especially those they disagree with and High Church Anglican clergy so camp and given to vestments that they have practically nothing in common, doctrinally, theologically or ritualistically with their Low Church colleagues. Yet they hang together, casting occasional sneers and anathemas in each others' direction. And that is convenient, too, not least for the politicians who would have to disentangle a complex web of historic laws and rights if they ever want to disestablish the Church of England. In a more serious religious age, it took more than sixty years to disestablish the church in Wales between the 1860s and 1920, and no modern government would relish the amount of parliamentary time that would be taken up with unravelling the process in England. So, even though fewer than a million people, less than a fiftieth of the English population, attend an Anglican service on a regular basis – though unquantifiably more regard themselves as members of the church, despite rarely darkening its doors – it remains the state religion and the monarchy is an important element in propping it up. As the Victorian archbishop Edward Benson wrote in 1887, the English 'are not a church-going race, but there is a solemn, quiet sense of religion for all that in their sayings and doings'.

Certainly, it is true that whereas earlier monarchs used and manipulated the Church for political purposes, the current relationship between the two is based on the deeply serious and personal model developed only partially consciously by Queen Victoria. Some monarchs before her had been true believers: George III set an example by reading his Bible assiduously and attending matins every day at eight o'clock, at least while he was still able to do so. His golden jubilee in 1809 was almost an ecumenical affair across the kingdom, devoid

of the sectarianism of a century before, as *The Times* noted: 'The
cathedral, the abbey, the parochial church, the meeting house of the
dissenter, the chapel of the Methodist and the Catholic, and the
synagogue of the Israelite were all alike opened on this interesting
occasion.' But the old King's piety scarcely rubbed off on his sons, who
barely observed the rituals and tenets, except when it came to opposing
Catholic emancipation. Victoria, however, was different. She was
brought up by her German mother and German governess in the
Lutheran tradition and, once married to Prince Albert, absorbed his
own questioning, liberal, Lutheranism – while of course remaining
within the Church of England. Albert found the English church
difficult to understand and it had its own suspicions of him, especially
when he challenged the Bishop of Oxford to play a game of chess on
a Sunday, or suggested that his children did not really need to kneel in
order to pray. The Prince Consort's influence gave his wife a suspicion
of English Anglican church practices and especially of bishops and
ritualism: 'No religious act ought ever to be allied to pomp and show'
– which went down well up to a point with a British public that was
still suspicious of Romanism, though they liked a bit of a show when
it came to national celebrations. Sermons preached before her had to
be – shades of the current Queen – 'orthodox, short and interesting';
preachers had to wear a simple black gown – no vestments, or candles;
and their remarks were not to exceed 20 minutes in duration. The
royal family attended ordinary services in local parish churches when
they stayed at Balmoral and Osborne – a practice which continues
today at Crathie Church near the Scottish estate and at the village
church in Sandringham. When clergy attended the Queen at Balmoral
they were not allowed to bring their wives with them – and that is a
tradition that also endures under the present Queen more than a
century and a half later.

Victoria's early experience of the Church of England was not inspiring. She disliked old Archbishop Howley, the man who had forced a ring onto the wrong finger at her coronation and who mumbled his way inaudibly through her marriage service two years later. 'He has an unfortunate manner, a hypocritical, cringing manner but I don't think he is so,' her prime minister Melbourne reassured her. The dean of Windsor was not much better: he tactlessly congratulated her when she gave birth to her first son 'for saving us from the incredible curse of a female succession'. Perhaps he had forgotten who he was talking to. But Albert's sturdy, moral seriousness rubbed off on her and she became a devout figure, particularly after his death. Under his guidance, the royal family self-consciously became a model for the Victorian middle classes and central to that was their religious observance: dutiful, stiflingly serious-minded and devout. The Queen conducted Bible classes at Buckingham Palace for the children of the servants and paid somewhat Lady Bountiful-type visits to the poor and sick. 'Do not be put about. I come not as a Queen but as a Christian lady!' she announced once when paying an unexpected visit to a sick and depressed woman living in a cottage in Windsor Great Park, doubtless cheering her up with the command: 'Put your trust in Jesus and you will soon be in a land where there is no pain. You are a widow, so am I and we shall soon meet our loved ones!' No wonder Disraeli on his death bed refused to see her on the grounds that the Queen would only want him to take a message to Albert. She carried out these philanthropic duties on a regular basis throughout the 1860s and 1870s, even as she was refusing to attend to public obligations and, when they were reported in the press, she received adulatory coverage. The royal touch was even deployed, as when she visited the East London Hospital in 1876 and was shown to the bedside of a little girl who had been run over. The Queen noted in her journal that the child had said she thought she would get well if she saw the Queen and Victoria dutifully shook hands and stroked her cheek. It was a touching incident, duly recorded in *Punch* with a cartoon captioned 'Her Best Title – Queen of the East'. Perhaps 'Queen of People's Hearts' did not occur to the caption writer. Sadly however, the child later died, so the royal healing powers had their limits.

This piety was noted approvingly by Bagehot as appealing to the public's 'diffused feeling'. 'A family on the throne is an interesting idea. It brings down the pride of sovereignty to the level of petty life ... We have come to believe it is natural to have a virtuous sovereign and that the domestic virtues are as likely to be found on thrones as they are eminent when there,' he said. Admiration for the royals' exemplary life made it easier to 'reverence' – or at least look up to – them. By and large, that has continued. To his mother's despair, Edward, the Prince of Wales, was scarcely a model of domestic propriety, yet he observed and sponsored the more flamboyant styles of worship and churchmanship that developed out of the royal celebrations of the latter years of his mother's reign. Indeed, one of the first ostentatious religious ceremonies linked to the Crown was the thanksgiving service which was organised at St Paul's Cathedral in 1872 following his recovery from a serious bout of typhoid exactly ten years after his father had succumbed to the same illness. That service, of which the Queen had initially disapproved but which she eventually attended, was strongly supported by William Gladstone's government and was echoed and emulated in churches around the country. It came at a time of mounting public criticism of the Queen's continuing withdrawal from public life and had the effect of killing off the nascent republican movement which had been gaining ground. Almost literally so: as the diarist, the Revd Francis Kilvert noted when he visited London some weeks after the Prince's illness: 'During the most critical days ... a friend ... was present one night amongst a great crowd when an unfavourable bulletin came from Sandringham. The crowd had been patiently waiting some time and when the sad bulletin was posted and read a great groan of dismay ran through the people. One man exclaimed: "Serve him right!" Immediately, the infuriated crowd seized him, stripped him naked, knocked him down and kicked him up and down the street like a football till the police burst in and rescued him just in time before he was killed.'

Charles Dilke, the Liberal politician and leading parliamentary republican, with spectacularly unfortunate timing was starting a national speaking tour against the monarchy just as the Prince was taken ill and, although he went on with it, faced demonstrations and near riots at many of the halls where he spoke: in Leeds one man was killed in the mayhem. 'What a sell for Dilke this illness has been,' chuckled Lord Henry Lennox to Disraeli. When Dilke sponsored a Commons debate a few months later to establish an inquiry into the royal finances, it was lost by 276 votes to two.

Edward, Prince of Wales was influential in another way even before he finally came to the throne thirty years later: in promoting the monarchy as sponsors of charity and philanthropy. Indeed his mother had scarcely given him and his brothers and sisters any other outlet for their energies. He might not be able to see government papers, or participate in official meetings with ministers, but he was allowed to go round visiting (and opening) hospitals and town halls, and meeting welfare organisations and charities. By encouraging the Prince to do this, Prime Minister Gladstone hoped that it would help to raise the moral tone of both the Prince and his court, and while that was going too far, Edward did quite enjoy the ceremonial aspects of the job and the benevolent attention he received. He could make a speech, tap a foundation stone with a silver trowel or attend a banquet and be thought better of by the public because of it. He might say that he did not like being 'a puff to the object in view', but it required very little commitment or concentration on his part. Other members of the royal family also fanned out across the country performing visits or serving on philanthropic committees: the prince's wife, Alexandra, made hundreds of outings to children's and women's charities, giving away 20 per cent of her annual income each year to hospitals and other good causes at a time when the state itself had no role in social provision. She even met and got to know Joseph Merrick, 'the Elephant Man', at the London Hospital.

Eventually, the Prince himself went further in 1884 by agreeing to sit on a royal commission investigating housing conditions among the poor. This was something that would be thought much too political today, but then it was encouraged by the prime minister (still Gladstone) and the Queen herself. The prince toured the roughest tenements in Clerkenwell and St Pancras incognito and was shocked by the destitution and squalor he was shown. 'We visited some very bad places,' wrote Lord Carrington, another member of the commission, 'But we got him back safe and sound to Marlborough House in time for luncheon.' A few days later, the Prince made a speech in the House of Lords calling for drastic action to improve conditions – but by charities and housing associations, not government. In 1892 he sat on another commission looking into the conditions of the aged poor, but again shied away (as did the commission) from recommending a state pension – that would have been much too socialistic – in favour of private philanthropy and self-help.

These were, however small, steps in the right direction, showing the royal family's concern for and interest in social welfare, and they were motivated, at least so far as Queen Victoria was concerned, by a sense of Christian duty and obligation – a *noblesse oblige*. Among her last acts in her dying months was to knit scarves for the troops sweltering in

South Africa during the Boer War and to send them bars of chocolate in tins embossed with her portrait – although sadly these mostly melted in the heat before ever getting to the front line. As importantly, the royal example helped to stimulate philanthropy among members of the public – and not only the wealthy. During her golden jubilee in 1887, more than two million women contributed to a Queen's fund which raised £80,000 to set up a training institute for district nurses and at the diamond jubilee ten years later there were numerous local fund-raising efforts to provide hospitals, infirmaries, institutes and libraries across the empire. The residents of Jodhpur in India even raised money in her honour to provide fodder for their own starving cattle – an action which Lord Curzon, the viceroy, assured the Queen led to the cattle having 'as grateful an appreciation of your Majesty's birthday in their dumb, unreasoning fashion, as can any of your Majesty's human subjects have done the same night'.

These are all traditions which have continued as public demonstrations of usefulness and generosity by members of the royal family. A 1964 Mass Observation survey found that members of the public were more than twice as likely to meet a royal doing charitable work than in any other context. The connections with charity have been continued by all members of the royal family in the past hundred years. They have helped to raise funds by giving themselves or, more usually, tapping up wealthy friends and other donors aspiring to honours or reflected glory. Edward VII was a master at this and noticeably unsnobbish about it, enlisting the support of Jewish tycoons at a time when some members of his entourage regarded them as beyond the social pale: men such as Sir Ernest Cassel who wrote a cheque for £200,000 for the King to use for benevolent purposes, or the Glasgow-born grocer Thomas Lipton whose donations brought him an invitation to stay at Sandringham and a baronetcy in 1902. Prominent among Edward VII's charitable causes was the establishment of a fund originally to help support hospitals, which eventually became and remains nearly 120 years on, the King's Fund, the medical think-tank. When the Jewish financier Samuel Lewis died and left the fund £250,000 in his will in 1901, his widow was persuaded by Horace Farquhar, the master of the King's household, to make over an extra £10,000 a year from the residue – and she gained a seat at the following year's coronation and a hamper of game from Sandringham as a result. As the historian Frank Prochaska noted: 'Charitable donation could be a short cut to a shooting party or a Palace investiture ... nothing puts a person more quickly in the court calendar or on the social map than signing a big cheque for a royal cause.' Or, as the courtier Lord Esher remarked at the time: 'In these days everybody expects that for every effort he makes in the cause of charity, he should be rewarded.'

It was not just philanthropists either, but the mayors and corporations of towns receiving royal visits and worthy members of the community who received medals, too (as they still do). This was not only a way of showing appreciation for worthy causes but also a means of securing the support and allegiance of the working classes who might otherwise be tempted into thinking that the royal family were wastrels and layabouts, and thus seduced into socialism, or worse, Bolshevism. If the philanthropy did some good in improving the working and living conditions of the poor, so much the better. Prochaska says when the King visited a humble dwelling he wanted to see a picture of himself on the wall, not one of the pioneering Labour leader Keir Hardie. Hardie himself referred derisively to George V as 'a street corner loafer ... destitute of every ability', adding that 'the life of one Welsh miner is of greater commercial and moral value to the British nation than the whole royal crowd put together' – to which the King responded peevishly by calling him 'that beast'. The royal answer to such subversiveness was to redouble their visits to deprived areas such as the East End of London – what they and their court liked to refer to as the 'democratisation' of the monarchy. The development of what became known as the Duke of York's Camp – bringing together teenagers from factories and public schools for summer holidays together, 'oiling the wheels of industry with good fellowship and understanding', was one initiative of the 1920s, the National Playing Fields Association, providing sports facilities, was another from the same period. None of this was particularly cynical: after the King's death in 1936 a network of King George's fields was set up across the country: there are still nearly five hundred of them and the association, renamed Fields in Trust in 2007, has had the Duke of Edinburgh as its president since 1947.

It would be wrong to assume that the monarchs of the twentieth century were not entirely sincere in their religious beliefs, with the probable exception of Edward VIII. Despite his training, he once asked the archbishop of Canterbury: 'Who appoints the bishops?' Seemingly unaware that, technically, he did. Stanley Baldwin told his niece, a Catholic nun, wonderingly following the abdication: 'He had *no* spiritual conflict *at all*...He is extraordinary in the way he has no spiritual sense; no idea of sacrifice for duty. *That* point of view never came before his mind...He has no religious sense. I have never in my life met anyone so completely lacking in any sense of the – the – well, what is *beyond*. There was simply no moral struggle. It appalled me.' Nevertheless, during their discussions, the worldly prime minister had suggested that the King might follow the example of some of his predecessors and just keep Mrs Simpson as his mistress. But Edward would not agree to that – his heart was set on marriage and if that meant abdication because of who she was, so be it.

Religious ignorance was certainly not how Edward or his brothers had been brought up. George V had an almost touchingly naïve faith

– not so remarkable given his own upbringing and the era in which he lived – and it was both devout and pugnacious. The Bible was 'a wonderful book but there are some very queer things in it.' He attended church at Sandringham as an ordinary parishioner: 'But I bargained that I should not be expected to take the bag round' – the collection – 'I drew the line at that.' When he could not find his favourite hymns – 'Abide with Me' and 'The Day Thou Gavest Lord is Ended' – where he expected to find them in a new hymn book, he exclaimed in exasperation: 'I'll have all the bloody books burned. I'm not defender of the faith for nothing.' As in his grandmother's (and granddaughter's) time, visiting preachers were told by Lord Stamfordham that sermons should last no more than fourteen minutes – 'If you preach for less, the King may say you are too lazy to prepare a sermon, if you preach for more . . . (he) may say that the man did not know when to stop.' At Buckingham Palace the King kept a map into which little flags were stuck showing where his children had made visits for charitable purposes.

George VI had a similarly robust and straight-forward faith – 'He believes it, you know,' his wife confided to Lord Reith, the director-general of the BBC – and demonstrated it in the Christmas broadcasts. This was particularly evident in the broadcast he made to a fearful nation on Christmas Day 1939, just after the start of the Second World War, when he poignantly and appositely quoted from a poem shown him by his daughter. Called 'God Knows', it had been written many years before by a sociologist at the London School of Economics called Minnie Louise Haskins and the excerpt read in his faltering but determined voice became famous: 'I said to the man who stood at the Gate of the Year, "Give me a light that I may tread safely into the unknown." And he replied, "Go out into the darkness and put your hand in the hand of God. That shall be better to you than light and safer than a known way."' Haskins said later that when she heard the broadcast she thought the words had sounded familiar, but they would not have been chosen had they not resonated with the King himself – and his daughter.

The young Elizabeth already had decided views. Aged ten, she was asked by the archbishop of Canterbury Cosmo Gordon Lang whether she would like to walk in the garden at Sandringham with him and she replied: 'Yes, very much, but please don't tell me anything more about God. I know all about him already.' Her father's coronation the following year was, apparently, 'very, very wonderful (but) at the end the service got rather boring as it was all prayers.'

Her piety is very much bound up in her religious belief. The Queen, like her present-day subjects, probably does not believe that she was chosen by God, but she certainly believes that he guides her and gives her personal authority and responsibility; it is not only a calling but a sacred duty that has devolved on to her shoulders and informs all her official actions. There is no question of frivolity in all of this: it is central to her personality and intellect. Both she and her husband are quietly devout and knowledgeable, able to quote the Bible from memory and sing the psalms without reading in a way that perhaps no future monarch will do. This piety has been coming out increasingly in the Queen's Christmas broadcasts in recent years, since the millennium. Some have suggested that she has felt increasingly able to express her deepest feelings and beliefs following the deaths of her mother and sister in 2002. Others believe that the openness to a more explicit expression of faith is due to the influence of the Duke of Edinburgh, telling her to go for it. Just as likely, she feels the need to emphasise her sense of Christian values in an increasingly secular, multireligious society which rarely listens much to talk of spiritual matters.

Among the less well-known duties of the Lord Chancellor, the country's most senior law officer, is the administration of the oath of homage to new Church of England bishops in the presence of the Queen. The bishops have to swear allegiance to her as supreme governor of their church in a formal ceremony attended also by the cleric who holds the quaint post of clerk of the closet. Lord chancellors themselves have to be Anglicans to administer the oath – Michael Howard, who is Jewish, was not allowed to do this – and it is a duty which requires a certain amount of dressing up. One said to me: 'I had a morning suit with two waistcoats – a black one and a grey one – and the first time I chose the grey one for the ceremony. Afterwards a flunkey came up to me and said: "You do know, don't you, that grey waistcoats are only for weddings or Ascot?" I did not make that mistake again.' He added: 'What always struck me was that the Queen not only has a very strong personal belief, but also an encyclopaedic knowledge of the Church of England. She was able to converse very directly with each new bishop about the issues in their dioceses and about where they had been incumbents before.'

Reminding a mass audience, exhausted and replete with Christmas lunch, on the one occasion of the year when she has a few minutes to address them unmediated by the government or even her own advisers, that religious faith lies at the heart of the festival is undoubtedly important to her. The 2000 Christmas message reads almost like a sermon: 'For me the teachings of Christ and my own personal accountability before God provide a framework in which I try to lead my life. I, like so many of you, have drawn great comfort in difficult times from Christ's words and example. I believe that the Christian message ... remains profoundly important to us all.' Certainly, the palace was surprised by the strength of public reaction and approval the first time she made that explicitly religious appeal at the heart of her broadcast. It has been noted ever since that there have been no complaints from members of other faiths and why should there be? The message is always clear, ecumenical and anodyne: a plea for tolerance and mutual respect between faiths. But every year has contained explicit statements about the anniversary of the birth of Christ and the spiritual meaning of the festival, as if her audience needs reminding what it is all about.

This might seem commonplace and natural, but it has not always been so, even in more religiously observant periods. George V's first broadcast, on Christmas Day in 1932, contains scarcely a reference to God. The old King wheezed and cleared his gravelly throat – no second takes, the broadcast was live – as he read the words written for him by Rudyard Kipling and the short speech is entirely concerned with wonder that the sound of his voice could penetrate the furthest recesses of the empire 'through one of the marvels of modern science'.[17] It is very vivid, evoking listeners cut off from the outside world 'by snows, deserts or sea' whom only voices out of the air could reach. But religious references are absent, as they were three years later for his last Christmas broadcast a month before he died. Perhaps he thought that such piety was unnecessary, or even slightly demeaning. There is no such reticence from his granddaughter.

It can be unnerving for those called upon to preach to the royal couple during their holidays at Balmoral or Sandringham and to look up and see the Queen gazing solidly at them from a few feet away and, even more so, the Duke beside her assiduously taking notes. Neither the Queen nor the Duke have to look up Biblical references. They are

---

17 The King read the first Christmas broadcast from a small cubby-hole under the stairs at Sandringham, sitting at a table covered with a thick cloth to muffle – not entirely successfully – the sound of rustling paper and his tapping hand. He complained that having to make the broadcast quite spoiled his Christmas, but he was persuaded to repeat the exercise each year thereafter. The Queen made the first televised Christmas broadcast in 1957.

moreover very well informed about current religious debates, in the Church of Scotland, just as much as the Church of England – no need to tell them what a bishop is, or, north of the border, about wrangles within the kirk.

Dr Ian Bradley, reader in practical theology and church history at St Andrews University, has preached at Balmoral. The specifications for those staying over the weekend are exact. As per Queen Victoria's instructions a century and a half ago, wives are not invited. You drive up on a Saturday afternoon and receive a briefing from the minister of Crathie church. At the big house, your bags are taken from you and your clothes unobtrusively packed away by a valet (a £10 tip is specified). The bedrooms do not have en suite bathrooms and you may notice that the clean, white cotton sheets are neatly patched. Tartan carpeting covers the floors. On Sunday morning a retail opportunity will be meaningfully given you in the Balmoral shop: a tweed bag (prices from £33 to £90) or cushion (£33) perhaps, a bottle of malt whisky (£39.95), a dangly corgi pendant (£11) or a golf towel embroidered with the castle crest (£15).

And then there are the meetings with royalty over the weekend. On the Saturday evening, there will be pre-dinner drinks, with guests summoned over from across the drawing room to chat to the Queen, who may be sitting at a table playing patience as she does so. Bradley found himself discussing dogs – a favourite topic – and, as one does, dieting: 'How very tedious,' replied the monarch robustly. If the weather is wet, dinner will be a black-tie affair indoors, but if fine it is likely to be a barbecue up in the hills of the estate. Bradley found himself being driven alone by the Queen to this, chatting away inconsequentially to the elderly lady behind the wheel of the Land Rover, as if to any other elderly woman on a drive. But the venue is not just any barbecue: this one will have food cooked by the Duke, servants present, and washing up afterwards organised by the Queen. It is one of her few menial tasks and Margaret Thatcher caused no end of merriment when she once insisted that she should be doing it instead – an incident never quite forgotten. You can see why such private moments of normality – or as near normality as possible – might be cherished.

On the Sunday morning, after a presumably nervous and restless night for the preacher, there will be a trip across the estate by car, then the sermon, then back at the castle the cross-examination over lunch. About forgiveness, the Duke will say beadily, does that extend to someone like Mugabe and if so how and why? Nor does the discussion end when the preacher drives away afterwards. Bradley's conversation with the Duke continued through correspondence, on the topic of religion and the environment, for some time afterwards.

Will this sense of religious earnestness continue into the next reign? Prince Charles is not as profound or as serious a thinker as his father. He has an antiquarian interest in the *Book of Common Prayer*, but does not quote unaided and at length as his parents' generation do (the Duke also has a perhaps surprising interest in the work of modern poets such as Larkin and Eliot and quotes them too – but 'Don't tell anyone,' he barks, as if people might think him a cissy). The Prince's interest in the cadences of the seventeenth-century prayer book can be set beside his radical ideas of the monarchy's future relationship with faith more generally. Charles's most original public thought about his coronation was, more than twenty years ago, that he might wish to pledge himself to be not a defender of *the* faith, but a defender of faith in a way that would be appropriate for modern, multicultural Britain. In a 1994 television documentary interview with Jonathan Dimbleby, he said: 'I personally would rather see it as defender of faith, not the faith because it means just one particular interpretation of the faith, which I think is sometimes something that causes a deal of a problem. It has done for hundreds of years. People have fought each other to death over these things, which seems to me a peculiar waste of people's energy, when we are all actually aiming for the same ultimate goal, I think. So I would much rather it was seen as defending faith itself which is so often under threat in our day where, you know, the whole concept of faith itself or anything beyond this existence, beyond life itself is considered almost old-fashioned and irrelevant.' Such words were enough to cause conniptions to Archbishop Carey and some Church of England conservatives, always sensitive to the church's slightly precarious relationship with modern secular society. This was all said long before the rise of militant Islam, or indeed the militant (but less bloody and more refined) Atheism that rose partly as a response to it in the early years of the twenty-first century. Were the Prince's remarks perceptively acute or do they bear a quaintly, nostalgic air? It is hard to think that everyone is aiming for the same ultimate goal these days unless there is a hitherto unrecognised al-Qaeda sleeper cell lurking deep within the good old Church of England. In fact, the Prince appeared to row back slightly in an interview in 2015, to say that he had been misunderstood: he would still be a full member of the Church of England, but appreciated that he presided over a multi-faith country and would promote religious harmony (it would have been a surprise if he had said he intended to promote religious *dis*harmony). Prince Charles has for many years shown an intrigued interest in Islam, its spiritual philosophy, art and design; no one can accuse him of ignorance or disdain. One of his favourite expressions is the Sufi phrase: 'Although there are many lamps, it is all the same light.' This is not something that religious hardliners of any description would accept: to them theirs is the only light. The Prince, however, says his prayers every night to his Anglican God.

Discussions have been discreetly continuing for many years about what form the next coronation service might take, or even whether there should be more than one. Coronations are not set in an immemorial, unchanging tradition, but have constantly evolved over the centuries – in any case, very few people now alive actually participated in the last in 1953, certainly closely enough to notice any changes. Many of the most significant declarations at the start of a new reign actually take place at different times and different places to the coronation itself, so that the monarch is already firmly in place by the time the formal ceremony happens at Westminster Abbey, usually more than a year after he or she ascends the throne. To start with, the succession is proclaimed from a balcony at St James's Palace within hours of the previous monarch's death, to forestall rivals. Then, at a later stage, when parliament meets, there is the royal declaration to the assembled Commons and Lords. Formerly, this was a somewhat blood-curdling oath, originally formulated at the time of the Popish Plot in 1678, denying the Catholic belief in transubstantiation (the metaphysical doctrine that the Holy Communion wafer has been transformed into the actual body and blood of Jesus Christ) and asserting that the invocation and adoration of the Virgin Mary or any other saints and the sacrifice of the Mass are superstitious and idolatrous. It ends with the ringing endorsement of Protestantism: 'I do solemnly in the presence of God profess, testify and declare that I do make this declaration and every part thereof in the plain and ordinary sense of the words read unto me as they are commonly understood by English Protestants,' whatever the Pope might say or do. Even by the time of the accession of George V in 1910, however, this was regarded as somewhat unnecessarily over the top – Queen Victoria herself, who had made such a declaration, had declared: 'I cannot bear to hear the violent abuse of the Catholic religion, which is so painful and cruel to the many good and innocent Roman Catholics' – and the formal declaration was simplified. It needed an Act of Parliament: the Accession Declaration Act, but the three subsequent monarchs have only been required to tell the assembled parliamentarians: 'I do solemnly and sincerely in the presence of God, profess, testify and declare that I am a faithful Protestant and that I will, according to the true intent of the enactments to secure the Protestant Succession to the Throne of my realm, uphold and maintain such enactments to the best of my power according to law.' The Queen made this declaration to parliament in November 1952, nine months after she succeeded to the throne and seven months before her coronation, so clearly there was no absolute urgency about it by then but, unless there is a change at Charles's accession, it will still have to be made next time.

The formal oath at the coronation takes the form of a question-and-answer incantation with the archbishop of Canterbury in which the monarch, hand on Bible, promises to govern the realms according to their respective laws and customs and to cause law and justice to be administered in mercy. Then indeed, the Queen promised to the utmost of her power to maintain the laws of God and the true profession of the Gospel. As part of this she was asked: 'Will you to the utmost of your power maintain in the United Kingdom the Protestant reformed religion established by law? Will you maintain and preserve inviolably the settlement of the Church of England and the doctrine, worship, discipline and government thereof, as by law established in England? And will you preserve unto the Bishops and Clergy of England and to the churches there committed to their charge, all such rights and privileges as by law do or shall appertain to them or any of them?' To which she replied: 'All this I promise to do.'

That sonorous oath probably did not sound so quaint in 1953, when anti-Catholic prejudice was still about in some respectable quarters, as it does now. But how would it sound in a multicultural, multi-faith country in the second or third decade of the twenty-first century? It is more than a quaint rubric because it binds up the monarch and the country's government into a sectarian promise and entrenches the Church of England into its privileged position. Start tugging at the string and it starts to unravel a whole skein of ancient laws. Part of the deal, as Michael Scott-Joynt, the then Bishop of Winchester who has since died, told me is the maintenance of a presence in every parish, the upkeep of many of the country's most distinguished ancient buildings and their treasures, and mundane things such as maintaining rights of public access to church property, including cemeteries. These, of course, could be legislated around, given parliamentary time; but is it something that ministers would wish to do if they don't have to?

The likelihood is that King Charles III will swear the oath, but that his coronation at the abbey will have multi-faith elements, or at least invitations to different faith leaders, unlike in 1953. An alternative might be to have a variety of accession services around the country: a crowning at Westminster, a multi-faith affirmation at York or in Edinburgh a little later, and maybe the anointing of William as Prince of Wales at Carnarvon after that. That seems to be Charles's current wish, but it offers hostages to fortune: would the country be happy with seemingly endless expensive ceremonials, with the purpose of enhancing the status of the new King, particularly if they occur, as may be possible, during a period of economic recession or stagnation? For that matter, would all parts of the kingdom welcome such ceremonies? Do the Scots wish to be reminded of their vassalage, or the Welsh of their English prince? Then there would be the inevitable visits to the realms across the seas: in the 1950s there was the virtue of novelty, and a beautiful young queen and her dashing husband who had not been seen much and certainly not in the flesh; but would the Commonwealth countries be so excited by the sight of an elderly king they have encountered many times before? Would he perhaps remind them of their reasons for wanting to become a republic? Would everyone get bored? One great ceremony might be popular but several risks alienation and offers plentiful scope for disruption.

Despite his inherent conservatism Rt Revd Chartres is dismissive of concerns about a multi-faith service. For him it will still be a Christian one. 'It's just words, words, words,' he told me. 'There is no major problem with the coronation. We can simplify the oath to show we have moved beyond the fractures of the seventeenth century – why not go back to the oath taken by King Edgar at Bath in 975? The important thing is it is absolutely vital that politicians are kept out of devising the ceremony or we'll have some awful, Blair-like management-speak about mission statements and transparency – they can fix something else up for themselves afterwards. What we need with the service is to weave new patterns of Britishness into the ceremony. I am not interested in Protestantism, I am interested in Christianity and that is what we should reflect.'

There might be something in using the words of King Edgar's coronation oath. The bishop will certainly have been consulted for his views and this may well be what is being actively considered. The oath was apparently devised for the King by St Dunstan, one of Chartres' predecessors in the tenth century as bishop of London and latterly archbishop of Canterbury (he was also an early abbot of Glastonbury). Dunstan was skilled at making a picture and forming letters according to his much later biographer Osbern, and you don't have to believe the stories about his ability to outwit devils in order to appreciate the simplicity of the words he composed. At his coronation, Edgar is supposed to have said: 'In the name of the Holy Trinity, I promise three things to the Christian people subject to me. Firstly, that God's church and all the Christian people of my dominions will be held in true peace.

Secondly, I forbid robbery and all unlawful deeds by all ranks of men. Thirdly, I promise and command justice and mercy in all judgements, in order that the gracious and merciful Lord, who liveth and reigneth, may thereby forgive us all through his everlasting mercy.'

That seems to cover most bases, though possibly the word 'Christian' could be removed for modern tastes, for that would still allow scope for use of the word God, in a slightly more ambiguous and ecumenical context, retaining a mystical, spiritual element. It has the virtue of brevity and simplicity, it offers fundamental protections and it is at least hallowed by time if it was first devised more than a thousand years ago. There is an historic ring to it. Would the Church of England object to such pre-Reformation rubric? Perhaps not. The Church is understandably nervous of diluting its privileged status and losing the market share it so jealously guards over issues such as the proportion of English marriages it conducts. But it might find it hard to object to something so simple and direct.

In any event, other post-Reformation, eighteenth-century complications remain, such as the bar on a member of the royal family converting to, or marrying, a Roman Catholic if they wish to remain in the line of succession, and no one is in a particular hurry to remove that. Such a provision, in the post-Glorious Revolution 1701 Act of Settlement, is now widely regarded as otiose and unnecessary, but it has not been repealed in Britain or the fifteen other realms which would have to do so in order to effect the change.

In 2001 I was part of a team at the *Guardian* that sought to find a person in line of succession to the throne willing to complain under human rights legislation that the Act of Settlement was discriminatory. The newspaper discovered in devising such a challenge that it could only be brought by someone who was personally affected by the perceived discrimination. Incredibly, there are more than seven hundred names of potential successors, ranging from minor British royalty, through European royalty, the aristocracy and, eventually, the hoi polloi, and we went steadily down through the list. All the first several hundred valued their links with the royal family too much – the occasional invitations, the infrequent meetings, the social cachet – to take up the gallant challenge proffered by the *Guardian*. But eventually we found someone, somewhere in the five hundreds. He turned out to be an antique dealer living in Monaco and he was up for it providing the newspaper publicised his business. The great wheeze was quietly dropped on grounds of inherent ludicrousness. A parallel attempt by the newspaper's editor Alan Rusbridger to challenge another ancient statute, the Treason Felony Act of 1848, which threatened life imprisonment for anyone advocating the overthrow of the monarch even by peaceful means, also foundered after Lord Williams of Mostyn, the then Labour attorney general, unsportingly refused to guarantee that Rusbridger would not be prosecuted if he did so, although the chances of it happening were evidently vanishingly remote. The prospect of the editor's martyrdom receded further when the Law Lords eventually ruled that the legislation had anyway been superseded by the Human Rights Act and was self-evidently not enforced since the newspaper had safely advocated a republic (attained by peaceful means) without being taken to court. Nonetheless, the 1848 act remains on the statute book.

Would a twenty-first-century Calvinist take over the mantle of the late Revd Ian Paisley and raise the spectre of Popery and, if they did so, would they gain any support in this realm of Britain? Maybe not now and almost certainly not in twenty-five or thirty years' time – the first occasion on which it would seriously be tested – if Prince George eventually falls for a good Catholic girl who he wants to marry. In that case the provision would be abolished in an afternoon – but, as it is a problem which does not yet arise, governments have chosen not to address it seriously. In the meantime, the anomaly that George could one day marry anyone who is a Jew, a Muslim, a Buddhist or an Atheist, but *not* a Catholic and yet still stand in the line of succession without a need to change the eighteenth-century law remains a quirk of history. Why address it at Westminster, or in the parliaments of St Lucia, Barbuda or Papua New Guinea, unless or until it eventually happens?

The precedence given to males in the line of succession has now been dealt with, an alteration given urgency and made in some haste in case Prince William and Duchess Kate's first child had turned out to be a girl in 2013 instead of Prince George. So the oldest child now succeeds without discrimination whether they are male or female. This too is a distant eventuality, given that the heir, Charles, the heir apparent, William, and the third in line, George, are all males, so a direct female heir is not a consideration that is likely to arise for at least four generations, maybe until the start of the twenty-second century. So that is a relief. A female archbishop of Canterbury may by then even be conducting the ceremony. Chartres, known to be at best ambivalent about women's ordination – he does not ordain women as priests, though he did not stand in the way of the changes to the church's rules – said slightly gloomily, using the old Latin title: 'I expect we shall have a *Sharon cantuar* before too long.'

He looked out of the window at the darkening autumn sky outside. 'Do you know what the Queen says when there's something she doesn't want to do? "Not in this reign". Well, I expect it will come.'

Chapter 7

'You have mosquitoes,
I have the press'

(Duke of Edinburgh to a woman in the Caribbean)

There is no accounting for what will make the news on a royal tour, though something has to do so every day to justify the expense of sending reporters across the world to cover it. Unfortunately, in strictly news terms, nothing much does happen: the Queen travels on a bus or views an exhibition, Prince Charles ruefully dons (or, more likely these days, refuses to don) another silly-looking hat or inspects an organic farm, Prince William kisses a grandmother during a walkabout. Very often, the news story is little more than writing an interesting caption to go with a photograph or a wry commentary to accompany some moving pictures. The message of the medium is that the royals were going about their business, looking interested in what they were being shown, or smiling at the greetings of the crowd. However ingenious the day's visits are: a visit to a factory here, a hospital there, here a rainforest, there a parade, local responses varying from polite to ecstatic (depending on which royal they have got: the Queen gets respect, Prince William gets adulation) they do tend to pall after a while, especially on organising news desks back in London.

We should not be too cynical (though it is remarkable how often royal correspondents are) for this is just members of the royal family fulfilling their age-old function of showing themselves to the populace. They are not – theoretically – here for us, though if we were not there they might eventually miss us and the publicity we bring. But the number of truly important or really newsworthy events is minuscule: at best for a reporter there can be a taking of the temperature of royal popularity or observation of how they comport themselves. However, to acquire even these small nuggets which, with ingenuity and a few puns, will make it deep into the news pages back home, the royal party's reporters and photographers will probably have hung about for hours behind a police cordon. They will have got there far too early because of security considerations in order to catch a fleeting glimpse of a distant royal personage who mostly will not be looking in their direction. Literally fleeting: how long does it take to get out of a car and walk into a building? I once calculated, having plenty of time to do so, that on a three-day visit to the US, the press waited 12 hours to watch Prince Charles and Camilla performing various official functions for less than 20 minutes. On that occasion – freezing November days in New York and Washington DC in 2005 – we were corralled in a pen opposite the memorial garden to British victims of the 9/11 attacks in Hanover Square, downtown Manhattan at nine o'clock in the morning in order to watch the brief visit which occurred shortly before 3 p.m. and was over by 3.10 p.m. At the time we arrived at the venue, the Prince's flight to the US was probably still somewhere over Ireland. I don't expect sympathy – there are many worse and more hazardous ways of earning a living even as a journalist – but it does help to explain a certain jaundiced approach to coverage.

Prince Charles, of course, can't understand why his umpteenth worthy visit to a clean water project, a farm or a rainforest is somehow not terribly newsworthy in itself while a photograph of him looking vaguely embarrassed in a Native American headdress or dancing awkwardly with a local tribeswoman clearly is. Why on earth does he think we're there?

I received a salutary lesson in what is, or might be, news on my first day covering a royal tour – in my case the Queen's official visit to Italy in 2000. She and the Duke flew into Rome late in the afternoon and so, knowing there would be little time to file an article for the first edition, I prepared a piece earlier: waffle about the importance of links between Britain and Italy as the main reason for the visit, the significance of improving trade and a little colour of what she would be seeing. There would be a meeting with the Italian president, a state dinner, a visit to the ailing Pope John Paul II in the Vatican and, on the last day heading home, a flight to Milan to view the restored Leonardo da Vinci mural of the Last Supper in the Convent of Santa Maria delle Grazie (the best bit of the trip as far as I was concerned). As usual with royal visits, because reporters could not individually cover all of it, the components of the arrival itinerary were split between us: each group reporting back on what had happened to the rest afterwards so that no one missed anything. A little pool went off to the airport for the arrival – 'I always do that,' said the *Sun's* correspondent Charlie Rae sagely, 'Quite often something happens.' I could not see what would be so thrilling in watching the Queen descending the aircraft steps, so I stayed to attend the official welcome in the courtyard of the presidential palace where at least there would be a colourful display of Italian cavalry and a guard of honour. Foolish me. The parade went off unexceptionably and, just as the royal party disappeared inside, Charlie and the rest of the airport journalists and photographers arrived, breathless but chortling. Fantastic! A good story and Charlie had seen it...the Italian baggage handlers had tried to load the Queen's dresses on to a portable hanger and it had collapsed under the weight, dropping some items (all of which were wrapped in cellophane) on to the ground. Naively, I could not quite see the newsworthy significance of this. The lady from *OK!* magazine nearly swooned: all those dresses, in the mud (of course there was no mud, it was on the tarmac), probably ruined, costing thousands, what a humiliation. Charlie had the perfect angle though: Italian incompetence (and by extension *European* incompetence) ruining the arrival. The others sucked their teeth and agreed: that was the story of the day. It was the only story worth filing, in various degrees of irony and condescension and outrage. We returned to our hotel to send our stories. Stubbornly, I stuck to my serious line about trade and amity but to cover myself I added a paragraph tucked late into the story – about sentence twenty-five – about the dresses being rescued after a baggage mishandling. Big mistake. The following morning when the Continental editions of the British papers arrived I discovered that the *Guardian* newsdesk back home had somewhat changed my story, leading off with copy from the Press Association news agency: now it was the dropped frocks that led the story and took up most of it and my supposedly heavyweight analysis of the trip's significance was relegated to a couple of paragraphs at the end. So much for my news judgement. No wonder the royals think we're odd.

On any foreign trip by the Queen and Duke of Edinburgh or Prince William and Duchess Kate – these are now the two sure-fire newsworthy royal couples – there will be maybe twenty British press photographers present, quite apart from the local media who will usually provide dozens more. Most of the British photographers are freelancers and will have paid handsomely for the privilege of joining the party. Alongside them, depending on the nature of the tour, there are likely to be between six and fifteen reporters from British media organisations, paid for by their employers. *The Times, Daily Telegraph, Sun* and *Mirror* usually send, the *Daily Mail* often, *Daily Express* more often than not, the BBC and ITN almost invariably, the Press Association always and the *Guardian* occasionally. There are sometimes freelance reporters as well, paying their own way and hoping to make the money back by selling articles and features. The trips are expensive: because of the nature of the daily schedules the journalists and photographers have to stay in the same, invariably expensive, downtown hotels, so that they can be rounded up quickly in the morning and their organisations will be charged by the palace for any bus or coach travel, or internal air flights if these need to be arranged. There may not be any alternative if the itinerary takes the royal visitors from one remote location straight on to another overnight. In July 2011, William and Kate on their first Canadian visit, finished one day's programme at Charlottetown on Prince Edward Island on the Atlantic coast in the late afternoon, and started the next more than 2,000 miles away at Yellowknife in the North Western Territory up in the Arctic Circle the following morning (travelling by road the distance is nearer 4,000 miles and would have taken several days). Such a trip costs the thick end of £10,000 so has to be worth it, for the photographers needing to supply striking pictures every day and for the reporters hoping to file worthwhile copy.

One veteran freelance journalist working for British tabloids told me ruefully that for many years his presence had been ignored and he had been excluded from travelling with the rest of the party, having instead to chase them by scheduled flights as if his presence was of no account even though he was selling stories to mass-circulation papers back home. That had some advantages in that he was not beholden to royal officials, who like to corral the press, but was also a counterproductive tactic on the part of the palace. 'The men in grey suits treated us like scum in those days,' he said. 'They did not want to talk to you: it was all "no comment, old boy" and they wouldn't even let you on the plane or allow you into briefings. Then they would complain about everything you wrote. In the end you gave up checking out stories with them because you knew what they'd say and if you'd already stood the story up, why would you want a comment from the grey men?'

In 2007 when Prince Harry was first deployed to serve in Afghanistan, the press office chose to warn only the British correspondents of the security embargo relating to his presence in the country, not freelancers or foreign media and their British-based contacts, so when the news leaked out it was published in an Australian magazine, then on an American news website and the Prince had to be hurriedly withdrawn from the country. Should the magazine and the website have been sensitive to the security implications for the Prince of publishing the news? Of course – but the press office might also have warned the freelancers covering the royals as well.

The cost is one reason why Charles finds he is less frequently accompanied on trips these days: his tours abroad tend to be stultifyingly dull and he does not make things any easier by ostentatiously shunning the media while on them. Royal correspondents and photographers covering the Prince's trip to the Gulf states in the spring of 2015 reported that, even though he travelled on the same plane as them and saw them every day, he never once acknowledged their presence or even said good morning. This trivial discourtesy is par for the course, but does not endear him. We know the public outbursts: as when he spluttered insults under his breath at the BBC royal correspondent Nicholas Witchell. This was in March 2005, shortly before the Prince's marriage to Camilla and he and his sons had gone to Switzerland on a skiing trip. In a quid pro quo to the media, so that the royal party might be left undisturbed for the rest of the trip, they had staged a photo opportunity in their skiing gear and had agreed to answer questions. Witchell's inquiry, asked to elicit a general sound bite for the evening news – a question actually cleared by royal press officers as fit to be asked the evening before, so it was hardly underhand or unexpected – was perfectly unexceptionable, about how the princes were looking forward to their father's forthcoming wedding; all part of the game of getting a broadcastable quote. It produced a startling, muttered outburst from Charles, apparently aimed at his sons sitting beside him, but was clearly audible to the microphones on the ground just in front of him. He exclaimed: 'These bloody people. I can't bear that man. I mean, he's so awful, he really is.' Charles seems to have been annoyed that the princes were asked their opinion of his wedding – at least, that is Witchell's explanation. But it was mean-spirited, peevish and rude on Charles's part – as well as remarkably stupid – and ruined (from the royal point of view though not the media's) a perfectly straightforward and benign occasion. An official who was there sighed: 'We warned Charles about the microphones. He knew they were there, right in front of him, but he clearly did not realise how powerful they are these days. I think he doesn't like Witchell because he is often so downbeat, as if he doesn't want to be there. He just took the question the wrong way. But it looked awful.' The official shuddered at the memory. The Prince's touchiness on this occasion had been increased by the French paparazzi photographers who had been dogging him and his sons on the slopes and at their hotel, and who were present at the photo call taking more pictures. Neither side was going to back off.

The story inevitably became all about Charles's tantrum and poor Witchell's embarrassment. An additional irony was that the BBC is scarcely the most intrusive of media outlets and Witchell hardly the most truculent of reporters – quite the reverse. Of course, the Prince did not deign to apologise then or later. It is to Witchell's professional credit that he has not let even a sardonic aside intrude in his subsequent reports about the Prince since. This was unusual only in being so public – and recorded. On other occasions, Charles deliberately turns his back or ducks his head when photographers want to take a picture, or snarls a snide remark. This may explain why he so often looks glum or bad tempered in pictures and, funnily enough it does not make him any more popular with the press, who are, after all, only doing their job, which is usually intended to show him in a good light. At a time of media cutbacks, his trips are increasingly ones to avoid. The Prince employs seven press officers and so perhaps feels he does not need to trouble himself.

Sometimes his remoteness, protected by an impenetrable bubble of advisers and officials who do not wish to disturb him, seems otherworldly and even callous. The press corps had an example of this during Charles and Camilla's tour to Pakistan in 2006, when several members of the local police force assisting in the visit were killed in an accident. The incident was ghastly – the car in which the four policemen were travelling slid in the gravel at the edge of an unprotected mountain road, teetered on the edge for a few moments and then toppled over a ravine and into a rushing river far below. The policemen could be seen trying unavailingly to scramble out of the car even as it slid. It was seen by the entire British media corps who were being driven along the same narrow and precipitous road to the remote village venue where Charles was due to open a new school. It was the convoy of press vehicles that the police car was attempting to overtake when it slipped off the road into the void. The Prince's party did not have to brave the same route: they travelled by helicopter. What made the incident even more pointless was that the reason for the police car's hurried overtaking was that they were carrying the British media's little cardboard accreditation passes for the event and had been ordered to arrive at the village first. A shaken group of journalists arrived later at the venue. We were conscious that we would have to travel the same route back later, in the dark. The Prince was told of the accident but showed no reaction, his spokesman explained, because the incident had not been officially confirmed. It is only fair to say that the Pakistani police reacted imperturbably, too: 'They died in the line of duty,' the commanding officer at the village said tersely.

Occasionally a story emerges which seems to illustrate a larger truth about someone – and in the Prince's case it was the yarn about the valet employed to squeeze out his toothpaste. That story and a similar one about the same valet having to hold a specimen bottle for the Prince to pee into have a slight truth in that it apparently did happen, briefly, in 1990 when Charles had broken his arm in a fall while playing polo. Most people in such a situation manage somehow on their own, but not it seems the Prince of Wales at that point in his life. The valet in question, Michael Fawcett, was formerly Charles's closest and most trusted servant, though he felt obliged to resign from the Prince's service in 2003 following a critical report about mismanagement in the royal household – only to be employed thereafter on a freelance basis by the Prince to organise events. In the words of the former royal press officer Dickie Arbiter: 'Fawcett has

hree royal generations: The Queen, Duke of Edinburgh, Prince Charles and Prince William:
l dressed up and somewhere to go. © *Anwar Hussein/Getty Images*

above: The ideal Victorian family: Prince Albert, the Queen and their nine children, an early informal photograph taken at Osborne House, 1857. © *Royal Collection Trust/Her Majesty Queen Elizabeth II 2015*

right: Queen Victoria, portrait by Bassano, 1882: with little tucks here and there to smooth the skin, remove a double chin or two and make the bust more shapely.
© *Alexander Bassano/Spencer Arnold/Getty Images*

left: The King who failed: Edward VIII gazes haughtily at the camera.
© *Hirz/Getty Images*

left: George V speaks to the empire, 'from his home and from his heart', via microphones encased in walnut wood.

right: Eighty years on, the Queen's Christmas broadcast is slightly more informal.

above: If the crown fits: George VI and his family on the Buckingham Palace balcony following his coronation in May 1937. His elder daughter Elizabeth (second left in front of her mother) is already perfecting the royal wave. © *Popperfoto/Getty Images*

below: Same balcony seventy-eight years later, different cast, with one notable exception, and only one tentative wave. © *Keith Hewitt/GC Images*

left: A royal duty: happier with his stamps or at the races, King George V nevertheless presents the FA Cup to Manchester City's captain Sam Cowan in 1934. City had just beaten Portsmouth 2-1. © *Keystone/Getty Images*

above: A willing annual obligation: the Queen looks forward to the racing at Ascot week, in the carriage procession with the Duke. © *Chris Jackson/Getty Images for Ascot Racecourse*

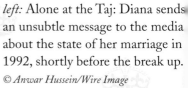

left: Alone at the Taj: Diana sends an unsubtle message to the media about the state of her marriage in 1992, shortly before the break up.
© *Anwar Hussein/Wire Image*

below: The Way Ahead: The Queen takes tea with Mrs Susan McCarron at her Glasgow housing association flat in July 1999. © *Dave Cheskin/PA Archive/Press Association Images*

above: The Way Ahead 2: The selfie generation takes a picture: why bother to see the real thing when you can look at her, slightly obscured, on your iPhone later? © *Peter Macdiarmid – Pool/Getty Images*

right: Prince Harry is rather ore at home with selfies (and paper crowns): in Australia 2015. © *Chris Jackson/Getty Images*

above: William, Kate and Harry (and Beatrice, left) cheer their cousin Zara Phillips on to a silver medal as an eventer at the London Olympics 2012.
© *Carl Court/AFP/Getty Image*

left: Long to reign over us? Prince George, aged sixteen months, sits for his first formal portrait on the steps of Kensington Palace, December 2014. He may not always find the camera so friendly.
© *The Duke and Duchess of Cambridge/PA Wire via Getty Images*

been there for so many years, so close in times of stress, knowing all the ins and outs and all the warts.' This and other stories, such as that the Prince takes his own, soft leather toilet seat with him when he stays somewhere on visits, and a supply of Kleenex Velvet toilet paper as well, and that he presents his hostesses with a list of likes and dislikes (likes include soft-boiled eggs, fish, game, pasta, soft cheese, dry Martinis and Laphroaig whisky; dislikes include coffee, chocolate, nuts, garlic, curries, pork, oysters and blue cheese) might be thought unexceptionable, except for the prince's well-aired concerns for the lives of ordinary people. Similarly, his architectural interests, given full rein in the Poundbury model village outside Dorchester in Dorset whose design and street layout he has supervised, also give rise to a suggestion of hypocrisy. At Poundbury the residents find their houses sited extremely close together to facilitate the good neighbourliness and community spirit that the Prince senses has been lost elsewhere, but which he does not seem to feel ever applies to himself. His staff at St James's Palace are encouraged to cycle to work to save the planet by cutting carbon emissions, yet the Prince often uses official cars, including an armour-plated Bentley, in preference to the Jaguar limousine, modified to run on biodiesel from used cooking oil, which he, with his ecological concerns, might otherwise have been expected to prefer (except he does not like the headroom, apparently). Armour plating might be necessary since the Rolls Royce he was travelling in to the Royal Variety Performance was trashed by demonstrators in 2010, though he and Camilla were unhurt. These stories get told with a certain glee and are occasionally rebutted, or explained away, by his spokesmen, but they resonate precisely because of the difference between appearance and reality.

It is easy to tell which members of the royal family the press likes: the Queen, Prince Harry, the late Queen Mother; and who they loathe: Charles, Andrew, Edward; those who stop, smile, pose and sometimes banter, and those who snarl, grimace, glare, sneer and turn away. The latter group do not seem to realise the connection between their behaviour and the coverage they receive – though you'd think they might, after all this time. Interestingly, one who has seemingly learned the lesson is Princess Anne, who used to receive an awful press when she glowered and swore at journalists and who no longer does so now she appears somewhat more benign – though perhaps that has something to do with the fact that she is much more rarely in the national spotlight these days. It is not to be expected that the royal family would actively court or enjoy the attentions of the media. Some of them have not been well treated in the past, though often for indiscretions they have brought upon themselves. But the media is crucial to how they are perceived by the public and they cannot expect inherent or unearned deference: that happened too often in the past – and even if the Press could be muzzled or relied upon for discretion and obsequiousness (and the events of the past twenty years have shown they can't be) then social media would soon spread an alternative version. Prince Charles's behaviour does not much matter now, but it hinders him getting such messages across as he wishes to convey and may signify a great deal when he becomes King. A series of similar misjudgements as in the Witchell episode will scarcely assist his reputation and may even prove catastrophic to the institution's standing in the public eye. The monarchy is supposed to sprinkle hope, optimism and stardust, and a gloomy, peevish, hectoring old man will not do that. The media are interested in him not particularly for his views or his profound commitments to a number of causes, but because of who he is and what he will become. He has to learn that he needs the media even more than it needs him.

This ought to come as no surprise to any member of the royal family since there are phalanxes of press officers to service the media and smooth the way: Buckingham Palace has a team of seven, the Prince himself has his separate team, there is a press adviser for princes William and Harry, there is a press team for the Royal Collection – the Queen's paintings and treasures – and a press officer in Scotland for when they head north of the border. It is clearly the largest communications unit that the royals have ever assembled – and they have been at it a long time. The first royal press officer was actually appointed in the reign of George III. Then the King was annoyed at inaccuracies in the newspapers and wanted them rebutted. The post was initially known as the court newsman: the appointee being responsible for sending the court circular of official engagements to the press. The appointment was ambiguous however, since the man was paid partly by the court and partly by the newspapers when they used the paragraphs he supplied. It was also virtually hereditary, being held by three generations of the Doane family, until the appointment of Thomas Beard, a journalist and friend of Charles Dickens, in 1864.

Newspaper interest in and comment on the royal family had started well before then. As early as the 1720s there were qualms about newspaper coverage and how to make it more favourable to the King. The historian Linda Colley quotes a letter to the press in 1723 in her book *Britons*: ''Tis pity but some way could be devised whereby His Majesty's speeches and all other loyal papers might be dispersed more publicly through the nation . . . The news coming only to some particular houses in market towns, the vulgar commonly take things by hearsay and live all their time in ignorance.'

The first to suffer from public criticism for his lifestyle was inevitably George IV who resorted to bribery. He was not unusual in attempting to pay off unfriendly newspapers and cartoonists: as early as the 1790s the government was paying out £5,000 a year from secret service funds to keep loyal newspapers sweet. But the character of the monarchy had changed by the 1840s, with a young, happily married Queen on the throne, surrounded by a growing family. The lack of scandal did not dissuade the press from intruding, precisely because of the public fascination with the model royals – so like the home lives of their own dear families, or at least what they aspired them to be like. The newspapers found they had a ready readership for royal gossip and a public agog for details of the royal family's lives, what they looked like, how they dressed and what the inside of their palaces looked like. This could only expand as controls and taxation on papers were lifted in the 1840s and 1850s, so reducing costs and cover prices and as the newly developed rotary printing presses (so admired by the Queen during her visits to the Great Exhibition in 1851) cranked into operation, enhancing the number of copies that could be printed for each edition. The spread of the railways meant that the papers could be on almost every breakfast table in the land each morning. Newspapers were selling for a few pence rather than shillings, more people were literate enough to read them and more could afford to buy them. Circulations rose exponentially: the *Daily Telegraph*, for instance, founded in 1855 (ironically, to air its founder's grievances against the Queen's cousin the Duke of Cambridge) soon halved its cover price to a penny and saw its circulation soar from 27,000 to 141,000 within a year, and to more than a million within a decade or so.

Selected members of the press were given passes to cover the Queen's wedding in 1840 and journalists were soon resorting to undercover tactics to obtain more inside information. In 1844 one Rumsey Forster of the *Morning Post* managed to insinuate himself among the crew of the royal yacht *Victoria and Albert* on the journey back from the Isle of Wight to the mainland. He was spotted by Prince Albert and chucked into a small rowing boat being towed along behind the yacht. When the boat passed the mudflats near Portsmouth, Forster was ejected and forced to wade half a mile through the mud to dry land, soaked and filthy. The *Daily Mirror*'s reporter Ryan Parry, who worked as a footman at Buckingham Palace for two months in 2003, at least escaped that fate and his newspaper was allowed to keep the syndication rights to the pictures he took, which included a shot of the plastic Tupperware containers in which the Queen and Duke kept their breakfast cereals. The newspaper did, however, have to pay the Queen's £25,000 legal costs when the palace took the nearly unprecedented step of suing for breach of confidentiality – a commercial bargain as far as the paper was concerned.

Modern tabloids had nothing to teach the gentlemen of the Victorian press about intrusion. The equipment was different but the methods were much the same. *Punch* satirised the *Morning Post*'s reporter for sitting in a bed of nettles in the Scottish Highlands for hours, hoping to spot the Queen wandering past – much as the *Daily Mirror*'s royal correspondent James Whitaker hid in the bushes in the Caribbean to catch a glimpse of Princess Diana 130 years later. A coachload of reporters was driven off the road as it attempted to follow the royal family on holiday in 1873, Victoria laughing heartily at their discomfort as she passed. *Chambers' Edinburgh Journal* in 1845 wrote of the horde of penny-a-line freelancers stalking Victoria: 'They described with painful minuteness every inch of her journey, giving facts, however small, wherever they could get them and substituting surmises when facts were not to be obtained. No respect had they for royal privacy; and the colour of the royal gown or bonnet, or of the royal spouse's hat and hat-band and shooting jacket were carefully noted from day to day – always with a view to the three half-pences that were thus to be acquired.

Every place that Her Majesty passed, or obtained even a glimpse of in passing, became of consequence immediately in their eyes.'

One of the first details royal reporters are still given by press officers at events these days is precisely what the Queen or the Duchess of Cambridge is wearing, what shade of colour it is and, as importantly, who made it. The readers want to know, it cannot be classed as a state secret and, dotted like sultanas in a Christmas pudding, the relevant facts are always slipped into the reports. The choice of outfit can then be admired, copied or suitably sneered at subsequently by the columnists. Thus, the Associated Press's breathless report (carried in the *Daily Mail*) in December 2014 that, during a visit to New York the pregnant duchess wore 'a hot-pink Mulberry coat, black tights and black stiletto-heeled pumps, over a black dress from maternity designer Seraphine', followed three days later by the newspaper's columnist Jan Moir who said that the Duchess and Prince William were like 'a couple of dreary suburbanites, a Mr and Mrs Bland who trundle around the world in mumsy dresses and dad-trousers . . . somehow (managing) to look as if they are attending a golf club dinner in the Home Counties just after they have finished the weekend shop at Waitrose.' Nothing quite so snobbish as a newspaper columnist come to judgement.

In its assessment of how much freelancers might earn, *Chambers' Edinburgh Journal* may have underestimated the amount of money the freelance stalkers could make in covering the royals: it was said that the London papers would pay them £1,000 a year for their coverage – which, for a penny a line, represented a considerable word count. And it was worth it in circulation terms: *The Times* nearly doubled its circulation from 60,000 to 108,000 on the day after the Prince of Wales's wedding in 1863: a clear profit of about £800.

In 1848, a journalist named Jasper Judge managed to obtain copies of sketches by the Queen and Prince Albert showing their children and close friends. They had been intended for private circulation and had been printed under conditions of great secrecy. Judge and a London publisher of scurrilous texts named William Strange planned to put the drawings on public exhibition and had to be taken to court in order to stop them. The judge inevitably sided with the royals, denouncing a sordid intrusion into the family's private life: '. . . into the home – a word hitherto sacred amongst us – into the home of a family, a family whose private life forms not their only unquestionable title to the most marked respect.' Queen Victoria herself of course did not hesitate to intrude on her own life, as the publication of her book *Leaves from the Journal of Our Life in the Highlands* in 1868 and its sequel *More Leaves* in 1884 demonstrated. The books, containing the Queen's artless sketches[18] and gentle accounts of holidays in Scotland – the grammar and spelling tidied up for publication by Sir Arthur Helps, the clerk to the Privy Council – did phenomenally well, such was the public's appetite for royal information. The first sold more than 100,000 copies and was even translated into Hindi and the profits from sales were donated to charity. The Queen evidently hoped that such books would not only inspire her subjects with the simplicity of royal tastes and the condescension they bestowed on their servants but would also remove the need for any further biographies intruding into her private life.

That was a vain hope, but the highland journals and the discreet editing of her letters for publication in the years following her death by Viscount Esher and Arthur Benson, served to create a near-idyllic

---

18 Of the Queen's etchings, the Scottish poet and translator Sir Theodore Martin wrote: 'Of them it is enough to say that the drawing is not remarkable and that, as etchings, the difficulties of the art have not been overcome.' Modern art critics have tended to be similarly sniffy about Prince Charles's more accomplished watercolours of the Cairngorms.

and consequently false image of a sweet-natured Queen and her winsome domestic life. As the future Lord Stamfordham, then Edward VII's deputy private secretary, wrote to them: 'Her memory is loved and venerated by all English speaking people . . . and if I were the king, both from the point of view of son and mother and also for the sake of the monarchical idea and "culte" I would publish nothing which could tend to shake the position of Queen Victoria in the minds of her subjects.' Only with the publication of Lytton Strachey's irreverent biography in 1921 did the ice around the Queen's reputation begin to crack – much to the outrage of George V, and the extent of Esher and Benson's deliberate censorship of Victoria's image has only become generally known with the publication of Yvonne M. Ward's PhD thesis in 2014, published in book form as *Censoring Queen Victoria*.

The Queen's successors naturally wished to profit from an idealised image of the monarchy and not to see anything published that might tarnish its perfection, however false a picture that might convey. Journalism was – is – less easy to control, even if its tone is largely deferential and adulatory. Here was the nub: for the Victorian court, journalists were not only intruding, but also showing disrespect. The air of snobbery remains strong in palace circles even a century and a half later. 'There was a day,' wrote the veteran journalist T.P. O'Connor in 1887, 'when any allusion to the personal appearance, the habits, the clothes or the home and social life of any person would have been resented as an impertinence and almost an indecency.' By the late 1840s, however, several of the national newspapers had their own accredited royal correspondents, allowed access to events though usually kept as discreetly out of the way as possible as they tended not to wear court dress. When the Princess Royal married Prince Frederick Wilhelm of Prussia in January 1858, six reporters were allowed into the Chapel

Royal to cover the event, but were screened off behind a red silk curtain. One hundred and fifty years later, the media are allowed to sit for royal services in the south transept of Westminster Abbey, appropriately or otherwise in Poets' Corner, which does allow occasional distant glimpses of what is going on, though not the high altar – but at least television screens are also provided these days so that the journalists can see what is happening out of their sight, just like the rest of the world.

This proximity, but non-proximity, is a constant feature of royal reporting. Journalists assigned to the beat are writing about an institution and its personalities that they can see but never touch, nor usually speak to. Unlike almost every other specialism that is reported on journalists cannot interview the monarch or, except in limited, strictly controlled circumstances, a member of the royal family. This also tends to go for their senior staff: it is rare for a private secretary to speak to the media, certainly on the record, and background briefings are rare too. There are seldom opportunities to meet privately or socially either. This is not conducive to grown-up or informed reporting and is one reason why the stories are so often either trivial or – a favourite palace word – unhelpful. It also assists the palace in denying stories or denouncing them as inaccurate, even when both sides know them to be true.

But very occasionally these days, there are formal receptions for the media – at Windsor Castle once before the Queen's golden jubilee in 2002 and then again in 2011 at Buckingham Palace shortly before the diamond jubilee. They have both been crowded events, calculated to impress on the royals how right they are to have as little to do with the media as possible, with hordes surging obsequiously around the Queen and Duke, and on the latter occasion around the Duchess of Cambridge, too. There is a rich seam of unintentional humour and the Queen teases the media moguls milling around her as a way of getting her own back. At the Windsor reception in 2002 she asked to be introduced to Dominic Lawson, then editor of the recently redesigned *Sunday Telegraph*, only to question him when he appeared, not for advice on a pressing issue of the moment, or to congratulate him on the scintillating nature of his paper, but as to why he had moved the crossword puzzle from the page on which she was used to finding it.[19] Meanwhile, the Duke beadily approached a group from the *Independent*, which is famously reluctant to cover royal affairs at all. 'Why are you here?' he asked the editor Simon Kelner. 'Because I was invited,' the hapless hack replied. 'Well, you didn't *have* to come,' the Duke snorted back. The Duke also found himself at one stage fallen among *Guardian* writers and was asked by the columnist Polly Toynbee whether he ever read the paper. 'No fear,' he replied, but he would probably have said that to all the female columnists.

Such presumptuousness in questioning would have been unthinkable only a few years earlier. For the first sixteen years of the Queen's reign, her press secretary was Commander Richard Colville who was known as 'the abominable no man' to the ranks of the media, for his reluctance to give them any assistance or information whatsoever. A former naval officer, he preferred to divulge no more than was in the formal court circular of the Queen's previous day's activities. In this, despite the best efforts of Clive Wigram in the 1920s to open up the monarchy, Colville was clearly following general precedent after he became press secretary in 1947. It would be inconceivable for any palace press officer to last twenty years in the job today, as Colville did before his retirement in 1968 – but then he did believe in going home, if possible, in mid-afternoon and remaining

---

19 The puzzle was subsequently restored to its previous place in the paper. Who says the royals have no influence over the media?

incommunicado until the following morning. In the words of the gentlemanly royal biographer and journalist Kenneth Rose, a man who would have found it difficult ever to be either offensive or impertinent: 'There was nothing breezy about Colville, at least in the performance of his duties. Press inquiries were met at best with guarded courtesy, sometimes with impatient disdain, never with good humour...it was particularly unfortunate that Colville's costive reserve coincided with a widespread quickening of interest in the monarchy. Lacking previous knowledge of the press, he seemed to make no distinction between journalists in search of scandal or sensation and those – the majority – who needed little encouragement to stimulate and strengthen loyalty to the Crown. All were made to feel that their questions were impertinent if not downright vulgar.'

Colville went further, writing to the Press Council, the newspapers' then regulatory body, that the Queen was entitled to expect that her family would attain the same privacy at home as any other family was entitled to enjoy. This was in the period when the Queen's Scottish former nanny Marian Crawford was cast into outer darkness by the royal family for having the temerity to write an anodyne account in 1950, *The Little Princesses*, about Elizabeth and Margaret growing up as children. Crawfie had the limited and temporary consolation of the book becoming an international bestseller, but the lifelong humiliation of being regarded as a betrayer by her former charges: as Margaret said when asked about it: 'Crawfie? She snaked.' In answering Colville, however, the council, not known for its robust defence of press freedom, responded reasonably: 'The private lives of public men and women, especially royal persons, have always been the subject of natural curiosity. That is one of the consequences of fame or eminence or sincere national affection. Everything therefore that touches the Crown is of public interest and concern.'

As Rose says, Colville's period as press secretary coincided with an increasing interest in royal events: Princess Elizabeth was just getting married, then she was having her first babies, then her father was gravely ill and then she herself was succeeding to the throne, and before long her sister would be hoping to marry Group Captain Peter Townsend – more than enough stories to interest the public and be of significance to the Crown. Townsend himself was bitter that he received no help, guidance or advice from the Commander, beyond being told that he was on his own. Instead, as the affair reached its climax in October 1955 – would Margaret break free and marry the man she loved, even though he was a divorcee? – Colville's reticence made matters worse. He deigned to make a statement that no announcement concerning the princess's future was 'at present' contemplated, which naturally only fired all the more worldwide interest in the story and increased the speculation that he was trying so ineptly to extinguish.

In the post-abdication world after Edward VIII stood down in 1936, the British media was determined not to be caught out again. Then, no newspaper had dared to break the unofficial embargo, fearful of official displeasure or, more directly, the possible effect of disclosure on their advertising revenues if outraged companies withdrew their business. Editors seem also to have been waiting for *The Times* to take the lead, but Geoffrey Dawson, the editor, wanted Baldwin, the prime minister, to tell him what he wished to see printed. This complicity created then and ever since a conscious determination by the media never to be caught like that again. Twenty years on, Colville could hold the line – 'I am not what you North Americans call a press officer,' he told one Canadian journalist – and, although the young Queen must have approved his ineptitude, it was an attitude to the outside world that could not last.

Within a year of Colville's retirement in 1968, the royal family had sanctioned the most extraordinary turnaround in their attitude to the media, by agreeing to take part in a television documentary about their lives. Called *The Royal Family*, the 90-minute programme, shown on both the BBC and ITV, and subsequently in 125 other countries including the US, was supposedly an intimate and natural fly-on-the-wall type programme showing the Queen, Duke and their children going about their lives in a completely artless fashion. It was, a former courtier told the historian Ben Pimlott years later, an attempt to buy popularity. As such, it succeeded for its time as an unprecedented insight into the family. There were scenes of them greeting the American president Richard Nixon and engaging in stilted conversation with him, a sequence of Prince Charles playing the cello, the Queen buying sweets for the young Prince Edward at a village shop in Scotland and the family enjoying a barbecue on a loch side at Balmoral with Prince Philip doing the cooking. The programme had been the idea of Lord Mountbatten – probably, he usually claimed credit for any initiative – whose son-in-law Lord Brabourne was a documentary film-maker and it was enthusiastically backed by William Heseltine, the private secretary who had been a press officer in Australia and so came from a less hidebound background, and by the Duke of Edinburgh himself. The Queen was more ambivalent but went along with the project; her passivity and pragmatism is something many palace officials comment upon.

Intended to be studiously informal, the programme was in fact carefully contrived and controlled, with a huge ratio of film shot to the amount finally broadcast. It presented the royals as they wished to be seen. There were no potentially off-putting scenes of members of the royal family shooting game and the conversational moments were both formal and anodyne. On one celebrated occasion when the Queen was being filmed chatting to some Commonwealth heads of government she was startled by the sudden appearance of a long microphone, which was promptly dealt with by a royal protection officer who leaped in to give it a karate chop.

The documentary was greeted with wild enthusiasm, on the basis that nothing of the sort had ever been seen before, showing the royal family as real, breathing human beings (though of a rather self-conscious and ponderously refined sort) and that, of course, had been its intention: a counteract in the swinging sixties to the impression that the whole institution was too pompus and remote. This had been exemplified (and much commented upon) a couple of years earlier in October 1966 when the Queen had decided not to rush to the scene of the Aberfan tragedy when an unstable nearby spoil heap in South Wales had slid down a mountainside and engulfed the local village school, killing many of the children and their teachers inside. The terrible event, in many ways a retribution from Britain's industrial past, became vivid and visceral as television pictures from the scene were beamed around the world and, as would come to be expected at the scenes of later disasters, political leaders and, indeed, Princess Margaret's husband Lord Snowdon and the Duke of Edinburgh soon visited the scene to pay their respects. But not the Queen; she thought her presence would be a distraction from the rescue effort and could not see that her attendance might bring comfort to the bereaved. She was also, possibly, understandably reticent in the face of so much grief – as she would be thirty years later following the death of Princess Diana – and her perceived lack of empathy was taken by some in the press as an example of the palace's remoteness from ordinary folk. Appearances were deceptive however and when she did eventually go to the village a week later her visit was appreciated. 'She really feels this very deep. After all she is the mother of four children.

We had four too and now we have only two,' one woman told reporters. The Queen remains of a generation that does stoicism better than emotion.

'The monarchy was falling behind the times. There was a need for a positive exercise and there was a realisation that the way you did it was by television,' said Ronald Allison, then the BBC's court correspondent, who subsequently became the Queen's first press secretary to have journalistic experience in 1973. In other words, the intention ran counter to everything for which Commander Colville had striven for over twenty years. There were other purposes as well: it was a period in which deference to institutions was increasingly challenged and the staid old ways were ridiculed. Informality and innovation were the watchwords, though there were limits to that so far as the royals were concerned. There was a decision that the Queen should knight the elderly returning round-the-world yachtsman Francis Chichester in public, at Greenwich, not in private at the palace, using the sword that Elizabeth I had used to knight Sir Francis Drake four hundred years before. If this seems a minor matter now, then it was regarded as a bold and modern thing to do for the first time, in full view of the cameras. Chichester, a wizened old salt and rather curmudgeonly character, was hardly as glamorous (or as bold) as his piratical Tudor predecessor, but his voyage had caught the public imagination and started a trend for solo round-the-world sailing.

More important than this though was the fact that Prince Charles was reaching adulthood and needed to be projected as the heir to the throne. He was young, certainly, rather more problematically dynamic and could almost be presented as dashing – a suitable candidate for a modern monarchy. It was a hard task – the long-haired, rebellious hippy years had passed the Prince by. Charles was at one of the most aristocratic colleges in Cambridge, dressed in tweed jackets and corduroy trousers, and was short-haired and over-protected. The nearest he got to raciness was at an undergraduate review when he awkwardly imitated the Goons, from his favourite radio show, which was by now not only off-air but slightly dated. The solution was not only showing him as a 'normal' adolescent in the documentary – his interventions in family conversations were generally ignored by his parents, so that was an authentic touch – but also to invest him formally as Prince of Wales at a spectacular ceremony at Carnarvon Castle in July 1969. The ceremonial, largely devised for the occasion, took place under a large Perspex canopy designed by Lord Snowdon, Princess Margaret's husband, and Charles was crowned by his mother with a very 1960s-looking gold coronet trimmed with ermine, looking 'like a candle-snuffer' when placed on his head, it was unkindly said. The event, too, proved popular, especially as it was given a slight whiff of danger by some half-baked bomb attacks beforehand by Welsh Nationalists, two of whom contrived to blow themselves up in the process.

There were those within the palace and in stuffier conservative circles outside who said that the royal family's attempts to be 'with it', especially the family documentary, were doing precisely what Bagehot had warned against – letting daylight in on the magic. 'I don't think that by the late 1960s you could have continued as if nothing had ever happened,' said one subsequent royal communications director. 'It was something that was inevitable. They could not continue to hide away. And the Queen saw that.'

There could certainly be no going back: it was a path which led inexorably to the spectacular wedding of Charles to Diana twelve years later and the equally spectacular break up of their marriage – and those of two of Charles's siblings – in the 1990s. The upsides of being accessible: the humanising of the monarch and the evolving informality of the palace were countered by the downsides: media intrusiveness and public interest in the personalities behind the previously impenetrable palace walls. What else could they have done? 'To those who say "it started the rot", it is possible to reply, "how long could the curtains be held in place?"' Allison told Pimlott. The royal soap opera had begun...

Chapter 8:

'I think we're a soap opera'

(Prince Charles to Jeremy Paxman)

*T*he attempt to present Prince Charles in the 1970s as something he manifestly was not: a handsome action hero who also happened to be the most eligible young bachelor in the world, was largely a creation of the British press, but not entirely so. There was some collusion from the palace and especially from the Prince's 'honorary grandfather', his great-uncle Lord Mountbatten, who was determined to mould him for kingship, preferably in his own image and with himself as kingmaker. Charles, a sensitive, somewhat shy, unselfconfident soul, had had to endure the sort of rugged upbringing he loathed: Gordonstoun public school followed by a time (which he enjoyed more) at a similar remote establishment in Australia, then a lonely undergraduate life at Cambridge and a period of training as a junior officer in the Royal Navy. While it was probably a more varied sequence than previous princes had undergone (with similar lack of enthusiasm) it was still a rarified and socially narrow experience, every attempt at fostering normality somehow isolating a young man born to be King. The difference was that each outing was now accompanied at every step by an obsessive media interest, for he was the first young, male heir to the throne for fifty years – and every attempt to show Charles to be a normal young man underlined the fact that he palpably was not.

In November 1948 at the time of Charles's birth *The Times* had editorialised: 'This child from the moment of his birth becomes to many peoples the symbol of their common aspirations for an even more splendid realm and Commonwealth than have been handed down to them by the virtue and prowess of their ancestors.' And so the weight of expectation continued, especially once he had become the heir to the throne at the age of three – and has continued ever since for more than sixty years. Few people spend all their lives, the best part of seven decades, in training and waiting for their life's real work to begin, or knowing that their destiny depends on the timing of their mother's death. Much of the royal soap opera of the past forty years has indeed been centred on Charles, his future and the obsessive question of what sort of king he will be.

By the mid-1970s, the active search was on for a royal bride, not only among the media but within the royal family itself. Once Charles left the navy in 1976 and especially once he had incautiously told an interviewer at the time that he thought thirty – two years hence – would be a good time to marry, the quest was on.[20] But who would want him, with his staid middle-aged tastes and his esoteric pursuits, such as hunting, coarse fishing and polo? While a dynastic marriage to a neighbouring, cousinly European royal family was no longer thought necessary, a suitable bride could not just be anyone: there ought to be

---

20 An exasperated (and possibly tipsy) Prince William confided something similar to a reporter from the *Sun* who he bumped into at a nightclub while on a skiing holiday in Klosters in 2005: 'Look, I'm only twenty-two, for God's sake. I am too young to marry at my age. I don't want to get married until I'm at least twenty-eight or maybe thirty.' And so it came to pass: he was twenty-eight when he married in 2011, though by then he and Kate Middleton had known each other for nine years.

at least something aristocratic about her – otherwise how could she know what would be expected? Marrying into the House of Windsor was, the Prince said, a sacrifice no one should be expected to make. It would be a constricted, goldfish-bowl life, governed by frustrating conventions and traditions that seemed dated by the 1980s, as perhaps he knew and his wiser girlfriends understood. But, every time the Prince was seen in the approximate vicinity of a potentially eligible young woman: Davina Sheffield, Sabrina Guinness, Lady Jane Wellesley, Anna Wallace, Lady Sarah Spencer, Princess Astrid of Belgium (though, as a Catholic, she rather ruled herself out), the cameras would click and the speculation revive until even the columnists grew weary of the possibility of writing something fresh. It went on for nearly five years. In all this, remarkably it now seems, no one particularly noticed the real love of his life, Camilla Shand, who had given up waiting for him to make up his mind and gone off to marry the army officer Andrew Parker-Bowles instead. The Prince's courtship with her in the early 1970s had been too brief and discreet, and had occurred before the media was really focused on the great bride hunt. He had not forgotten though and evidently neither had she.

The chief pander was the ever-ambitious Mountbatten who laid on his private estate at Broadlands outside Romsey for secret weekend trysts and was not slow to push his granddaughter Amanda Knatchbull forward as a potential spouse and future Queen. Such soul-destroying, passion-killing, attention must have been excruciating for both the Prince and his girlfriends, especially knowing that any publicity would strain friendship and kill romance stone-dead. It was hardly the Prince's fault that his coming of age coincided with a ferocious tabloid circulation war and a desperate competition for scoops that would ditch the opposition and bring what could be classed as good news to the reading public at a gloomy and demoralising period of national life.

At a time when the royal family was opening up more to the public, doing walkabouts at the Queen's silver jubilee in 1977, competing at the Olympics as Princess Anne had done the previous year, the Prince's self-conscious quest for a wife was bound to become an obsessive royal story. There were several coincidences of timing in this, all baleful from the Prince's point of view. Tabloid newspaper competition was intense – bingo was the great contemporary circulation catch, with Rupert Murdoch's *Sun* pitted ruthlessly for readers against Robert Maxwell's *Daily Mirror,* but there was also the nearly perfect coincidence that the American soap opera *Dallas*, the endless and improbable fictional tale of intrigue, lust and shenanigans among a rich Texan oil family, was also a hugely popular weekly event. If the US had the Ewings, the Brits at least had the Windsors, with the added advantage that they were real people whose lives could be constructed as an artefact to mimic the soap. The proprietors did not mind; Maxwell was desperate to make money and beat his rival, and Murdoch knew a good story when he saw one – and, as a chippy Australian, did not care too much for the British monarchy as a system of inherited privilege. In Kelvin Mackenzie, too, he had an editor at the *Sun* after his own heart: ruthless, hard-driving and reckless. Deference, even to the monarchy, was dead: the newspapers could point to the occasions when they had bowed to the palace's wishes and kept their readers in the dark. The royals were fair game to be pursued ruthlessly like any other. In *Sun* newsroom-speak each scoop was 'whacking the Germans'. It was prurient and also fun (for the newspapers themselves and, presumably, their readers) but there was also a legitimate public interest in who the heir to the throne would marry and how the dynasty would carry on – at least, that was the excuse. 'Kelvin MacKenzie was extremely difficult to deal with,' one palace communications secretary of the period told me. 'He was simply frightful and rude: he didn't care. At least Piers Morgan, when he was editor of the *Mirror* would ring up and warn us when something was going in the paper – and he would often ask confidentially whether his reporter's story was true before publication. He was much more courteous and civil.'

Both papers and their smaller rival the *Daily Star* put dedicated correspondents on the case, with the *Sun* demanding of its reporter Harry Arnold an exclusive a week, preferably for Monday mornings when the weekend news was otherwise dull. As MacKenzie once told a bemused Arnold: 'Don't worry if it's not true – so long as there's not too much fuss about it afterwards.' The convention was that the royals might grumble, but they would not sue and so any story was a free hit. If they complained – well, at least they had noticed the paper and the denial might make a sniggering news story in its own right. The era of newspaper forelock-tugging and obsequiousness was over.

The palace got used to dealing with bizarre stories. This one came from one of Arnold's successors. 'The most ludicrous one I ever had was just before a Greece v England soccer match,' said one palace communications official of the period. 'The *Sun* rang up and asked whether it was true – because they had it on very good authority – that the Queen Mother had died and her body was being kept in a deep freeze so they didn't have to announce her death and distract attention from the match. I think he asked it with a straight face but he probably knew it was rubbish. Anyway she lived for some time after that…'

In the circumstances, it was almost bound to end badly, though how precisely it would do so was not at all clear, certainly not when, almost miraculously, Charles's choice appeared to settle on a teenager named Lady Diana Spencer – another *Sun* scoop after its photographer Arthur Edwards spotted the couple chatting at the Braemar Games. Finally, at the age of thirty-two in 1981, almost desperately, Charles had chosen a potential bride. She, understandably, appeared star-struck, like the winner of a game show prize or at the very least the heroine of the *Cinderella* tale, though without the cinders: young, pretty, demure and virginal, with an aristocratic background, but without a racy past, and even a semblance of ordinary, modern life in a shared London flat and with a job at a children's nursery. The press was rather charmed by her diffidence and shy smile when cameramen mobbed her as she went to work, and were even more so when she posed holding a child and the sunlight behind her made her skirt appear translucent. She appeared, said Charles's biographer Jonathan Dimbleby, to have fallen in love with an idea rather than an individual. But, better than that, she had the youth and glamour to brighten up the institution with the infusion of new, revivifying blood.

Charles just appeared relieved. That they had virtually nothing in common and had hardly met or spent any time together did not, at the time, detract from the fairytale. In her favour for the Prince she seemed to like the countryside and laughed a lot at silly jokes. That he seemed wry, rather than love-struck and was nearly – not quite – old enough to be her father, was overlooked. As he had once told an interviewer: 'Marriage is something you ought to work at. I may easily be proved wrong but I intend to work at it when I get married.' Charles was accordingly just being Charles when he swallowed after being asked what it felt like to be in love and replied offhandedly 'whatever love means – put your own interpretation on it'. Very few questioned the match. He told friends: 'It is just a matter of taking an unusual plunge into some rather unknown circumstances that inevitably disturbs me but I expect it will be the right thing in the end . . . it all seems so ridiculous because I do very much want to do the right thing for this country and for my family, but I am terrified sometimes of making a promise and then perhaps living to regret it.' Too many princes perhaps have got married for the sake of the country and it was unfortunate that very few people were foolhardy enough to urge him not to go ahead. As it was, even on the verge of the wedding he seems to have been wondering whether he could duck out of it. As was Diana. But when a BBC camera crew attending the wedding rehearsal spotted that she was in tears, the corporation quietly destroyed the footage; there was no question of broadcasting it or even storing it for future reference – that would have played the tabloids' intrusive game and undermined the fairytale.

But even by the time of the royal engagement, it was probably too late to back out. The church was booked, the press was squared, the middle classes quite prepared – too bad that the Prince had never been sent out to govern New South Wales like Hilaire Belloc's Lord Lundy – and the souvenir mugs, tea towels and commemorative brochures were being churned out. Lady Di haircuts were all the rage and the crowds turned up in their tens of thousands, sleeping out along the route to St Paul's Cathedral to catch a glimpse of the new princess. Nothing could deflect the fairytale wedding and indeed it became – with Ian Botham's heroic cricketing feats against the Australians – one of the best news events of the year, certainly in comparison with the economic slump, widespread unemployment and rioting in the streets, which were also occurring that summer. Against this background, street parties, a televised grand wedding, a hot and sunny day, a parade through the streets of London and even the shower of more than four thousand gifts from well-wishers, including many ordinary citizens, appeared to be proof of how welcome a distraction a royal event could be. There was even a perfunctory balcony kiss for the crowds – though Charles had to ask his mother's permission first: 'I am not getting into that caper,' he had said – and naturally the *Sun*, which had an informant in place on the balcony, was able to report him saying it. And, just to confirm, a lip reader watching the television reported the same thing.

Newspaper sales soared away. The media's interest was not going to decrease now that the pair had married. The tabloids might be disdained by the palace, but they could not be ignored and they were essentially playing the royal game by embroidering the story of the heir to the throne's marriage. They felt themselves invulnerable and in charge for there was no comeback, either from the royals or their readerships, whatever they did. The permutations would be unending: next, a royal baby, then its sex, then its upbringing. As early as December 1981, Michael Shea, the royal press secretary, called in editors for an informal chat at Buckingham Palace to ask them to back off from harassing the Princess. The Queen herself put in an appearance at the meeting to say that the girl should be left alone to get used to her new role. The headlines were captured by her exchange with Barry Askew, briefly at that time editor of the News of the World. Askew suggested the Princess was fair game for photographers once she stepped outside the palace and added that if she wished to go out to buy a packet of wine gums she could not avoid being photographed. If she didn't like it, why did she not just send a servant out to buy them instead? That, said the Queen grimly, 'is an extremely pompous remark, if I may say so'. It came to something when the Queen could berate the editor of the News of the World for superciliousness, and within weeks Askew's brief and crass tenure at the newspaper was over. But less noticed was that MacKenzie himself had refused the palace's invitation to attend, saying he had an important meeting with his proprietor. He had no intention of stopping the stories: the Sun's circulation at this time was well past the four million mark (the Mirror's was above three million).[21]

Over the coming years, the untrained Princess would learn how to manipulate the media in a way that left her husband and the rest of the royal family standing. Soon she was joined as a royal bride by Sarah

---

21 In 2014, the Sun's circulation was just over two million, the Mirror's less than a million.

Ferguson, who married Prince Andrew. The daughter of Prince Charles's polo manager, the galloping Major Ron, Fergie was definitely someone with a past: she had had lovers and she was bouncy, indiscreet and good fun – another breath of fresh air for the royals, it seemed. The Prince, too, had a past – his previous girlfriends, such as the American actress and photographer Koo Stark, had been lovingly described by the press.

The second royal wedding duly took place in 1986. For a very short while, it seemed all was well as the royal family emerged blinking into the light of daily, mass-circulation publicity. The younger royals even seemed to ride the wave, writing (or in some cases plagiarising) books and putting in increasingly demotic and populist appearances: none worse than the ghastly televised game show which came to be known as *It's a Royal Knockout*, organised by Prince Edward, the Queen's youngest son in 1987. The event, a version of a long-running television game show in which competing teams took part in ludicrous competitive games – usually involving knocking each other over with inflated balloons or pushing their opponents into water to the accompaniment of frenzied commentary by hysterical commentators – was organised for charity and featured a number of junior royals, including Princess Anne who was old enough to have known better, dressed in medieval-style costumes taking part in similar stunts. The whole sorry spectacle was compounded by twenty-three-year-old Prince Edward petulantly publicly berating the assembled press for not agreeing how wonderful the whole occasion was. The Prince had earlier in the year let the side down by humiliatingly dropping out of the Royal Marines during training, to the evident displeasure of his father and the resigned acceptance of his mother, so had little leeway for indulgence from the media, and was duly jeered and criticised over the whole event. The show was the royal family's ill-judged and demeaning attempt at populism for the television age and such a stunt was not repeated. 'If you ask me,' said one former communications director of the period, 'the lowest point for the monarchy was not 1992, but the . . . *Royal Knockout* programme. That was the moment when it all started to go wrong. It made them all totally accessible, fooling about on television and it was that that gave the media licence to start investigating every other aspect of their lives.' It had all got out of hand.

The royals it seemed had swung from haughty reticence to crass populism without any intervening period of discretion, egged on and abetted by an increasingly intrusive and raucous media which knew absolutely no discretion at all. This was not only letting daylight in on the magic but keeping the floodlights poking through the curtains every day and all night. Perhaps things might have settled down, despite the intrusiveness. The palace was now employing more media-aware advisers, no longer retired military men who had had no experience of dealing with the press. Now they tended to be former diplomats rather than journalists – the former BBC man Allison had been a one off – men such as Charles Anson, the press secretary between 1990 and 1996 through most of the rough years, who had at least been the press officer in the Washington Embassy during the Falklands War and in Downing Street in the winter of discontent before going into public relations in the City of London. Even so, they were constantly caught out by the latest revelations and their increasingly pained attempts to deny the stories that were emerging weekly and often daily were often ignored because the stories so regularly turned out to be true. The spokesmen were hamstrung, not only because the stories were so personal – and so extreme – but also because they were not supposed to comment on happenings beyond the royals' public duties. Their job was, above all, to safeguard and promote the institution and the monarch. There was no rule book to deal with allegations of marital disharmony and they frankly did not know how to begin responding. Often the journalists had better sources than they did – and the gentleman diplomats scarcely felt able to ask the royals themselves to confirm the stories. Accordingly, they floundered and were always on the back foot defensively. When reporters from the *Sun* noted the first signs of estrangement between Charles and Diana, working out that the couple had not seen each other for a month, the bland (and untrue) response from the palace press office was that the Prince was merely absent because he was helping the Queen Mother to write her memoirs.

The serious press and broadcasters were drawn in, because the stories were too good – and seemed too significant – to remain unreported. But the intrusiveness was apparently getting too much for Diana – or at least that was how the palace accounted for her increasingly erratic private behaviour, rather than the oppressive effect of her husband's indifference and the stuffiness of palace protocol. It was in this frenzied climate that both Charles and Diana's marriage and Andrew and Sarah's broke down in 1992. The marriages had been faltering for some time: Diana disillusioned and increasingly wilful, her husband neglectful, self-obsessed and jealous; the senior royals baffled at her seeming refusal to partake happily in their rituals. Meanwhile, Andrew and Sarah were also going their separate ways in very tabloid fashion, Fergie having been photographed by the *Daily Mail* canoodling with a Texan called Steve Wyatt[22] and then, later in the summer, by the *Daily Mirror* which published photographs of another American, her 'financial adviser' John Bryan, sucking her toes while the couple sunbathed beside a pool in the south of France. Some previous royal marriages had been disasters,

---

22 The Wyatts were a true *Dallas*-type dynasty from the oil business, though in Houston farther south, Steve's pop – shades of J.R. Ewing – being described in the *Houston Chronicle* as 'meaner than a junkyard dog'. Perfect for soap opera, if not royalty.

ending in estrangement if not usually divorce, but none had done so under the relentless gaze of the world's media, for it was not just the British press that recognised an interesting royal story. The paparazzi of the world were also training their lenses on Princess Diana. Less restrained than the British media, magazines abroad were regularly reporting imminent disasters for the whole family, fatal illnesses, deaths and divorce. And eventually they came to pass.

The fiction that all was sweetness and light between Charles and Diana was excruciatingly exposed in *Diana: Her True Story*, a book published by the young journalist Andrew Morton in the summer of 1992, written with the Princess's assistance, though that was strongly denied at the time. This was a royal marriage laid bare as none had been before (with the possible exception of that of George IV and Caroline nearly two hundred years earlier). It detailed Diana's attempts at self-harm, her estrangement from a cold and indifferent royal family, and her husband's infidelity with Camilla Parker-Bowles. The denials only made things worse. The press had colluded in keeping things quiet and had allowed itself to be misled too often in the past. There was no longer an implicit deference or reticence, and now the book had been published the story it told could not be ignored – there was too much circumstantial detail for that.

The Princess was at the centre of the deceit, though it quickly became clear that she was stoking the crisis rather than trying to quench or downplay it. There was the famous photograph of her sitting alone and apparently deserted in front of the Taj Mahal, taken during a trip to India in February 1992 – a symbolism that was, as she well knew, eloquent – and, after Morton's book came out, there were ostentatious meetings with some of the friends used as sources for the book, with journalists and photographers pre-warned to be present. Contrary to the public impression of cold and heartless royals, there were solicitous attempts by the Queen and Prince Philip to foster a reconciliation, which were doomed to failure. With Diana crying her eyes out during one meeting, the Queen asked her son if he could explain what was the matter: 'What and read it all in the newspapers tomorrow. No thank you,' he replied.

During the course of that year, all three of the royal children's marriages broke down (Prince Edward would not get married for another seven years). Anne and her first husband Mark Phillips divorced in April – she then married the naval officer Timothy Laurence, a former royal equerry, in a quiet, private ceremony in Scotland (the church there allowed remarriage services for divorcees) during December 1992 – and Charles and Diana formally separated in November. Three royal marriages, supposedly fairytale romances, greeted a few years earlier with great hoopla and much ceremonial, ended in a year. None of these breakdowns was discreet or tasteful. In addition to Fergie's mishaps, Anne's husband, the former show jumper 'Foggy' Phillips[23], had fathered a child during an affair with a New Zealand art teacher. And then came the tapes. The *Daily Mirror* had the toe-sucking pictures and the *Sun* then retaliated with the 'Squidgy' tape, a recording of a mobile telephone conversation a few years earlier on New Year's Eve 1989 between Diana and her very close friend of the time, a car salesman called James Gilbey, who was a member of the gin company family. This had allegedly been obtained by a radio ham and the newspaper had discreetly filed it away in a safe for just such an emergency as a rival's scoop. In it Gilbey can be heard referring to Diana as 'Squidge' and she unburdens herself of the complaint: 'Bloody hell, after all I've done for this fucking family.' The *Mirror* retaliated a

---

23 A nickname supposedly coined by Prince Charles because he thought his then brother-in-law was thick and wet.

few months later with a rival tape, also illicitly recorded, of a telephone call between Charles and Camilla during which the heir to the throne, whose interest in spirituality was well known, pondered on the possibility of being reincarnated as his mistress's tampon 'just to live inside your trousers'. How the tapes were made and subsequently obtained has never been satisfactorily explained. The idea that an amateur might accidentally tune in to such conversations, immediately recognise the voices and their significance and then record and sell them, seems extremely far-fetched. On the other hand, GCHQ or the royal protection service might have done so...[24] No matter who was responsible, inquisitive and prurient subscribers could dial special premium-rate telephone lines to hear the tapes in all their gory details for themselves and, by doing so, boosted the newspapers' profits. Anything went as the royal marriages frayed.

It is fair to say that royal revelations have never been so intimate. In a poisonous atmosphere, there was little palace advisers could do or the communications team could have said, given the stark evidence of what the royals were up to, but they were lied to as well. When the Queen's private secretary Sir Robert Fellowes rang his sister-in-law, Diana, to ask whether she had colluded with Morton's book, she denied it and the chairman of the press complaints commission, the hapless and naive Lord McGregor, was then authorised to issue a statement sanctimoniously condemning 'the odious exhibition of

---

24 The security service has always denied any involvement in the tapes, but Sir Robert Fellowes, the Queen's private secretary at the time, told the Diana inquest in 2008 that the palace had held discussions with them about whether anything 'nefarious' had occurred: 'The main strand of thinking in Buckingham Palace . . . was that this had happened and what action should be taken to ensure that it did not happen again.' Of course, given the tabloids' history of making generous surreptitious payments to officials in the palace and in key organisations such as the police and armed forces, it is perfectly possible that someone in public office was tempted.

journalists dabbling their fingers in the stuff of other people's souls'. When the truth emerged that Diana had indeed assisted Morton with authorised disclosures made through her friends and even on tapes slipped to the author, Fellowes offered to resign, but this was refused. Perhaps McGregor would have been better advised to work out – like a professional journalist would have done, or even the rest of the country – that the likelihood the book's revelations must be undeniably true, or they would never have been published in such detail. The royal family were certainly victims of press intrusiveness and competition, but they undoubtedly brought the trouble on themselves by their behaviour. The tabloids at this time were sailing recklessly close to the wind in their circulation wars, but the stories were a gift to them. There was a sense that almost any story, however unlikely, would almost certainly turn out to be true and could be printed, and that an official denial counted for nothing. A royal communications officer of the time told me: 'We did not know what to say. If we said a story was rubbish, the next question was, how do you know? I would steer editors – I could pick up the telephone and speak to any of them – but you had to be careful not to stand up stories. Frankly, some of the journalists had better sources and better access than we did. In the end, if someone rang up and said: "Do you know Diana has been paying night-time visits to see down-and-outs under Waterloo Bridge?" I'd have had to have said, "That sounds quite plausible." We became almost inured to surprises as their private life and the marriage became the issue.'

Everyone knew the royal family would not dare to sue because of the embarrassment. If the British press did not print it, foreign papers would and the British were not going to be caught out again as they had been at the time of Edward VIII's abdication. In case they needed any reminding, the freelance paparazzi photographers who flocked round

Diana every time she appeared in public – and usually when she flitted out of Kensington Palace in private as well – were proof that the story would go on giving. The paparazzi provoked and insulted the Princess, harassing her mercilessly, milling around and chasing her to obtain intrusive pictures of her crying or losing her temper – the so-called loon shots – screaming abuse in her face just as they would Kate Middleton twenty years later. By such despicable means, they made a very good living from papers and magazines in Europe, Australia and the US. British newspapers and magazines used their pictures, too. It was remorseless and there was little to stop or deflect it.

On top of all this came the Windsor Castle fire in late November 1992 when a workman's spotlight, placed too close to a curtain, set a large part of the building alight, destroying nine state apartments and damaging about a hundred rooms. This in turn set off the spark which led to the Queen being asked to pay tax. The fire left the Queen, who was at the castle that day, distraught. She was pictured standing outside the blazing building, dressed in a long mackintosh and headscarf, looking desolate as servants and builders, supervised by Prince Andrew, scurried about rescuing paintings and furniture. Most of the treasures were saved but many rooms were destroyed or badly damaged, and seeing her ancestral home go up in smoke capped a wretched year for the Queen. The building and its contents were not insured. With misplaced gallantry, John Major's government, drastically misjudging the public mood, immediately announced after the fire that it – in other words the taxpayer – would pick up the £20 million bill for repairs and renovation. They might have got away with it but, on top of the ostentatious royal shenanigans in the marriages of the previous twelve months, public sympathy was running at a low ebb, especially in the middle of an economic recession. A murmur of aggravation rapidly grew into a storm of criticism. As one commentator noted, in normal times the castle was the Queen's private residence, but when it burned down it was somehow the nation's responsibility to restore it.

Palace advisers of the period tend to blame the Major government for being slow in arranging the changes because Tory MPs were afraid that Conservative voters would react badly. Fellowes approached Her Majesty with some trepidation in the wake of the fire to broach the subject again and found her for the first time amenable to paying tax. What else could she be in the circumstances? When the announcement was made, however, it inevitably appeared to be – and actually was – in response to the hostile public reaction to paying for the fire. It had been, as she croaked through a heavy cold in a speech at the Guildhall in the City of London a few days after the fire, an *annus horribilis* – not a year to look back on with undiluted pleasure. She may have meant the year more generally, in which Britain had been bounced humiliatingly out of the European exchange rate mechanism and the recession had deepened, but it certainly came out more personally in the circumstances. 'One's Bum Year' as the *Sun* characteristically had it for those of its readers who had not benefited from a classical education and did not know their *annus* from their anus.

To cap it all off, the paper then claimed a scoop in leaking the transcript of the Queen's Christmas broadcast a few weeks later. Trivial in itself, the paper did it not because the speech contained anything shocking, unexpected or even newsworthy, but essentially just because it could. The paper's executives felt there was nothing to fear from the Queen. Copies of the transmission tape went out in advance to all broadcasting organisations, as always under strict embargo for Christmas Day and the maintenance of confidentiality was important to the Queen, whose one occasion of the year it was to address the population directly. The leak, by a technician, did not just cause anguish to the monarch, but real anger and there was a sense that the tabloid had at last gone too far. For the first time, the palace sued for breach of copyright and eventually, and with ill grace, MacKenzie and the *Sun* apologised and paid damages to charity. But when MacKenzie eventually left the editorship a year later it was not because of upsetting the royals, but for upsetting the readers.

The marital separations and the decision to pay tax did not end the royals' torment, or draw a line under the marriages. Princess Anne and Commander, later Vice-Admiral, Laurence disappeared largely from tabloid view, the Princess diligently pursuing public duties and her husband his naval career at the Ministry of Defence, latterly in charge of its property portfolio, rarely appearing in public together. Andrew and Fergie's divorce was amicable, though she periodically resurfaced to complain about being snubbed by the family or to bemoan the financial settlement that left her short of cash and resorting to the indignity of soliciting money from wealthy friends, including her former husband's American sex offender friend Jeffrey Epstein, writing children's stories and representing Weight Watchers in the US.

But Charles and Diana's marriage was not resolved happily. The Princess, who had rapidly learned how to manipulate the press who followed her so devotedly, by flattering, cajoling and befriending them, did not go quietly. She had her favourites, usually the most handsome ones with whom she could flirt – one of the reasons why she had picked out Morton – and also, cannily, the most strategically placed such as the charming and highly professional Richard Kay of the *Daily Mail* to whose readers she appealed directly through his articles. She met Kay discreetly but hardly privately outside her gym and in his car, parked in side streets and he conveyed her views equally discreetly and devastatingly accurately in his newspaper. She used the press much more deviously than the palace, or her husband, has ever done. One press officer of the period told me: 'I could talk to Richard because he was decent but he did not talk to me about Diana – he did not need to, because he had better access to her than I did.' If the Prince and his friends thought the Princess was 'off her rocker' as they frequently complained among themselves, she certainly, cunningly, knew all about working the media. If it was difficult for the disinterested to know where the truth lay, or who was in the right, the image conveyed was of a deeply dysfunctional marriage and, worse and humiliatingly, a rancorous and disreputable family. Naturally, the one who seemed most to blame was not the sweet and beautiful Princess with her fluttering eyelashes and well-honed simper, but her grumpy, middle-aged husband. The royal facade had cracked. Newspapers and their readers took sides as the relationship collapsed.

The Prince, however, got his retaliation in first by authorising and collaborating on an official biography and documentary by Jonathan Dimbleby in 1994. What was meant to be a book about the Prince's good works, of a sort that might have worked when Dimbleby's father Richard was 'gold microphone in waiting' penning royal hagiographies in the 1950s, turned into a disaster for Charles when he was persuaded by the journalist to talk about his adultery with Camilla. The book was clearly written from Charles's standpoint, but it also showed how early his marriage had broken down, quoting him in November 1986 writing: 'How awful incompatibility is and how dreadfully destructive it can be for the players in this extraordinary drama. It has all the ingredients of a Greek tragedy...all I want to do is to _help_ other people.' The book was duly serialised, as Morton's had been two years earlier in the *Sunday Times* – hardly a tabloid but also owned by Rupert Murdoch. In the accompanying BBC documentary, the Prince admitted that his marriage had irretrievably broken down and that he had been seeing his 'friend for a very long time' Camilla. The admission removed any lingering doubt in even the most loyal supporters' minds that the stories had been true and the palace's denials worthless and self-serving. Andrew Parker-Bowles, who must have known what was going on, promptly sued his wife for divorce.

What was even worse from the Queen's point of view was that Dimbleby's researches through the Prince's letters and papers, freely made available to him, had laid bare his unhappiness with his parents since he had been a child, how his mother had been cold and distant, and his father harsh and bullying. Since Charles had checked the text before publication, he had obviously not objected to such intimate family resentments being published. Perhaps he did not realise that it diminished him even more than anyone else. All the whispers and gossip about his jealousy, self-obsession and self-pitying, rancorous nature were given credibility. 'Find out about the man for yourself!' announced the blurb, supplied by the Prince's friend Jonathon Porritt, on the front cover.

Diana vowed revenge and duly delivered it the following year with a devastatingly manipulative interview for the BBC's *Panorama* programme in November 1995, which caught the palace with no more than a few minutes' warning and was lucratively shared by the corporation around the world, 'to men and women so cut off by the snows, the desert or the sea that only pictures out of the air can reach them', as George V might have said. There were three people in the marriage, Diana famously confided to the interviewer Martin Bashir, whose career was thereby made, 'so it got pretty crowded'. She wanted to be a queen of people's hearts, she claimed, and sententiously she hoped that Charles might one day find peace of mind.[25] It was a

---

25 The *Panorama* programme had an unintended consequence for the BBC, too: there was royal retaliation – the Corporation found it lost its highly prized exclusivity over recording the Queen's Christmas broadcast: thereafter the honour was shared out with ITV and latterly Sky, each taking turns.

remarkable performance, fully serving her purpose. Had television been invented in the Prince Regent's day, it was the sort of show that his estranged wife Caroline of Brunswick might have attempted, or Catherine of Aragon as Henry VIII's attention started wandering in 1530 – though she would have risked the block, as would Bashir of course. No question of that in the late twentieth century but any hope of reconciliation was doomed, and to end the farce the Queen instructed the pair to begin divorce proceedings immediately in the best interests of themselves and the country.

Divorce did not end the rancour or the briefing. Now even the Queen was drawn in, finally appalled by the Princess's behaviour. Diana briefed Kay that it was the palace that demanded as part of the negotiations she surrender the Her Royal Highness title – quite the reverse of the truth, as she herself had proposed it. For the first time the press secretary Charles Anson was instructed to issue a specific and categorical denial: a sure sign of the breakdown of trust. It did not stop Diana: a few months later, after the marriage was dissolved, somehow the confidential details of the financial settlement: £15 million, largely paid by the Queen, also appeared in the newspapers. Despite the fundamental breakdown in relations with the royal family, she lived on in the apartment she had shared with her husband at Kensington Palace and her private secretary continued to work from the office he occupied with the prince's staff at St James's Palace. She could have had police bodyguard protection too, but spurned it because she thought the officers would be spying on her.

The Princess had a twin-track strategy (though she may not have thought of it like that): there was the sniping, manipulation and harassment, which continued right up to her final holiday on Mohamed Al-Fayed's newly bought yacht *Jonikal* in the Mediterranean in August 1997. There she alerted selected photographers where she might be seen kissing the tycoon's son Dodi.[26] Then there were also the ostentatious charity appearances that last summer, such as the auctioning of her dresses in New York for the American AIDS Crisis Trust and the trips to the minefields of Angola and Bosnia in January and August of that year. This was by no means doing good by stealth: it was, as she coolly told Tony Blair 'going for the caring angle'. She might have auctioned the dresses for the British charity at a less star-studded occasion and photographers accompanied her on the African trip, but the publicity undoubtedly raised public interest in both issues and established her, as intended, as a campaigner for good causes. She may even have enjoyed being described as a loose cannon by Tory MPs for her outspokenness on the landmines issue.

All frivolity came to an end, however, with the terrible car crash in the Pont de l'Alma road tunnel by the River Seine in Paris in which she and Dodi died on 30 August 1997. They had been driven recklessly at high speed into the tunnel by Henri Paul, the deputy head of security at Al-Fayed's Ritz Hotel, who had been told to drive them back to the Al-Fayed apartment just after midnight after they had dined at the

---

26 It is thought that Diana wanted the photographs taken and published to get back at her previous lover, the discreet London-based surgeon Hasnat Khan, from whom she had recently split after eighteen months and whom she had told friends was the love of her life. This was disputed by Mohamed Al-Fayed at the inquest ten years later: 'All this baloney. It was just a casual relation with this guy, a friend but nothing serious. You cannot say marry someone like that, lives in a council flat and has no money ... what you are saying is just bullshit.' Al-Fayed insisted the real relationship was with his son who she had only just met and that she had been killed in a far-reaching criminal conspiracy by the entire royal family, the British and French police, British diplomats, the secret services, the French ambulance service and the French investigators, because she was pregnant and had planned to marry Dodi who was, like Khan, a Muslim. It was a conspiracy that would have had to have been organised in the few minutes between the couple's decision to return to the apartment and leaving the hotel. In any case, Diana was not pregnant and her friends testified that she had had no intention of marrying Dodi. After an inquest lasting 94 days, hearing 278 witnesses, the jury did not find Al-Fayed's explanation convincing.

hotel. Paul, on prescription drugs and three times over the legal alcohol limit, had not expected to be working, let alone driving, that evening and was not used to the powerful Mercedes saloon that he was given to get them home. He took off fast and ostentatiously, apparently to elude the paparazzi who had gathered on motor scooters outside the front of the hotel, and entered the tunnel three minutes later at twice the speed limit: 105kph (65mph) as opposed to the permitted 50kph. The tunnel has a difficult camber and a bend in it and the Mercedes probably clipped a Fiat Uno before swerving into a central pillar and bouncing across the carriageway into the concrete side wall. A Paris taxi driver picking me up from the Gare du Nord a few hours later said bluntly: 'Only a fool would drive into that tunnel at any speed. Everyone knows that. The man must have been drunk or stupid.' He got it right long before the endless investigations came to the same conclusion. Paul and Dodi were killed outright and Diana died in the Pitié-Salpêtrière Hospital a short while later from massive injuries. The sole surviving passenger was the only one wearing a seatbelt at the time, the private bodyguard Trevor Rees-Jones, who was nevertheless badly injured. The news was broken in the early hours to the rest of the royal family who were on holiday at Balmoral, and Prince Charles went off to Paris to accompany Diana's coffin back to England that night.

The accident convulsed much of the British public that week with shock and grief: the sudden, tragic death of a beautiful young woman who they thought they had come to know intimately over the previous seventeen years provoked an hysterical outpouring of mourning that for several days created a spectacle that fed upon itself as bouquets of flowers and fluffy toys piled up, 5ft deep in places, for hundreds of yards around the gates of Kensington Palace.[27] Blame and recrimination focused initially on the journalists and photographers who had pursued the Princess, and whose words and pictures the public around the world had enjoyed for so long in the magazines and newspapers that they had bought. But it swiftly turned, directed by the press themselves, on the royal family and it was this that provoked the biggest crisis of the Queen's reign.

27 The ostentatious sentimentality had in fact something of a royal precedent: when George IV's daughter, the heir to the throne, Princess Charlotte Augusta, died suddenly in childbirth in November 1817 there was a similar outpouring of grief. 'No public event in my time ever produced such a universal union of spontaneous sympathy,' wrote William Darter, who published his memoirs well into his eighties much later in the century. 'All business was suspended, blinds were drawn down to the windows of private houses and even the poorest of the poor wore some humble token of sympathy.' The law courts and Royal Exchange shut for a fortnight and eventually manufacturers petitioned the government to shorten the period of official mourning for fear of going bankrupt. Doubtless teddy bears and bouquets of flowers would also have piled up had anyone thought of it at the time.

Chapter 9

'Speak to us, Ma'am'

(*Daily Mirror* headline, 4 September 1997)

Where were the royals? Why were they not sharing the nation's grief? Why was the Royal Standard not flying at half-mast from the flagpole on top of Buckingham Palace? It was easy enough to blame Charles – many tabloid readers over the years had already done that following the break up of his marriage – but now for the first time the Queen was in their sights as well. It was a disconcerting, even frightening, moment for the palace. This all played into the soap opera narrative that Diana herself had shamelessly promoted in the previous few years: of a remote, cold-hearted and insensitive royal family who had driven her out, now to her death, and were sheltering behind the walls of their Scottish castle, not even breaking their holiday to be with their hurting, weeping people. In an attempt to smoke them out, the tabloids sent threatening messages in large type all over their front pages: 'Show us you care' trumpeted the *Daily Express*, 'Where is the Queen when the country needs her?' demanded the *Sun*, adding in an open letter on its front page: 'The Queen's place is with the people. She should fly back to London immediately and stand on the palace balcony.'

There was no suggestion of what she might do when she got there: wave? Wear sackcloth and receive the throwing of rotten tomatoes? Burst into tears? Crave forgiveness?

In fact, the royals had a perfectly good explanation for their absence. The Queen thought it more important to protect the Princess's adolescent sons by keeping them away from the maelstrom of ostentatious grief developing in London, and the family was in no condition to go south and confront the mob. As with people of their generation and class, they thought it was natural to do their grieving in private: moreover, as the people best placed to know what Diana had been really like, they – especially the Queen – could not bring themselves to share false sentiments. There were anyway practical issues to sort out: should the funeral be a discreet and private one away from the crowds – should the Queen herself even attend it in the circumstances? She does not normally attend public funerals, making an exception previously only for Sir Winston Churchill thirty-two years earlier. But, if it was to be a public funeral, where should it be held and who would take it?

As for the flag, the Royal Standard was never flown when the Queen was not in residence at Buckingham Palace and only at half-mast following the death of the sovereign – couldn't people see that? Royalty moves slowly, by tradition and precedent, and even an obvious change requires stately consultation – and time was one thing they did not have. Anyway, the palace was closed down for the summer, the dust sheets out and workmen in carrying out repairs and routine maintenance, so it was not then in a fit state to be occupied before the Queen was due to return. One senior official, serving at the time, told me: 'The Queen said, "What good am I going to do, sitting in Buckingham Palace when up here I am looking after my grandchildren?" There is no doubt that the cost of opening it up again played a part, too. Then the press went absolutely berserk. You know the flag issue was unexpectedly difficult, people chipping in such as historians like Lord Blake, writing articles didn't help either – he ought to have known better. It was a complication we didn't need.'

All these considerations were irrelevant, of course, especially as the clamour mounted. The Union flag would indeed be flown over Buckingham Palace for the funeral – a not-so-hard decision as it turned out and a gesture repeated since without the earth shaking. The obligation on a sovereign and royal household that wished to survive was to be with their people, comforting *them* rather than being comforted themselves. After more than a century creating the notion of a middle-class monarchy in tune with the nation, sharing its interests and empathising with its sensibilities, it could scarcely hide now, especially as the public mood – or at least that reflected on the tabloids' front pages – was growing mutinous. Even loyal papers were muttering. And there was also pressure from the newly elected Labour government whose prime minister Tony Blair made a virtue of his powers of instantaneous empathy: she had been the People's Princess he had said with a catch in his voice on the morning of Diana's death. Empathy is not necessarily an emotion that comes readily to the Queen, nor is she willing to fake it. A cabinet minister of the period told me: 'The palace was deep in shock. They were acutely aware of what might come out. Number Ten moved in to fill the vacuum, though it caused friction at the time.'

How febrile the public mood actually was is difficult to assess. There was certainly passion and even hysteria among the crowds who took the trouble to take flowers to Kensington Palace and queued up for many hours to sign the books of condolence that were opened, and their grief was certainly exploited and publicised as a sort of half-guilty displacement by the press, but most of the country kept calm, though sad, and carried on. The mood of the crowd in London was not really insurrectionary, but it was vaguely menacing and disturbing, and the royal family's popularity was shaken. The government's advice was that the Queen really had to come back to London, which she did with some trepidation on the Friday. But she need not have worried: she was greeted warmly and sympathetically by the crowd outside the palace gates when she and other members of the royal family came outside to meet them and inspect their tributes. Just as Queen Victoria's unpopularity had melted away when her son was dangerously ill in 1871, the Queen was back and had become the grandmother of the nation once more. The visit was unannounced and informal: no one threw anything and no one barracked. And that was reflected in the live television broadcast she made that evening just before the six o'clock news. The 'live' decision was a late one, taken with the Queen in order to maintain the sense of spontaneity and immediacy so, ironically, that it would not appear staged or distant and this was enhanced by seating the Queen in front of a window looking out over the Mall, so that the huge crowd could be seen milling about in the distance, obviously unedited, their muffled sound rumbling in the background, picked up from a microphone on the balcony. The Queen is a very experienced if not relaxed broadcaster but, on this occasion, her seriousness and concentration, peering through large spectacles to read the prompter, matched the subject matter. The speech, largely scripted by Sir Robert Fellowes and Geoff Crawford, the Australian press secretary, was only three and a half minutes long but it managed, gracefully, to thank the public, to mention the other victims of the crash and their grieving families, to pay an honest and sincere tribute to the Princess without being mawkish, sentimental or insincere, and to promise that lessons would be drawn from what had happened to her. No one who had known Diana would ever forget her. It had been a remarkable life, cut too short.

Credit for the most striking phrase: 'What I say to you now, as your Queen and as a grandmother, I say from my heart,' was claimed by Blair and his communications director Alastair Campbell. Whoever was responsible, it hit absolutely the right note by reminding the audience that she was a person as well as a monarch, who had been affected by all the grief and emotions of the previous six days. 'We have all been trying in our different ways to cope,' she said, justifying the stay at Balmoral. And shrewdly, from the individual to the universal, there was a plea for the next day's funeral to be conducted with dignity and restraint, implicitly without demonstrations or dissent: a chance to show the whole world that the British nation was united in grief and respect. The speech went quite some way to defusing the tension and indeed the next day did go off peacefully. The two princes, flanked by the Duke of Edinburgh, Prince Charles and Diana's brother, Earl Spencer, walked solemnly behind the coffin, unmolested, past weeping crowds. The adolescent boys in particular were a picture of stoicism and dignity: the sort of pluck before such sentimental emotion that the British most admire; had they themselves broken down in the face of so much ostentatious grief, it would have been entirely understandable but also somewhat diminishing. The funeral service itself was an uneasy mixture of aristocratic pomp, Anglican ritual and very Diana-ish 1990s sensibility, with only the rancorous and defiant tribute by the Princess's brother Earl Spencer – a man with marital issues of his own – to inject bitterness into the occasion. The Queen must have heard the wave of applause from the crowd outside when his words were relayed to them by loudspeakers. By then, however, the worst was over: the coffin was loaded into a hearse for a flower-strewn journey back to the Spencer family home at Althorp in Northamptonshire and the immediate crisis was on the wane. The crowds dispersed, the moment passed and life went on.

But the soap opera was not over. Although the British press was chastened by the Diana saga, at least for a time, the following years yielded more twists to an undignified royal tale. The heir to the throne had been wrong-footed in his relations with Diana. He had very little understanding or appreciation of the press or of its importance to the royal family's image (nearly twenty years on, many would argue that he still does not). So he hired someone he thought did. This was a time when Prince Charles's communications staff, particularly his callow spokesman, a young man in his early thirties called Mark Bolland were accused of rather too openly briefing against Buckingham Palace and the other royal siblings in a way that was familiar in the world of Westminster politics but not in royal circles. Bolland – unusually for a royal adviser a comprehensive schoolboy educated in Middlesbrough and a chemistry graduate from York University – had been recommended to Charles when he was working at the Press Complaints Commission at the time of the Prince's divorce from Diana in 1996, and was quickly promoted to deputy private secretary the following year.

Known to the two adolescent princes as 'Lord Blackadder' after the devious (and hapless) television comedy character played by Rowan Atkinson, Bolland had two priorities in representing the Prince. His task essentially was firstly to reconstruct Charles's public image and latterly gradually to rehabilitate Camilla Parker-Bowles, the other woman, 'the third person in the marriage', who was widely regarded, especially by loyalist royalists, as the person ultimately responsible for destroying the marriage. The advice to Charles was sensible: to concentrate on public service and good works, including being an obviously good father to his two adolescent boys. The stories presented to the press were evidently genuine: Charles, William and Harry clearly did get on well together in the face of adversity, though the Prince of Wales was scarcely a lone parent, cooking the supper and making sure the boys did their homework and got to school on time – they were both boarding at Eton, after all. The photo opportunities, however, showed them together, coarse fishing or skiing, on outings and tours. They were somewhat strained occasions in the presence of the hated media, but they conveyed what was intended – and a chastened press was not going to pick the stilted pictures apart or present them in anything other than a most positive light.

Stories were strategically placed for maximum impact, however, with little regard to sensitivity. The first deeply private meeting between Mrs Parker-Bowles and William eleven months after his mother's death appeared in full technicolour detail, right down to her nervous cigarette and comforting gin and tonic, within days over seven pages in the *Sun*. How did it acquire such intimate knowledge? Bolland denies it was him, and it was certainly not the most sensitive way of pushing forward the adolescent boy's prospective relationship with his future stepmother. Both William and Harry felt they were used over certain stories: they could hardly publicly complain about having their private lives manipulated to create a necessarily false picture – in William's case over that first meeting with his father's mistress, the woman his mother had blamed for breaking up her marriage – but it was not likely to endear the media to them or reconcile them to the roles they were expected to play.

Where Bolland came unstuck was in choreographing Prince Charles's relations with his parents and siblings. There was a most unpalace-like aggression which chimed with the rough political spin doctoring of the period, with its bullying, briefing and partisanship. Bolland perhaps did not fully appreciate that this highly personal form of attack was not the right way of going about things in the context of a royal family. There was aggressive leaking to selected newspapers, usually *The Times* and *Daily Mail* or its Sunday stablemate, the *Mail on*

Sunday, with each of whom Bolland had friendly contacts, but not to the *Daily Telegraph* whose editorial line was openly hostile and even disdainful towards Bolland.

If the leaking of William's first meeting with Camilla was potentially harmful to relationships within Charles's family, some leaks were counterproductive to harmonious family relations and served only to isolate the Prince without protecting him from damaging stories. It also caused the near breakdown of relations between the Queen's communications department at Buckingham Palace and her son's at Clarence House a few hundred yards away. The palace press people were again regularly forced to respond to comments and allegations out of the blue as they had been during the so-called War of the Waleses, in Diana's time. There was mutual suspicion and no coordination of diaries between the two sides so that one event attended by the Queen or another member of the family might unexpectedly be upstaged by something the Prince was up to.

One official at Buckingham Palace dealing with the media at that time, told me: 'We didn't trust Bolland and we did not give him any sensitive information because we thought it might end up in the press. His commitment to the Prince of Wales did not seem to extend to the rest of the royal family, except the Queen. It was as if everyone else could be thrown to the wolves and the Duke of Edinburgh for one was very hurt and upset by it. Well, you can't operate any institution, briefing against each other, like that.'

Another palace official of the period said: 'What was being done was actually undermining the institution for the future, so ultimately damaging the prince himself. It was taking the worst lessons from political spin doctoring: undermining your potential rivals. But the palace isn't a here-today, gone-tomorrow operation on a five-year electoral cycle, it is here to stay. We did not retaliate. The Queen does not believe in spin doctoring. We needed to play a straight bat. But it was difficult, damaging and hurtful.'

There was also manipulation of stories from Clarence House. When the *News of the World* in late 2001 threatened to expose Prince Harry for experimenting with soft drugs during underage outings to the Rattlebone Inn at Sherston, near Highgrove, the story was massaged into one of the young Prince's repentance. Charles, it was said, as a caring father had given his younger son a good talking to and then sent Harry on a visit to a south London drug rehabilitation centre to cure him of his bad habit. He had never done drugs since, 'a good friend' told the paper. Actually, the Prince's tour of the drug rehabilitation centre had preceded the pub visit by two months, so perhaps the effect of that visit was not quite as profound as the paper had informed its readers. The *News of the World* did not mind: it had its scoop, could pose as a champion of the public good, helping the young Prince back on the straight and narrow and had a tale of royal redemption. The press adviser had also limited a highly damaging story so that it was over in a couple of days, once other newspapers had reported it. Unusually, Bolland was quite willing to discuss his work once he had left the Prince's employment, though he blamed the newspaper for over-zealously manipulating the sequence of events rather than himself for inspiring it: 'Presenting the centre as the great solution to the problem was something that I was embarrassed about. It was misleading to present the centre as the solution,' he told the *Guardian* in an interview in 2003.

Then there was the story of Prince Edward's Ardent film company, which was caught out defying an embargo on media organisations filming Prince William while he was a student at St Andrews University. The Prince had reluctantly agreed to a photocall on his arrival at the university only on the understanding that all the cameras, photographers and television crews would not only leave the vicinity afterwards but also pack their bags, get out of town and not come back. When he spotted the crew from Ardent the next day he was accordingly furious. The crew claimed that they had stayed behind innocently to take some location shots of the local sights but that was not how it was presented to the media. The Ardent company was little more than a vanity project for the Queen's youngest son, which during its brief existence somehow only made hagiographic films about the royal family, but it was left humiliated and bruised – and so, particularly, was Edward – by the fury that erupted around it. Perhaps the crew had either thought the embargo did not apply to them, or were just incompetent. They were sent packing, but it was the brutal, public and highly personal condemnation as the story was briefed to the media that caused trouble at the palace. That the Prince's uncle's company had breached the embargo on staying in town was bad enough, but the story was lavishly detailed in the briefing – Charles had rung his little brother three times to bawl him out, it was said – and the publicity effectively finished off Ardent. Was it true, Bolland was asked in the *Guardian* interview that, as reported, Charles had called his little brother 'a fucking idiot'? 'I doubt I used that language but it's probably got my fingerprints on it,' the spin doctor replied insouciantly.

There was no doubt that some curious stories appeared at about this time. Sophie, the Countess of Wessex, Prince Edward's wife, then working in public relations, was caught out by a secret recording made by an undercover reporter working for the *News of the World*, and posing as a potential client in which she boasted of her royal connections as a way of showing her influence and access to the family. This made a story, but other indiscreet comments about individual politicians were not published there and inexplicably surfaced in the rival *Mail on Sunday* instead. In an attempt to distract from the adverse publicity, the Countess then gave a formal interview to the *News of the World* which only made matters worse. As part of a general defence of his character and the state of their marriage she asserted that her husband was not gay. This palace-facilitated interview, apparently designed to head off the revelations contained in the secret recording, had the reverse effect of that intended, since the original comments were leaked anyway and the facilitated interview opened up a new public humiliation. The palace evidently had much to learn about modern media manipulation.

The closest the Prince has come to outright political partisanship concerned his covert support for the countryside march in London in September 2002, which attempted to rally the rural community against Labour's plans to ban fox hunting, an activity in which Charles had for many years actively and enthusiastically participated. On the eve of the march, which attracted 400,000 supporters, a letter from him to the prime minister was leaked to friendly Sunday newspapers in which Charles passed on – and appeared thereby to endorse – an anonymous Cumbrian farmer's complaint that farmers were more victimised than black or gay people. The letter was never disavowed. The espousal of victimhood and Charles's accompanying alleged assertion – claimed by the *Mail on Sunday* to have been overheard by an unnamed senior politician – that if fox hunting was banned he might as well leave the country and spend the rest of his life skiing, did not have a tangible effect. It just sounded petulant. The Labour government did, eventually and cack-handedly, ban fox hunting and unsurprisingly Charles did not emigrate. Hunts continued almost as before, pursuing scent trails, not live animals. They did not close down as they had threatened, their hounds were not slaughtered and some foxes mysteriously continued to be slain by hunts, but the Prince no longer joined them.

The heir to the throne seemed almost as loose a cannon as his former wife had been. Was it true he was speculating at dinner about the succession and what he would do as King? Was he really dabbling too publicly in political issues? Bolland says that he tried to stop the dissemination of the Prince's views, for instance the criticisms he made about the countries he visited, but the Prince would insist on sending the journals he wrote about his trips out to a range of friends, acquaintances, ministers, diplomats and even occasionally journalists. But when Charles wanted it to be known that he was taking a stand, as when he ostentatiously boycotted a state dinner for the Chinese president in 1999 – 'appalling old waxworks' was his opinion of the country's gerontocracy when he attended the handover of Hong Kong in 1997[28] – the media were told in advance that he was doing so because he disapproved of China's treatment of the his friend the Dalai Lama.

In the end, Sir Michael Peat, the palace's Mr Fix-it of the period, the old Etonian accountant (and member of the Peat Marwick accountancy family) who was the treasurer of the royal household, was sent across to St James's Palace to sort things out in 2002 and became Charles's private secretary. Peat, a slight figure but one who could adeptly wield feline claws, had already conducted an extensive survey across the road of the royal household's expenses and slimmed down its expenditure. Now he had to sort out the Prince. Bolland soon left the royal service, without any public honour. Unlike most former royal servants he did

---

28 When the contents of the Prince's China journal 'The Takeover of Hong Kong or the Great Chinese Takeaway' were leaked in the *Mail on Sunday* eight years later, in November 2005, Charles for the first time initiated legal action against the newspaper. There was a final falling out with Bolland who gave a witness statement in support of the *MoS*, though it was never aired in court. In it, 'Lord Blackadder' confided that the Prince was indeed a politicised figure whose 'very definite aim' was to influence opinion: 'He saw that as part of the job of the heir apparent. He carried it out in a very considered, thoughtful and researched way. He often referred to himself as a "dissident" working against the prevailing political consensus.' In the circumstances it was perhaps unsurprising that Bolland was cast into outer darkness, unlike some others of the Prince's former employees who have found themselves called back into royal service as consultants and aides.

not go quietly. Besides the *Guardian* interview, he was awarded a column in the *News of the World*, unburdening himself of harsh and regular personal criticism of his former employer. One official told me: 'We had to move away from the previous spinning culture. It was out of control. It was just harming the institution it was supposed to be promoting. The Bolland era had to end and it was clear that a very different path had to be taken.' Bolland told the *Guardian* later: 'The Prince is not a terribly strong person. I just think he lacks a lot of confidence. He doesn't have a lot of self belief. He doesn't have a lot of inner strength. It's one of the very sweet and lovely things about him that he's a humble man.' This is not the usual language of palace officials, at least for quotation and Bolland also went off to prosperity running his own public relations company in the City. He had, after all, been named Public Relations Professional of the Year while still in the Prince's service – but the palace's first attempt at aggressive spin doctoring had not ended happily for the heir to the throne.

One issue Bolland had tackled successfully, however, was that of the Prince's relationship with Camilla Parker-Bowles – the 'non-negotiable' in Charles's life. That was the motive behind the leaking of William's meeting with her in 1998: the implication being that if they were getting on, the public would be reassured, too. The question of remarriage was far away in the aftermath of Diana's death, though it was a long-term goal, and the Prince could not even be seen in public with his mistress. The so-called 'Operation Mrs P-B' was undertaken deliberately to create public acceptance of her as the Prince's future wife. Her emergence into the light was carefully choreographed: the press was informed that they would be publicly seen together in January 1999 leaving a birthday party at the Ritz and photographers turned up en masse to photograph the event. The first chaste public kiss came a further two and a half years later in June 2001 at a reception at Somerset

House for the National Osteoporosis Society and it would be another four years after that before they married. Even then, some Diana loyalists were unhappy, but by the time of the marriage in April 2005 most people accepted the wedding – after all, most Britons know divorced people, have been divorced themselves or have experience of them in their families.

Although the palace's officials saw off vexatious legal challenges from a high Anglican vicar and others, the event was beset by a series of glitches of a sort that many wedding preparations experience between engagement and altar, but which, since they happened to the royal preparations in the full light of publicity, added to the uncertainty and general merriment. Because Mrs Parker-Bowles was a divorcee who was remarrying[29], the marriage service itself could not be conducted as planned at St George's Chapel in the relative privacy of Windsor Castle, but would have to be a civil wedding in a register office – the first ever for an heir to the throne (the lord chancellor helpfully resolved the legal question of whether a future monarch and supreme governor of the Church of England could marry in a civil ceremony, conveniently in the affirmative). Perhaps the registrar could conduct the ceremony inside the castle? That was the original plan but that, too, was scuppered: if the castle was licensed to conduct civil weddings, it would have to accept bookings from other couples, too. This might be an appealing prospect for ordinary mortals but would be distinctly unwelcome to the royal family, which understandably did not want to be besieged every week with marriage parties cluttering up the state rooms.

The solution was to hold the civil part at Windsor Guildhall, the seventeenth-century town hall designed by Sir Christopher Wren, which served as the local register office, its only drawback being that it was

---

29 There was no bar to Charles remarrying in church since his first wife was dead.

outside the castle walls on the High Street and so relatively accessible to any protester who wished to make a scene, either about the heir to the throne and future defender of the faith resorting to a non-religious, bureaucratic civic ceremony or to the fact that he was marrying a divorcee. These manoeuvres were complicated enough although, unlike most couples, Charles and Camilla were scarcely organising the event themselves. But then there was an unexpected added difficulty. The previous weekend, Pope John Paul II died and the Prince was despatched to Rome for the funeral, which was held at the Vatican on the day the wedding was supposed to have taken place, so it was postponed for twenty-four hours. In the end, all passed off peacefully on both occasions though, perhaps distractedly, the Prince found himself shaking hands in St Peter's Square with the ageing Zimbabwean tyrant Robert Mugabe who mischievously insinuated himself close by in the VIPs' section and thrust his hand in Charles's direction. The Prince grasped it without looking to see who its owner was.

For the wedding the following day, the royal party arrived in closed limousines and scuttled into the Guildhall, then out again afterwards. Behind the castle walls there was indeed a private blessing service in the chapel, conducted by the archbishop of Canterbury Rowan Williams, followed by a reception for invited guests and by all accounts it was a very happy party. 'It was a wonderful, strangely egalitarian occasion, just like an ordinary family wedding' one of the guests told me. 'The Queen made a very happy, funny speech, unlike anything she's ever done in public. I found myself saying, 'Do you know Andrew?' introducing Phil Collins to the Duke of York. *Phil Collins! The rock star...*' Prince Charles was at last married to his long-time lover and became visibly more relaxed and cheerful because of it.

There were still some ticklish issues, most notably what title Camilla would have now she was married to the Prince of Wales and, more sensitively, once he became King. The immediate solution was for Camilla not to usurp the blessed Princess Diana, but to attach herself to one of Charles's subsidiary titles and become Duchess of Cornwall to his Duke. For the long term, it was suggested that she should become Princess Consort and also Her Royal Highness, but not Queen, when her husband becomes King. This again skirts the Diana issue and the sensitivity supposedly surrounding Charles's first marriage, but in fact the title is somewhat irrelevant since, as the King's wife, she will effectively be Queen. This is clearly what Charles would like – Camilla is less flustered by titles – but the manoeuvring towards it has been slow and crab-like, fearful of stirring up the Diana irredentists and causing palpitations to the Church of England. 'We have never had a grand campaign as such to "make Camilla queen",' one royal aide explained. 'That would be counter-productive, self-defeating and dangerous. Obviously time will heal all things. Camilla is clearly a tremendous asset and she is great for him and there is no hurry. She chooses to be known as the Duchess of Cornwall and everyone is happy with that.'

The Duchess brings a welcome lightness of touch to her sometimes gloomy consort, perhaps because she has not ever quite gone through the media firestorm in the way that Diana did. She does not upstage her touchy husband but is friendly and amenable towards the media. She even likes a gossip with them and gives the impression of enjoying the company of journalists, probably because she has friends who are journalists – and, after all, her son is one. Much of her life had been outside the royal bubble and she has a different outlook to those whose life has been spent inside it. 'She's very smart, she will have a drink with the journalists at receptions on tours and she enjoys the chit chat,' said one official. 'Her husband will be upstairs, working on his papers, worrying about the next day and she will stay downstairs talking.'

Both she and Charles know that, however agreeable a couple they are now, or will be in the future, the ghost of Diana will always hover just behind them. The third person in the marriage has been swapped. The Princess's legacy is that her former husband will never completely escape her toils and neither will his wife.

When the time comes, the Church will undoubtedly find itself flexible enough to conduct the service and welcome Queen Camilla: it would not be the first time it has accepted a royal mistress and its former archbishop of Canterbury has, after all, already blessed the marriage. The unwritten constitution has its advantages in flexibility and no one is going to go to the block for objecting to a title. The *Mail on Sunday*'s telephone opinion poll in April 2015, ten years after the wedding, suggested the country was still deeply divided over whether she should become Queen. But will people notice when the day eventually dawns, apart from making it a talking point during the longueurs of the coronation broadcasts and an opinion piece or two in the news pages before the ceremony? If Camilla indeed becomes Queen it will be an indication of how close she has come to public acceptability. If most of the population now accepts second marriages for themselves, maybe they are unlikely to be mystically poleaxed by the sovereign and his wife taking the obvious titles.

There was a general sense of haplessness about the royals during this period, however, most exemplified by the humiliating farce of the royal butler trials at the end of 2002. They arose out of a suspicion that the servants were getting out of control, almost as though they were taking advantage of a decaying institution and making off with the family goods, as if from some dying Dickensian household. It started when someone spotted one of Charles and Diana's more conspicuous wedding presents from 1981: a jewel-encrusted 2ft-long model of an Arabian dhow, given to them by the Emir of Bahrain, for sale in the window of a Mayfair jeweller's shop. There were other gifts which had apparently been disposed of as well – hard to notice in households which received so many, especially with no proper record kept then of what they were and who had given them – and, when police raided the Cheshire home of the Princess's former valet Paul Burrell, they found more than 300 items of Diana's in the loft: mainly small items such as CDs, but also dresses and other clothing, letters and even a ceremonial sword. Apart from perfunctorily informing Prince Charles and asking whether he wanted to prosecute, the police pressed ahead with bringing the case to court, alleging that he had been selling her property, though they never produced any evidence of this.

Burrell went on trial at the Old Bailey on charges of theft and it was not until two weeks into the hearing, just as he was about to give evidence, that the Queen suddenly remembered that he had told her during an interview following the Princess's death four years earlier that he was looking after papers for safe keeping. The trial was brought to a shuddering halt – if the Queen herself knew that he was holding the Princess's property and was acquiescing in that, he could hardly have stolen it – and Burrell was acquitted. He jubilantly announced outside the court in tabloid-speak that the Queen had come through for him – and promptly sold his story to the *Daily Mirror*.

Another long-serving former palace butler, Harold Brown, was also acquitted a few weeks later, for the police could not sustain a case against him in the light of what had happened in the first trial. The items were quietly restored and Burrell himself went on to have a lucrative if relatively short-lived career, advising on etiquette and trading on his memories of the Princess, primarily on American television. The whole affair left a distinctly odd taste: the two men were clearly innocent, but why had the Queen suddenly, conveniently, remembered a conversation she had held long before and how come

Burrell had not thought to highlight it to the police who had interrogated him before coming to trial – not to mention, what was Clarence House doing, allowing its servants to quietly sell unwanted gifts? A subsequent internal inquiry, conducted by Peat, found that the royals did indeed dispose of gifts to their staff – items such as watches and bottles of champagne won at polo matches and the like, but also, on one occasion at least a gold ring (not *the* wedding ring), found in an envelope bearing the Prince's writing: 'There is a very good gold wedding ring here which someone in the office may find useful.' Indeed the practice had even become semi-formalised, organised through the good offices of the Prince's valet Michael Fawcett and some royal servants, who traded miserly pay for the privilege of serving the royal family, had been selling off gifts that they themselves had properly received. Peat's report pledged to tighten up palace procedures, though it did not find anyone particularly to blame for the disposals, or the cavalier way the palace had with presents. The report stated: 'Opprobrium cannot be attached to this because the rules were not enforced and he made no secret of such gifts,' and added that the procedure had been authorised by the Prince. Mr Fawcett was criticised, however, for what sounds close to bullying: 'His robust approach to dealing with some people combined perhaps with his having been promoted from a relatively junior position within the household undoubtedly caused jealousy and friction.' He resigned from the Prince's service, but was soon back, acting as a freelance adviser and organiser of parties and receptions for Charles at Highgrove. Mr Fawcett was subsequently appointed chief executive of Dumfries House, the eighteenth-century Palladian mansion in Ayrshire which the Prince had been instrumental in saving for the nation after it was put up for sale in 2005. He has also remained in close touch with Clarence House: still advising the Prince, still a highly influential figure in the organisation of Charles's life.

Gradually, under Peat's leadership, a grip was gained over Prince Charles's household. Once Bolland had left, there were no more damaging competitive briefings and leakings. A new director of communications, Paddy Harverson, was brought in to bring some control to the public relations strategy, which now focused on emphasising the Prince's good works as a form of rehabilitation. This was an altogether more professional appointment: tall, bald and bearded, he was jocular and self-effacing but could dominate by sheer size. Harverson was an interesting choice: a former junior *Financial Times* journalist with a London School of Economics degree in international relations, he had subsequently gone into public relations. As a fanatical Manchester United supporter, he had been placed in charge of that club's press office, representing possibly the only institution in the country more in the public eye, wealthier and more defensive and suspicious of the media than the royal family. To that degree, representing David Beckham and the Waleses was not so very different. Harverson was headhunted by Peat – at their introductory lunch together they discussed the respective merits of United and Arsenal, the club Peat supported, rather than the striking abilities of Prince Charles and his sons. Harverson admitted that he was not particularly monarchist in outlook, more agnostic, never having given much thought to the monarchy (and, at the *FT*, not having had to do so either). He had to be persuaded to take the job, but he was intrigued by the task of promoting a somewhat tarnished brand rather more proactively than had been the case before.

A deliberate strategy was adopted to draw attention to Charles's interests and activities: to show him in a more positive light, devoted to finding practical solutions to important and enduring national issues. Journalists found themselves taken on day trips to the estate farm at Highgrove, the Prince's country home near Tetbury in Gloucestershire, to listen to talks about organic farming and watch estate workers laying hedges; and then on to Poundbury, the model housing estate on Duchy land outside Dorchester in Dorset, to hear the Prince's American architect expatiate on how to create equally model communities. There were also tours to the Prince's Trust, the charitable organisation Charles had founded with his severance pay from the navy in 1976, to help youngsters mainly from deprived backgrounds learn skills and trades and to set up in business for themselves. The subordinate intention, beyond showing that the Prince was a good egg, was to demonstrate his engagement with the issues affecting the country he would one day rule: with non party-political causes such as housing, sustainability and deprivation. It was to present a story that showed Charles being proactive in developing a new role for himself as heir to the throne, not falling back on his privileges or sitting idly by waiting for his mother to die. There was no doubt about the Prince's diligence: 'He goes through the red boxes every day,' said one former aide who worked for him for a number of years. 'He is possibly the only man in the country who works through on Christmas Day. You can get calls from him up until midnight and before nine in the morning.' Actually, quite a few people have to work on 25 December of course, but you get the drift.

The official line was that Charles was to be a focal point of national unity, duty and service and that he could fulfil this role precisely because he was not a temporary fixture, like a politician seeking re-election every five years. It was, as one senior official engaged in the strategy said, a unique space that he could fill, free from the divisiveness and short-termism of party politics. And he was more engaged than his predecessor a century before, Edward VII as Prince Bertie, touring hospitals, putting on a concerned face and being guest of honour at grand fund-raising dinners. In contrast to Bertie's enjoyment of ten-course meals, Charles eats only once a day.

One former senior adviser to the Prince said: 'Our job was fundamentally quite different from that of the other royals. Charles has made his life: now he wants to make a difference. The Prince was keen for us to be more proactive: he wanted his spokesmen to go out on the media and explain what he was about. We knew the general direction of travel that he wanted to go in but we had to fend off the intrusions into his family's private life and that involved hand-to-hand combat with the media for years.'

It is possible to be sceptical about Charles's enthusiasms. One former palace official said to me: 'It is as though the prince and his brothers are looking for the approval of the Duke of Edinburgh. The Prince's Trust is the Duke of Edinburgh's Award Scheme writ large and even the environmental stuff is like the World Wildlife Fund. It is very difficult for them to disconnect from their father.'

But there is no doubt that the Prince is passionate about – and has exhibited – an extremely lengthy commitment to a great number of charitable ventures in the areas of his interests over decades. The Prince's Trust sponsors and funds a wide array of projects from anti-drugs initiatives to campaigns against bullying, it supports young people setting themselves up in business and it runs training courses to help youngsters apply for jobs. Nearly 60,000 young people, aged between thirteen and thirty, are helped in some way each year – it claims 750,000 have benefited since it was set up – and the trust has become a major charity in its own right, employing more than 550 people and seeking to raise £50 million a year. This is a major and highly beneficial achievement for a prince 'making a difference', but it is not the only one. There is the drawing school in Shoreditch, east London, seeking to improve the standards of draughtsmanship and offering programmes ranging from those for schools to MA courses; the traditional arts school (you can see where Charles's enthusiasms lie); the Prince's teaching institute, aiming to promote aspirations in pupils and career development in state school staff; the foundation for the building community and a number of others. The Prince is patron of more than four hundred organisations, from Age Cymru to the Woodland Trust, most of them highlighting his interests in architecture, complementary medicine, farming, the environment and sustainability. He is also patron of the UK branch of what is now the Worldwide Fund for Nature, formerly the World Wildlife Fund, of which his father was international president for fifteen years until 1996. These are all-absorbing and enduring interests. It is a far cry from his great-great-grandfather's penchant for opening hospitals and celebratory banquets – though Charles does those as well.

The potential downside of this public engagement by the heir to the throne is his tendency to adopt dogmatic positions on the issues that matter to him and privately to lobby ministers about them. Charles sometimes appears to forget that his personal enthusiasms ought not necessarily to carry more weight or bear more influence just because of who he is. He had always been a prolific letter and memo writer – Charles, unlike his sons and his father, does not use a computer – and tends to shoot off typed up letters or handwritten notes in his spidery black-ink writing. They range from polite thank-you notes, to personal condolences to the relatives of servicemen killed in Iraq or Afghanistan, or, for instance, to the parents of two little girls murdered by a paedophile in Cambridgeshire, to long-winded multi-page memoranda, arguing a case or outlining forthcoming potential problems. There is a constant stream to staff and contacts backed up by telephone calls late into the evening. 'He is computer illiterate so we get an unbelievable quantity of stuff,' one close associate told me. 'He spends an enormous amount of time writing notes: "I have had a thought..." followed by ten pages in black ink. When you get your own memos back they are marked in red Pentel to suggest amendments. In my area I should think he spends twenty to thirty hours a week. It is micromanagement: he has never learned to manage things. He rings up a lot but personally I tend to discourage being called late.'

The so-called 'black spider' letters to ministers are what have caused controversy. The upside of Charles's reliance on paper and pen is that his thoughts cannot be hacked, the downside that they form a permanent written record. Such letters are bound to be contentious, coming as they do from someone who is supposed to remain aloof from political engagement but who, because of who he is, is likely to have rather more access and influence than most other members of the population. The fact that the correspondence is confidential only increases concern about meddling. The Prince tends to shoot off such missives after he has heard or discussed something on a visit: anything from a particular complaint from a farmer, someone waiting for hospital treatment, the prevalence of plastic bags, problems in rural communities such as the lack of public transport or the closure of pubs and village shops, the lack of facilities and training opportunities for school leavers in the inner cities, to bureaucratic tangles. The messages get targeted at ministers who supposedly can do something about them and they are usually followed up by the Prince's private secretary to find out what has happened and what action has been taken. There is a badgering and even hectoring element to this – although often couched in mock-obsequious tones: 'at the risk of being a complete bore', 'please forgive me for repeating my growing anxiety' – and some of the advocacy on issues such as genetically modified crops, state education, military equipment and complementary medicine veers close to the political. The Prince believes he is operating in a public-spirited way, saying: 'If I don't raise it, who else will?' And he resents the lack of understanding of what he is trying to do: we know he thinks of himself as an outsider, smuggling in subversive messages, but he seems to lack an appreciation of why his letters might cause concern. Former ministers who have received the letters tend to shrug them off and none admits to having been unduly influenced by them. There is a slight sense that sometimes Charles does not appreciate all the complexities, or the politics. But of course the letters go to the top of the pile and naturally ministers read and answer them more carefully than those of other people: they know that if they don't, there will be even more. If ministers do find the pressure tiresome, they do not admit it and they defend the prince's right to lobby them. In a column for the *Sunday Mirror* in April 2015, Lord Prescott, the former Labour cabinet minister, wrote that, while not a raving loyalist, he had a lot of time for the Prince: 'Charles has an awful lot to offer this country. And if he wants to serve his subjects by helping young people into work, combating climate change and building sustainable communities, he can write as many damn letters as he likes.'

In 2005 the *Guardian* launched a Freedom of Information request to see a selection of twenty-seven of the Prince's black spider letters to various ministers in the then Labour government: in the departments of health, agriculture and business. It was ironic that the Prince's views on some issues such as GM foods might well have coincided with the newspaper's editorial position. But that was not the point: it was the constitutional aspect that worried the newspaper as it came out increasingly strongly if not necessarily always entirely coherently for republicanism. Its line wavered from calling for a serious debate about the constitution and the succession to a more jeering scepticism.

Such was the sensitivity about the letters that the request was refused and successive governments embarked on a decade-long rearguard action to maintain their confidentiality. When the High Court ruled in 2012 that the letters should be disclosed, the attorney general Dominic Grieve overruled the court on the grounds that publication of the Prince's 'particularly frank' views would 'seriously undermine his ability to fulfil his duties when he becomes King'. The dangerous precedent of a government minister overruling a court decision was only set aside three years later when the Supreme Court finally ordered publication. Some of the Prince's staff maintained that the letters were no more than courtesy missives and that defending their confidentiality was a matter of principle rather than because of the nature of what they contained. The palace was 'relaxed' about the appeal court ruling and anyway the letters were ten years old...but what did the attorney general mean?

When the twenty-seven letters were finally released in May 2015 they were indeed startlingly uncontroversial in their content, to the newspaper's barely disguised disappointment. They had focused on issues such as a badger cull, inadequate equipment for troops then serving in Iraq, the European Union's restrictions on the use of herbal complementary medicines and even the illegal fishing of the Patagonian toothfish and its deleterious effect on the 'poor old albatross'. They might almost have been written by a worried *Guardian* reader. This was scarcely the stuff of the divine right of kings, but a wider principle was involved: the government had spent £400,000 in legal fees to protect the confidentiality of the Prince's correspondence and the paper had expended ten years of effort to overturn it. 'A head of state with an opinion,' *The Times* severely noted in its editorial, 'Is called a president, not a prince.' A second tranche of letters, written between 2007 and 2009, released in June 2015, only reinforced the image of the Prince's lobbying on issues such as homeopathic medicine. Their wheedling tone – 'I cannot bear to see people suffering unnecessarily' – and the suggestion that the Prince's advisers might be seconded to work in government departments (he suggested that

that would be 'wonderful') could only be seen to be an exercise in direct influence. Despite the obsequious, even ironic, responses of Labour ministers – one signed his replies as a 'most humble and obedient subject' – there is little indication that, ultimately, they were swayed. Did the Prince recognise his humble servants' irony, or just accept it as his due? And who knows if he has an influence with his letters these days?

Unfortunately, even non-partisan issues tend to be highly controversial and the Prince seems insufficiently aware that he tends to skim the surface of issues that interest him and to consult only those whose views he shares. 'Does he lack focus?' one who has worked with him for most of the past twenty-five years mused to me. 'Yes, he does. He is not a great intellectual. He's got a butterfly mind. I suppose if you are going to be monarch you are going to have to do four or five things in a day, so perhaps it will come in useful. Perhaps it is best not to be too focused.' He did not sound entirely sure.

When Charles complained that the secretaries in his office could not spell as an example of the shortcomings of modern education, he tended to overlook the fact that many of them had been privately educated, and when he called in educationalists to discuss what was going wrong in state schools, they were often right-wing polemicists and commentators, rather than teachers or head teachers with experience running state schools. John Dunford, the former general secretary of the Secondary Heads Association, who had himself been a successful head teacher, told me: 'I think he listens to people who would have a traditional view of education and the rest of us generally ignore him when he speaks. He does absolutely sod all for state education. I am pretty certain he does not visit many state schools, though if you browse through Headmasters' Conference[30] publications you will see quite a lot of pictures of royalty opening buildings.' Nevertheless, the Prince has set up summer schools for teachers of English literature and history. Are they patronising in their assumptions that state schools do not teach such subjects adequately? Is there a subliminal message about the diminution of British culture and heritage, with which the monarchy itself is so bound up? Have the initiatives made a difference in state schools? Not obviously if Tory education ministers are to be believed as they bemoan school standards. All the Queen's children were educated privately, the sons at Gordonstoun, Princess Anne at Benenden and the grandsons William and Harry, too, in their case at Eton. There were certainly security reasons for this, but no disguising personal preferences either.

The same consideration applied to homeopathy, one of the Prince's long-term interests, where he listened only to those whose views he agreed with. Most in the medical profession are sceptical of the effects of 'natural' treatments, but the Prince has lobbied for them to be available on the National Health Service (though he and his family do not themselves use the NHS). As Professor Edzard Ernst, the world's first professor of complementary medicine at the Peninsula Medical School, attached to Exeter and Plymouth universities, told me, he believes he was frozen out by the Prince's circle when he expressed scepticism about some treatments: 'He took great interest when my chair was set up but I only met him twice, to shake hands for half a millisecond, not to have a dialogue. He stands for implementing complementary medicine at all costs, whereas I stand for therapies

---

30 The Headmasters' Conference represents the heads of the major private schools, though some of its members belong to the Secondary Heads Association to which state school leaders also belong.

which can be proved by sound evidence. His energy and influence could be used so much better. As it is used now it is detrimental to progress. He has started a discipline but he doesn't seem to have any understanding of the need for evidence. I have repeatedly been told he cannot tolerate advice which is not one hundred per cent in line with his opinion...I think his advisers are all sycophants.'

The Prince also upset many in the architectural profession. The needling of their *amour-propre* had started when he publicly criticised the design of the National Gallery extension as a 'monstrous carbuncle' in 1984, but his open championing of what could be called traditional architectural forms for public buildings, sometimes ersatz copies of eighteenth-century designs, all porticoes and pediments, irked the more progressive members of the profession. His interventions and occasional lobbying against designs, such as the redevelopment of Chelsea Barracks in 2010 by a company commissioned by the Emir of Qatar – why not something more old-fashioned, in imitation of the buildings of eighteenth-century Bath or Edinburgh? He asked, suggesting in his view more appropriate architects. It had a chilling effect and even occasionally undermined careers. As Sunand Prasad, a former president of the Royal Institute for British Architects, said: 'It [is] very wounding and not justified. It [has] closed down debate and has been destructive of individual careers. Everyone got cast in the same liberal mould. The prince has championed sustainability and stewardship of resources and it is fantastic that someone in his position should do so. But the debate has moved on: there's huge public interest in architecture, but people are buying modernist products, not classical ones.' Is it true that people want modern architecture rather than classical designs? The Prince's interventions do not seem to have prevented the modernist skyscrapers of central London and the City whether 'people' want them or not. Richard Rogers, whose company designed the Chelsea barracks scheme, insists that local residents and the Royal Borough of Kensington and Chelsea's planning department were happy with the modernist plans and the Qataris only pulled out because of pressure from the Prince. Perhaps what people really want in such areas though is affordable housing.

These interests were a descant to the coverage of the Prince's life, a source of an unchanging debate about Charles's role as heir to the throne and, as such, of declining interest to the media, only occasionally surfacing when the Prince says something that could be interpreted as particularly egregious. The Prince's wish to become an activist monarch can easily place him at odds with critics, irked by his determination to make a difference and suspicious of every public position he takes whether they might otherwise agree with him or not. What remains an unknown quantity is how far his frequently publicly stated positions can be subsumed when he becomes King. What if a future government legislates about something he is known to have previously opposed? Actually, he would clearly be expected to sign such a bill into law, but that might not preclude him expressing his opposition in private. As it is, the Queen and the Prince both have a right to consultation about future legislation which might affect their interests, though it seems that neither has vetoed bills because of it. To do so would cause a constitutional convulsion. Perhaps for the Prince as King to be known publicly to have concerns on an issue would be enough. Plenty of monarchs in the past have had robust views on many subjects, though they have been more able, usually, to express them privately – much harder to do so in the age of social media and freedom of information legislation. Pragmatically, will the public worry if the King expresses contrary views occasionally, or will they be more relaxed than the politicians and experts? Presumably it will depend on the issue, the timing and the terms in which those views are expressed – and whether the monarchy is gaining a reputation for meddling. Charles probably hopes that common sense will prevail – possibly so long as it is his common sense.

Media attention shifted in the early 2000s to his two sons who were now passing adolescence and emerging into adulthood. During their schooling at Eton – an institution conveniently close to Granny's castle and moreover one which was well used to dealing discreetly with the sons of the rich and famous – William and Harry had been shielded from intrusive publicity by the so-called 'pressure cooker' agreement with the chastened British newspapers. Editors were nervous in the light of the boys' mother's death, of being accused of intrusiveness and even more so of their prurient readers' potential displeasure if they were felt to have overstepped the mark. But now the princes were leaving school and emerging once more into the light: William to go to St Andrews University on the east coast of Scotland – a destination chosen not just for the excellence of its education but also its relative remoteness from the metropolitan media. Harry, less academically inclined, was to enter the army immediately. William, the heir to the heir, was naturally quiet and serious, and very conscious of his position; Harry, the younger spare, was much less so – hearty, unwilling to be constrained in public and also less selective in his choice of friends. He was the tabloids' perfect naughty boy for the continuing soap opera narrative and duly lived down to expectations. There was the light soft drug-taking, a drunken bundle outside a London nightclub and, most notoriously, the wearing of a homemade Nazi-style armband as part of a mock Afrika Korps uniform to a friend's fancy-dress party – a serious and fatuous error of judgement, albeit one made by a twenty year old. Understandably, the solution was his expression of contrition – again – and packing him off to the Royal Military Academy at Sandhurst. To satisfy any conceivable public thirst for information, the princes underwent occasional formal photo opportunities, as when William went up to university, or Harry (and later William himself) graduated at the public passing-out parade from Sandhurst. They also very occasionally gave stilted and stultifyingly dull interviews to carefully selected television correspondents. But while the pact generally held with British media in Britain, it could not be enforced with the foreign media or when the princes went abroad. When Harry went to Australia briefly to sample life at a Queensland cattle ranch, the farm was buzzed by photographers in low-flying planes trying to get pictures of the Prince, preferably being thrown from a horse. Much later, his first tour of duty in Afghanistan had to be cut short when it was reported in the Australian and American media. And it was not just the tabloids publicly buzzing around the princes: in the era of social media and phone hacking, as for many other celebrities, their lives were more on show than their predecessors' ever had been before and the controls were much less likely to be effective. Both young men were packed off into the military, a standard part of training for royal princes, William following his university degree with a spell in the Household Cavalry before training as a helicopter pilot with the RAF and a posting in the Air Sea Rescue Services, and Harry also in the Household Cavalry and then the Army Air Corps, flying helicopters.

But there was a limit to the protection from intrusion that could be offered. Both princes' phones were hacked and voicemail messages listened to, to reveal in the *News of the World* in 2006 the crass and tedious details of William's forthcoming meeting with ITN's royal correspondent to hand over some home movies so that a documentary could be made, and his appointment to see a knee surgeon – particularly stupid revelations since, when they appeared in print, there could be no doubt about how the stories had been obtained. The newspaper's royal correspondent, Clive Goodman, was a man under such intense pressure to obtain scoops that he evidently lost all perspective and paid for it by going to prison, and a newspaper which was so confident in its invulnerability that it sanctioned and paid for criminal acts in pursuit of trivia.

It was at about this time that the palace made a clear decision to focus its main drive for publicity on television, which offered better control and a chance to portray the royals as they wished to be seen. The pictures would be seen more widely than any newspaper story or even photographs would. There were good stories to tell, from the royals' point of view: the princes' visits abroad. William had reluctantly taken along a freelance cameraman on his gap year stay at an orphanage in Chile before going to university, but the results had been good, showing an apparently relaxed and ordinary young man playing with the children and undertaking menial tasks such as cleaning the toilets. It was certainly a different and more human view, fully underlining the intention of emphasising the Prince's willing engagement with normal – and public-spirited – life. The royals had not moved on from opening hospitals and other charitable good works but the sight of William cuddling deprived children inevitably underscored a side of him that seemed to derive directly and naturally from his late mother. Later, Harry would follow the same path with an ITV crew following him to Lesotho in southern Africa, this time showing the younger Prince romping with local children. Both princes were interviewed during their time abroad and appeared relaxed, or at least more relaxed than they actually were in the presence of a camera.

But the television exposure was double-edged when a BBC documentary series about a year in the life of the Queen in 2007 was compromised by the maladroit editing of the publicity material shown to journalists. This occurred in a sequence that seemed to show the Queen petulantly reacting to suggestions being made by the celebrated American photographer Annie Leibovitz and walking out of the photoshoot at Buckingham Palace. She certainly seemed a little exasperated by the photographer's demands that she should take off her crown for the formal portrait but the film was edited to show her walking away in annoyance after the exchange when the walking shot had actually shown her earlier approaching the photoshoot. The Queen *was* moaning, but about the weight of her Garter robes, not about her treatment by Leibovitz. The manipulation was crass and juvenile and the BBC's response to the criticism that followed was slow and confused. It scarcely helped the corporation's attempt to be restored to royal favour – a tenth-anniversary documentary about Princess Diana later that year was dropped in a loss of nerve – but the Leibovitz incident showed the palace, if it needed reminding, that filming could be as manipulative and distorted as anything in the press.

The army clearly suited Harry's personality and he enjoyed being one of the lads – Cornet Wales – instead of being constantly deferred to as a prince. He was even allowed to serve in the war zone of Afghanistan, a posting which had been denied to his older brother, who as second in line to the throne could not be risked. But he was also more accident prone than his brother, at least so far as bad publicity was concerned. There was the time in 2009 when he was caught (in his own mobile phone footage) calling a fellow officer a 'Paki': though the sequence had taken four years to make it into the public domain. The remark was clearly bantering rather than malevolent and had not led to a complaint from the Pakistani officer concerned, but there had to be an apology and a dressing down from the commanding officer: 'an interview without coffee' as it is known in the military. Again, three years later, when Harry cavorted naked in private with six undressed young American acquaintances during a game of strip billiards in a Las Vegas hotel suite in August 2012 – a case, he later admitted of 'too much army, not enough prince ... it's very easy to forget who I am when I am in the army'. His antics came to light when the pictures taken by one of those present were rapidly circulated to the world online. A grovelling apology – of course – followed though actually there was not much sign of public censoriousness back in Britain outside the tabloid editorial pages, because he was, after all, on leave before a tour of duty in Afghanistan. It helped that the Prince was understood to be doing serious work in the army. It was Harry being Harry again, a bit like Shakespeare's version of a previous Prince Hal, though at twenty-seven he was old enough to have known better. With the arrival of the Internet and social media and no constraints on access, the dangers would only get worse and the remedies less certain. In a television interview during a break in Afghanistan, Harry said resignedly: 'I don't believe there is any such thing as a private life any more. I am not going to sit here and whinge. Everyone knows about Twitter and the Internet and stuff like that. Every single mobile phone has got a camera on it now. You can't move an inch without someone judging you. It's an unstoppable force.'

All the more reason, perhaps, not to play strip billiards with a group of women you have never met before. How different from five generations back, when Prince Bertie's sexual initiation with the Irish prostitute Nellie Clifden while he was in camp with the Grenadier Guards on the Curragh in 1861, did not reach the public prints, though it was the gossip of the officers' mess and caused his father Prince Albert to have conniptions.

The demand for news, however trivial, was now insatiable, international and continuous, twenty-four hours a day. Occasional access for formal interviews and photo opportunities did not satisfy the craving: 'You would not believe the queries we received,' said one former press officer. 'When they went skiing, the French paparazzi would be buzzing around them, they'd be up in the trees, training their lenses into their bedroom windows. That sort of thing is relentless – and wearing.'

What really interested the press of course was who the boys would marry and the guessing game began again a quarter century on from the courtship of Charles and Diana. Even in junior adolescence, William had been mobbed by young girls in outbreaks of 'Wills Mania', so there was certainly an appetite for knowing whatever the supposedly most eligible young man in the world was doing. The Cinderella dream, of being plucked from the crowd by a prince remains surprisingly alluring: most adolescent girls must have known it was illusory, others thought it a joke on a day out to share with their mates, but a few – perhaps – do think it might really happen, like winning the lottery. How as a very young, rather shy, lad, do you cope with teenagers screaming 'marry me' and 'kiss me' and 'I love you' at short range (or even the 'I love Willy' T-shirts worn by two gay chaps to meet him in Sydney)? How do you feel when very little of your life, including its most intimate details, is kept secret? And how do you react, knowing that the same public obsessiveness hounded your mother and played a part in her terrible death? Although he usually appeared equable in public, William in particular developed a well-honed loathing of the media. He was aware that he could not react badly, or throw a tantrum or even exhibit aggravation and exasperation since angry pictures – so much more profitable than ordinary ones – would be flashed round the world within minutes. He knew too that the paparazzi would do their best to provoke him into just such reactions whenever he appeared, as they had his mother. They would be coming too close, being too intimate and cheeky and generally being obnoxious and they would do it as often as they could.

This was not the case with British staff press photographers who were polite and professional but the freelancers were another matter. He could cope, but would a girlfriend be able to do so? William's choice soon settled on his fellow St Andrews student Catherine Middleton, forever to be known as Kate, a name (and a spelling) she had never had before, and she too was soon subjected to the treatment. Middleton had an interestingly novel back-story for a prince's consort: her parents Carole and Michael had risen from lower-middle-class backgrounds – earlier members of the family had been coal miners in the north-east of England – to run a small mail-order business supplying children's party paraphernalia from offices in rural Berkshire, profitable enough to send their three children to private schools. It was not the sort of family that earlier princes would ever have considered marrying into[31]: commoners as royal brides have been extremely rare: there is Camilla, of course, but before that you have to go back to Mrs Fitzherbert, the secret wife of the Prince Regent, and Anne Hyde, who married James II in 1660.

Now, however, Kate Middleton became the apotheosis of the middle-class monarchy, the girl whose parents had started from nothing – an air hostess and a flight dispatcher at Heathrow Airport – and built themselves into somebodies. All the posh jibes at the royal wedding that the last time Carole Middleton had walked down an aisle so crowded she had been offering the passengers the choice of beef or chicken[32] were otiose. For more than a century the royal family had aspired to represent middle-class values and quite often failed in their private lives: now their brightest young hope had actually chosen a bride from those aspirant classes. And, apart from some discreet cashing in – who else was going to supply party pieces for the celebratory

---

31 In 1812, the Prince Regent consulted the lord chancellor, Lord Eldon, about what to do with his wayward teenage daughter Princess Charlotte. Eldon, whose family money came from coal mining in the north-east, advised the Prince to lock up his daughter, which drew the haughty response from Charlotte when she heard of it: 'What would the King say if he could know that his granddaughter had been compared to the granddaughter of a collier?' Two hundred years later it had come to pass.

32 By Marina Hyde, herself the daughter of a baronet, in the *Guardian*: a good joke but a somewhat snobbish one.

nuptials across the country, or who better to sign a lucrative contract for a book about arranging parties than the bride's attractive younger sister? – the Middletons have been the souls of discretion and respectability.

By the time the pair came to marry in 2011, Kate Middleton had proved herself resilient enough to cope with the pressures of marrying the second in line to the throne. It helped also that she and William had known each other for nearly ten years, had lived together, studied together, had similar educational backgrounds and attainments, shared similar interests and were both the same age, nearly thirty by the time of their wedding – all attributes that no previous British princes and their consorts had ever had: certainly not his father and mother. Nevertheless, Middleton had experienced the intrusion of paparazzi photographers at St Andrews – the pact that the palace had agreed with the British press had no effect on foreign camera crews, or a girlfriend if unaccompanied by the Prince. She had accordingly found packs of photographers dogging her footsteps when she walked about the university. Later, on her twenty-fifth birthday in January 2007, more than fifty cameramen and five television crews camped outside her London flat to take pictures as she emerged to get to her car and go to work. The pack was back, running after her, jostling her, screaming abuse in her face – 'slag, whore, bitch' – all intended to provoke a reaction of the sort that would make their day. This was long before she and William were engaged and before she had retreated from her original grace-and-favour job as an accessories buyer for the Jigsaw chain of retail shops which was run by family friends – she would later go and work for her parents' company, Party Pieces.

The palace did not provide police or security protection, but it did warn the media to back off with a threat to complain to the Press Complaints Commission. William wanted the palace to go further and take a case alleging harassment to the European Court of Human Rights in Strasbourg, which would indeed have been a first for the British royal family, but this was not pursued. Instead what happened was that the British press retreated tactically, led by Rupert Murdoch's News Corporation, which hoped to curry favour by promising not to use any paparazzi photographs of Middleton – a hypocritical pledge given that its *News of the World* journalists were busy hacking phones, including those of royal officials, at the same time. There was also the fact that the paparazzi were beginning to find the Prince's girlfriend just a little bit boring: she was notably cautious, did not go out much, wore smart, sensible clothes when she did, never appeared the worse for wear in public, did not even seem to have many outside interests and so, frankly, there was not much to photograph, especially when she retreated to her parents' home in the wilds of west Berkshire instead. She was, above all, sensible and conformist, even a little dull, but absolutely unfazed or visibly distressed by the attention she was getting. These, of course, were precisely the sort of qualities about her that appealed to the royal family and made her eventually quite suitable as a bride. Much more suitable, perhaps, than Harry's long-term girlfriend, the Zimbabwean Chelsy Davy, who dressed more provocatively, smoked and drank in public, and generally seemed to be having a good time and not treating the possibility of a long-term relationship too seriously: her on-off-on again, off-again friendship with Harry was in keeping both with his informal nature and the younger son soap opera narrative.

The wedding of Prince William and Kate Middleton duly took place at Westminster Abbey in April 2011 and was, in royal terms, a hugely successful occasion. Maybe as many as a million people crowded into central London, armed with their sleeping bags, picnic baskets, coats, blankets and Union flags to watch the processions – the satisfyingly round figure being just a Metropolitan police guess – and many millions more watched the live broadcast of the ceremonials over many hours in many countries. The figure of two billion viewers worldwide must also have been the roughest of estimates – about five times as many as were said to have watched his parents' marriage in 1981 – but, even so, it is hard to imagine that a third of the world's population were glued to their television sets for the occasion. Australian monarchists, however, did stay up late in the evening and Canadians got up early to watch and to hold discreet little receptions and parties. The American networks sent their star presenters. Royal commentators were out in force in their best frocks and morning suits ready to emote to whoever would employ them and, in the Abbey, the royal correspondents (even the *Guardian*'s) were togged out in formal dress[33] to view the proceedings. More than 8,500 journalists, broadcasters and technicians were on duty to cover the wedding. Only a handful of anti-royalist demonstrators turned up to vent their displeasure and they were corralled far away from the action, in Red Lion Square.

Inside the abbey itself, beside the relatives and personal friends, there were also celebrities, including the Beckhams and Elton John, politicians including the British political party leaders, and Commonwealth prime ministers such as the avowedly republican Julia Gillard of Australia – a veritable Madame Tussauds gallery come to life. There were uniforms – William in the scarlet dress uniform of the Irish Guards, his father in that of an admiral – and there was flummery and pomp and circumstance. The music was all English and traditional: Elgar and Vaughan Williams, Finzi and Delius, 'Guide Me O Thou Great Redeemer', 'Jerusalem' and 'Love Divine All Loves Excelling'. And there was a procession back from the abbey with the married couple in the 1902 state landau pulled by white horses, escorted by the Household

---

33 Hired on expenses.

Cavalry. There was even a slightly reticent kiss on the palace balcony after lunch, repeated in case any of the watching multitude or the photographers had missed it. The Battle of Britain Memorial Flight – a Lancaster bomber, a Spitfire and a Hurricane – roared overhead in commemoration of the country's finest hour forty years before the couple were born. The palace announced that the Queen had bestowed the title of Duke and Duchess of Cambridge on the pair at the time of their marriage and that the middle-class Berkshire girl would henceforth be Her Royal Highness in keeping with her husband's status.

The weather stayed fine, though cold and blustery throughout, and the day culminated in the spectacle of the couple pootling along the Mall in the Prince's father's ageing Aston Martin, festooned with balloons, all the way to Clarence House, 200 yards down the road from the palace. Thus the event passed off with joyous celebrations. The abbey had hosted, as television viewers could not avoid being told, sixteen royal weddings since the first between Henry I and Matilda of Scotland in 1100. There was no question of a reversion now to the privacy in which royal weddings had been conducted until the hoopla of Bertie and Alexandra's in 1863. This was also ceremonial as heritage and as a tourism event: a ten-hour showcase for the things that Britain prides itself on doing well and by which it hopes to attract foreign tourists. Prime Minister David Cameron explicitly said as much: 'A day when we see the new team. It was incredibly romantic and moving. It is a great moment for Britain, a moment when everyone is celebrating and it is being watched around the world where people will see lots of things they love about Britain.' If, as some supporters allege, the royal family is worth its weight to the economy as a tourist attraction, they played their part that day and a prince, known for his reticence and suspicion of the limelight, was put on display with his bride as a promotional symbol as well as a future monarch and a demonstration that the royal line was in good shape.

More than that though, the occasion finally drew a line under William's father's unhappy first marriage and was a demonstration that the institution had pulled through, regained its popularity and could be celebrated once more. The brand was back on top, more popular than ever, and secure in the knowledge that its young Prince – its best hope for the future – had come of age. Understandably, there had been some hesitation about pronouncing another fairytale wedding after the previous debacle, but this one seemed genuine enough.

Both princes had by now been groomed to deal with the media. Outwardly they appeared to have inherited their mother's friendly approachability. Inwardly they neither trusted nor appreciated the media's interest: in fact, they hated it, even when it was on its best behaviour. Nor did the princes differentiate between intrusive French magazines, British tabloids or the broadsheet media. Understandably, they loathed the sort of journalism that had deformed Diana's life and the photographers who had pursued her remorselessly, even into the Pont de l'Alma tunnel on her last journey, and they also saw no need to emulate her manipulation of the media. The exception to this was in publicising their good works, such as the charitable foundation working with children in Lesotho.

But they learned how to be at least relatively civil to the media in public. 'William and Harry are really nice lads,' said a former director of communications. 'They are fundamentally good kids with an excellent judgement and understanding of what is expected of them. Harry in particular is a natural. We did not need to do much training, beyond giving technical advice as to where cameras and microphones were, where to look and what questions to expect.

'The belief was very strongly that if we gave them too much preparatory coaching they would stop being natural. You don't want to stifle their personalities as that's their great asset. William has got better, but he is naturally self-conscious and you don't want to train that out because then you would be turning him into something he's not. When he is reading a speech, the slight awkwardness shows that he is authentic, not trained to be smooth like a politician. He is there by a lottery of birth but at least people know because of that that he has not had to change his principles or sell out to get to the top, so it does not make sense to try to make him appear to be something he is not.'

Accordingly, on royal tours now, William appears at ease with the requirements of the job, including walkabouts, so far as the general public is concerned, if not the media. Events can be conducted in jeans and casual shirts and are even touchy-feely: the Prince seemingly as easy hugging grandmothers from the grim Block, down-at-heel housing district in Sydney as meeting (in a business suit) the judges of the Wellington High Court in New Zealand the day before. At the Block that afternoon he happily posed for photographs with the ageing matrons who had turned out in their very best: 'Of course you can, my love...no worries,' and they in turn pronounced him a real, down-to-earth human being – inspirational, just like his mother.

'They have got us where they want us,' said one royal correspondent with a soupçon of bitterness. 'We turn up and do what they want. We are sooo supportive even when they sneer at us.' Not like thirty years ago, then.

Compare and contrast the admittedly ridiculous outrage on one of the Queen's visits to Australia in 1992 when the then prime minister Paul Keating was seen gently to touch her, putting his hand in the small of her back, to guide her as she met dignitaries. The Queen of course to the Maoris is the Great White Heron, a remote and symbolic bird on the verge of extinction. Touching is not what one does with monarchs, not since the ending of the practice of the King's evil, except for the gentlest shaking of hands (you touch her hand when she proffers it and certainly do not seize it, or shake it vigorously). Keating's successor John Howard and Barack Obama's wife Michelle also incurred some indignation in guiding the Queen. Her Majesty herself does not seem to mind, though hugging another octogenarian granny on a state visit is not quite her style. Times change and what once seemed outrageous to one generation, just appears to be stuffiness to the next and is embraced by the third.

In William's case there is empathy, too, in meeting survivors of severe bushfires in rural Victoria and, on a subsequent visit, the victims of the earthquake in Christchurch in 2010. He can 'do' charming, does not mind being teased and does not seem to get stressed or aggravated, so long as it is with the general public. There are certainly signs of a more relaxed and informal style than his father or grandmother's generations. Even sceptical Australians are impressed: after his first solo visit in 2010, the pro-republican *Melbourne Age* declared him an all-round good egg 'who may have done more to set back the republican cause than anything since the [failed] referendum in 1999'. Something similar happened on Prince Harry's first solo foreign trip to the West Indies in 2012, shortly before his Las Vegas hotel antics. There was a mock race in Jamaica with the champion sprinter Usain Bolt, including the Prince's emulation of the latter's famous lightning gesture, and also a hug for the island's pro-republican prime minister Portia Simpson-Miller. He told her she was his date for the evening, which produced a purr of pleasure and her admission: 'We are in love with him.' Republicans may sneer that these are easy, meaningless gestures and so they are. But they are also human ones, humanising and personalising the institution and inducing little bursts of pleasure in the recipients. They may not stop such countries ultimately becoming republics but they produce goodwill and just a little more benignity.

William and his brother are not sent out alone, of course, on public trips, though neither are they submerged by staff. On William's early visits abroad there was the princes' then private secretary Major Jamie Lowther-Pinkerton, the leathery, hatchet-faced, former Irish Guards and SAS army officer, glowering close beside him, ready glumly to receive the bouquets of flowers thrust into the Prince's hands and looking as if he would cheerfully leap into the crowd to strangle anyone showing signs of dissent with his bare hands. Also at the princes' sides is the former diplomat Sir David Manning, previously the British ambassador to Washington, brought in on a part-time basis to advise and steer them through the protocol and diplomacy shoals of the trips, an appointment sanctioned by the Queen. A small, slight, grey-haired figure, he can be seen standing looking quizzical on the fringes of the walkabouts.

There was also Miguel Head, the young press officer who succeeded Lowther-Pinkerton as full-time private secretary in 2013. 'Mig' Head first won Prince Harry's confidence when, as a junior press officer at the Ministry of Defence, he handled the fallout following the Prince's enforced withdrawal early from Afghanistan after his presence there was revealed in the Australian and US media. He was subsequently seconded to Clarence House in 2009 and proved to be a genial and helpful figure: only a couple of years older than Prince William he was relaxed in dealing with the media.

Kate Middleton has also gone through the gradual minding process. On her first tour with the Prince after their marriage, to Canada and the west coast of the United States, she did little more than smile in public and certainly did not speak officially. That would be too soon and too overwhelming, said Lowther-Pinkerton. Little gestures helped, such as the bright-red maple leaf fascinator she wore perched on the top of her head on Canada Day and the evident enjoyment she was deriving from her first official outings abroad were enough to draw enthusiasm from the monarchist crowds. On such occasions it is the size of the crowd that overawes opposition: it is the head count that matters. The media contingent when there is a public event, as opposed to mundane day-to-day happenings, can be overwhelming, too: on an overseas tour for instance there will be British press, British television crews, radio, national press, local press, local and national television, and radio networks, photographers, freelancers, commentators, feature writers: a whole gallimaufry of journalists all straining for a view and piled high with equipment; to use the jargon, a veritable goat fuck of internecine competition, all demanding to be kept happy. They would not be there if their editors did not think their readers, listeners and viewers wanted to see the royals. Boring or not, for the couple's spring tour to Australia and New Zealand in 2014, there were at least 450 accreditations, fortunately not all there all the time, but a considerable crowd. No wonder it is sometimes hard to see ordinary civilians through the melee, or to tell the sheep from the goats. No wonder, too, faced with such a mob, that the Duchess can appear stiff and head-girlish, eyes averted from the cameras: the swaying ziggurat of photographers and television crews must be terrifying.

Back home, the duchess was guided gently towards making her first public speech, nearly a year after the wedding – at the opening of a building at a hospice in East Anglia – and towards the charities whose patron she would become in keeping with her interests in the arts and child health. She did the research herself on the web, not relying on reports from aides. 'In the old days an army of grey suits would have written up reports on the charities for her,' one official told the *Sunday Telegraph* at the time. 'Now she can do the research herself on the Internet. Anybody who has met her knows she is a very nice young woman.' Even better from the royals' point of view, she was diligent and willing to learn, meeting Manning to be mentored about constitutional niceties, the workings of the institution she has joined and the duchy lands that her husband will one day preside over. This was not something that happened with Diana, or at least that she troubled to imbibe. The Duchess is more diligent about such things, has had a better education, comes from a more ambitious background and is older than her late mother-in-law was: indeed by 2018, she and her husband will be older than Diana was when she died. However, proof that paparazzi interest had not really declined following her wedding came with the publication in France in September 2012 of photographs of the Duchess sunbathing topless while on holiday at a private villa in Provence. The pictures had been taken by a French photographer using a telephoto lens from a public road half a mile away. The British press would not touch the photographs but they were published by the celebrity magazine *Closer* in Paris and subsequently sold to other magazines in Ireland, Denmark, Sweden and Italy. Other photographs have also appeared in the German magazine *Bild* and the pictures have also surfaced on the Internet. *Closer's* publisher and a photographer working for the magazine (though not, apparently, the paparazzo) were charged with invading the Duchess's privacy – but not until seven months later, long after publication and the profit had been made. It is the double-edged sword of royal publicity: the pictures would not be taken if there was not a public-consuming interest in buying the magazines and seeing them, but without publicity (just not *that* sort of publicity) the royal brand would be diminished. Ironically, with the British press's self-denying ordinance against publishing paparazzi pictures of the royals, we have in some ways returned to the situation in 1936 when the British public were kept in the dark. The difference of course is that that was a story of constitutional significance and the Duchess's breasts are not. Walter Bagehot's aphorism still holds true – it is just that he could never have envisaged the degree of sunlight that modern technology now affords. What will happen if one day a paparazzo's shot turns out to be newsworthy? How long then will the newspaper agreement last? William and Harry may wish to be ordinary in their private lives, unbothered, left alone to go to a pub for a pint or to go clubbing, but they are not: it is the price royalty pays for privilege.

The princes' encounters with the press are strained, with a sort of passive aggression. Sensitivities remain: on the Duke and Duchess's trip to Australia and New Zealand in the spring of 2014, with their baby son, photographers were asked to leave them alone for a day of privacy at Government House in Canberra. The British media complied, some of the Australians did not: and published inoffensive photographs of the couple strolling in the grounds and playing with the child. Initially warned off, the British contingent did not publish the pictures even after the Prince and his advisers decided they were unexceptionable and could be used. Where does this leave things? The Prince and the palace cannot control what the rest of the world sees and any attempt to stop them doing so even in another Commonwealth country of which he might conceivably one day be head of state risks stirring up a storm of protest and anti-monarchy chippiness. They just have to grin and bear it.

But the smiles are forced. The princes enjoy telling journalists how they have frustrated attempts to photograph them and the other little tricks they have played with false trails, disguises and deceptions. On his first trip to China in the spring of 2015, the Prince had to be reminded to acknowledge the presence of the media and was eventually persuaded to thank the British contingent for coming all that way to cover the visit, which he did through gritted teeth according to one who was there. It is a loathe/hate relationship on Prince William's side. And there is occasional peevishness, too, as when Harry sneered at correspondents who had loyally turned up to cover the Invictus Games for disabled war veterans, which he had spearheaded in London in September 2014. When William and Kate acquired a pet black cocker-spaniel puppy, the offspring of a Middleton family pet, the press office was given instructions not to confirm either the name or the sex of the shaggy little creature – apparently a reaction to the couple having been photographed unexpectedly on holiday on a beach in Wales. The animal's name was said to be a private matter even though journalists protested that they knew the names of every one of the Queen's corgis and always had. Then, some time later, the name slipped out when the Duchess mentioned it while speaking to a patient while visiting a hospital. For the record, the dog's name is Lupo. If a pet dog's name becomes a state secret, what else will he want to prevent the world from knowing? The Prince needs to be careful not to follow his father's example, as one tabloid correspondent said to me: 'Newsdesks are starting to say, "He's just a bald bloke in a suit. Do we need pictures of that?"' If the media is not there, how does the public know that the royals are still doing their job? If the brand is to survive, he will have to loosen up a little.

Chapter 10

'What does she do with it?'

(George Otto Trevelyan on Queen Victoria's wealth, 1871)

The history of Britain's monarchy could almost be summed up as the story of the Crown's attempts to secure more money from its subjects and parliament's periodic attempt to circumvent it. Nothing causes more potential for danger to the institution and its popularity than the public's resentment over the monarch's cost and rapacity. It has been at the heart of virtually every crisis in the institution's history. There has always been the gnawing feeling that royalty costs too much and demands ever more from its subjects – and aggravation from the monarch that they are being kept on too short a rein to reign properly, in the style to which they ought to be accustomed. The Victorian Liberal politician George Trevelyan's rhetorical question remains pertinent but is now somewhat more fully, but not completely, answered.

For much of the last hundred years, while playing its winsome card of being a respectable and responsible national institution, successive monarchs attempted to claw back concessions that their predecessors, especially Queen Victoria, had made over paying tax. By and large, too, they got away with it. They grumbled privately, lobbied regularly and negotiated ceaselessly with ministers to preserve and enhance as much public funding as they could obtain without the obligation to give any of it back to the state. Ministers usually allowed them to get away with it and declined to test the public's acceptance of royal revenues by allowing them to be debated openly in parliament. By this means, the contention that the monarchy had never paid tax came to be accepted as a convention by press, politicians and public quite erroneously until the fallout from the crisis of 1992. If the monarchy is now more open about its income and expenditure than it has ever been before, however, its cost still leaves it vulnerable. The British public like the monarchy but resent extravagance, particularly if they are having to pay for it and now that the annual accounts are published the media is acutely aware of every nuance that suggests a sense of entitlement.

The Queen's income comes from three sources: her investments, which are shrouded in secrecy, the Duchy of Lancaster, and the Crown Estate whose revenues go to the government which disburses the Sovereign Grant to the monarch. The presumption is that her shares are invested in blue-chip companies through a wholly owned subsidiary of the Bank of England called BOEN (Bank of England Nominees), set up in 1977, which holds securities and investments in British companies, specifically for heads of state and certain other high-worth individuals in sensitive positions who wish to remain anonymous. It does so on the understanding that they do not seek to influence the affairs of the companies in which they are investing. The company was initially exempted from making disclosures about its holdings and shareholders by James Callaghan's Labour government when it was established, but since 2011 it has lost that exemption and does have to file accounts. However, officially, BOEN is dormant and not trading as a company in its own right, which assists its opacity as its disclosures under the Companies Act are uninformative. Its latest accounts show no cash, no assets, no net worth and no liabilities, and undoubtedly its next accounts, due to be published at the end of November 2015, will show the same. But dormancy does not preclude the company from acting as a nominee shareholder, making investments on the investors' behalf and channelling profits back to them. When they are asked about this, the Queen's accountants always insist that her investments, like those of anyone else, are confidential and that she does pay income tax on the profits. Previously the nearest to an authoritative estimate to how much they are worth came obliquely from Lord Airlie, the former banker who was Lord Chamberlain of the Household in 1993 at the time the Queen started to pay tax, who said that the speculated figure of £100 million was grossly overestimated – but that was nearly a quarter of a century ago and shares and values can go up as well as down.

There is a regular guessing game to establish the Queen's private worth, made complicated by the assets she holds, which she could never sell: the Crown Jewels for instance, or the royal picture collection spread around the palaces. It is perhaps the greatest collection of old masters held anywhere in the world: 7,000 paintings, 40,000 watercolours, 150,000 prints: six Rembrandts, thirteen Rubens, twenty-six van Dycks, fifty Canalettos, thirty-three Gainsboroughs, eighteen Stubbs, twenty Reynolds, one Bruegel the Elder, one Dürer, one Vermeer, two Caravaggios, six hundred da Vinci drawings, eight Raphaels including his full-size cartoons, loaned to the Victoria and Albert Museum for tapestries to be hung in the Sistine Chapel, five Tintorettos, four Titians, one Monet... And that is before you get to the eighteenth-century French furniture, the three Fabergé eggs (left by the Queen Mother), three Canova statues, thirty-six Gobelin tapestries and the largest collection of Sèvres porcelain in the world. Through the list you can trace the chief royal collectors: Charles I, George III and George IV, Victoria (120 Winterhalters, one hundred

Landseers...) though perhaps royal art appreciation has petered out a little more recently.[34] When a visitor comes the royal archivists pull out items they might like to see from the royal collection: the Obamas in 2011 were shown one of the world's most expensive books – the double elephant folio volume of John James Audubon's *The Birds of America*, its going price at auction $11 million dollars[35] and a copy of the first edition of *Uncle Tom's Cabin* signed by the author Harriet Beecher Stowe. Do these belong to the state, or do these belong to the Queen since they were given to or bought by her ancestors?

Clearly, no one is going to be able to sell the Crown Jewels held in the Tower of London, or the occupied royal residences: Buckingham Palace, Windsor Castle, Holyroodhouse Palace in Edinburgh, Hillsborough Castle in Northern Ireland, or St James's Palace, Clarence House and Kensington Palace, all owned by the Crown Estate. But what about Sandringham with its 8,000-hectare estate in Norfolk and Balmoral and its 20,000 hectares in Scotland, both privately owned by the Queen, or Highgrove in Gloucestershire with 400 hectares, owned by the Prince of Wales since the Duchy of Cornwall bought it for him for £1 million in 1980; what would they be worth if put up for sale?

Then there are the Queen's private possessions such as her racehorses, the wine collection, the cars including the 1900 Daimler Phaeton, and her grandfather's stamp collection, which may be worth up to £100 million on its own account, including as it does one of the

---

34 The Queen herself has probably had her portrait painted, or has been formally photographed for a portrait, more often than anyone else in history: at least 854 times, according to the National Portrait Gallery. The Lucian Freud grumpy Queen is in the Royal Collection, as is a Warhol screen print and the Annie Liebovitz photograph that got the BBC into so much trouble – all highly valuable. The Rolf Harris perhaps less so.

35 As he showed the Obamas the Audubon, the Duke of Edinburgh genially flicked through the enormous pages without wearing gloves, as idly as other pensioners might browse through a seed catalogue.

rarest stamps in the world – the Mauritian Two Penny Blue of 1847, worth at least £2 million alone. Even so in 2015 the *Sunday Times* Rich List's estimate that the Queen was worth £340 million, an increase of £10 million on the year before not counting the unsellable assets, still placed her only 302nd in its calculation of the richest people in the country, a drop of seventeen places by its reckoning. The list now includes at least a hundred billionaires. If its compilers' calculations are roughly accurate, this makes the Russian-born businessman and philanthropist Len Blavatnik, owner of Warner Music, with his £13 billion fortune – allegedly the UK's richest resident – forty times richer than she is; Roman Abramovich twenty times richer; Richard Branson twelve times; and even Richard Desmond, owner of the *Daily Express* and various insalubrious magazines, four times wealthier. She is also far from being the richest royal: old King Bhumibol of Thailand was estimated by *Forbes*, the American business magazine, to be worth $35 billion (£23 billion) in 2009, so very roughly seventy times the Queen's wealth; Prince Hans-Adam II of Liechtenstein racked up $6 billion (£4 billion) in the magazine's estimation thanks to his family's ownership of the duchy's LGT private banking group; and even Albert II of Monaco was held to be worth $1.4 billion (£886 million) because of all the property his family owns in its tiny toehold on the Mediterranean.

The £340 million is the Queen's private wealth, which keeps her from penury, but then there is also separately the surplus of the historic Duchy of Lancaster estate, which has been in the possession of the Crown since 1399, when the Duke of Lancaster Henry Bolingbroke seized the Crown to become Henry IV. As all her predecessors have been since then, the Queen is the Duke of Lancaster, among all her other titles, and this separate estate is technically administered for her by the Chancellor of the Duchy of Lancaster, a government post currently held by the Cabinet Office minister Oliver Letwin, but one which is answerable to the sovereign rather than to parliament (though he does answer questions about the duchy in the Commons). It is no small property either, encompassing 18,454 hectares of prime agricultural land across the country, from North Yorkshire grouse moors[36] to parts of the Peak District, farms in Lincolnshire and Northants, a golf course in South Wales and most of the Lancashire coast. The prime urban part of the duchy's holdings is the Savoy estate in central London, between the Strand and the Embankment, including the Savoy Hotel and Somerset House. The Queen cannot sell these properties but she can take the income from them, which has been taxable since 1992. The Duchy does not, however, have to pay corporation tax. In 2014, the estate was worth £442 million – a 14.6 per cent growth over the previous year, giving a surplus of £14.5 million of which the Queen received £13.6 million after tax. This income is handled by the keeper of the privy purse: a quaint medieval term conjuring up the image of a small reticule from which the sovereign counts her pennies, but which these days is an office in Buckingham Palace administered by her Scottish accountant Sir Alan Reid. Actually, there *is* a privy purse and it is red and gold, the size of a large fabric satchel or shoulder bag: a new one is embroidered with the monarch's initials and the royal crest and given to the current keeper at the start of every reign, to carry at the coronation. The George V purse hangs in a glass case on the wall in Reid's corner office on the ground floor of Buckingham Palace – it was apparently bought when the widow of the holder of the office in the King's day fell on hard times and had to sell it. What do they keep in it? 'Mars Bars,' said Sir Alan laconically. 'It was such

---

36 Goathland whose Victorian railway station is often used for filming historical dramas and was used in the *Harry Potter* movies is part of the duchy's Yorkshire estates.

a long coronation service that the keeper kept chocolate bars in it to hand out to the choirboys to keep them going. I hope he timed it so that it didn't interfere with their singing.'

Sir Alan is the very image of a Scottish accountant: small, precise, grey-haired and bespectacled, he is charmingly accessible and was one of the palace employees who agreed to an on-the-record interview for this book. He was formerly chief executive on the management consulting side of the accountancy firm KPMG and first came to the palace at Lord Airlie's invitation to give a presentation on business practice with the blunt message that the household must change or would be changed involuntarily. Appointed aged fifty-five, thirteen years later he is still there. 'In my village everyone assumes I must be a *Telegraph* reader, holding this position,' he confided. 'Actually, I have always read the *Guardian*.' This may make him the first senior palace employee to read the paper since Lord Stamfordham a century ago.

Prince Charles as heir to the throne benefits from an even older estate than the Queen's. His household is funded from the revenues of the Duchy of Cornwall, the hereditary estate, which have gone to the heir to the throne since 1337 when Edward III gifted the estate to his son, the Black Prince. He cannot sell it off either. These days it consists of 53,154 hectares spread across twenty-four counties, mainly in the south-west, from the Isles of Scilly to the Cotswolds and Herefordshire, with land also in Wales and the Manor of Kennington in south London, which also once belonged to the Black Prince and now includes a large slice of Lambeth, south of the river, including Guy's and St Thomas's hospitals and the Oval cricket ground. The agricultural estates of the duchy, as with other royal land holdings, qualify for EU common agricultural policy payments: in 2013 the Duchy of Cornwall received more than £160,000, according to the Department for Environment, Food and Rural Affairs' website. The capital value of the estate, including property and investments, was nearly £900 million in 2014, from which the Prince received £19.5 million to fund his public duties and pay for his 130-strong household: gardeners, valets, cooks, secretaries, not to mention his press officers. He paid £4.19 million in tax on that income – a reduction of £250,000 on the previous year thanks to the government's reduction of the top rate to 45 pence.

Then for the monarch there is separately the Crown Estate, comprising a rich variety – in all senses – of other properties, gathered by successive monarchs between the eleventh and eighteenth centuries, whose surplus goes to the Treasury under an agreement whose roots go back to 1760. The 139,000-hectare estate includes all of Regent's Street and half of St James's in London, Ascot racecourse, Windsor Great Park and Virginia Water, sixteen retail parks from Newcastle to Swansea[37], the Cambridge Business Park, assorted marinas, wind farms, gravel and sand extraction sites, potash and salt extraction sites, estates and forests from Glenlivet in the Cairgorms to Dunster in Somerset, a number of golf clubs, more than half the UK's coastline and the seabed from the low water mark out to the 12 nautical mile offshore limit. The Crown Estate's offshore wind farms alone generate five gigawatts of power: equivalent to about five per cent of the country's electricity. Her Majesty can't sell any of this either, nor does she get the income directly. In the 1980s Prince Charles discreetly campaigned to claim back the estate to increase the Crown's independence from government, but that was never going to happen, for a very good reason. It is part of the constitutional monarch's dependence on the government in parliament that the estate's money goes to the national coffers and some of it is

---

37 These include major interests in: Oxford's Westgate Centre, the Princesshay in Exeter, Bluewater near Gravesend, Touchwood in Solihull, Crown Point in Leeds, the Aintree Shopping Park in Liverpool, Ocean Retail in Portsmouth and even the Bath Road shopping Park at Slough, which the Queen can see on a clear day from Windsor Castle.

then disbursed to the sovereign. The revenue is not the Queen's personally but, as it always was, a contribution to the cost of running the country: it is not just the money that has historically been handed over but the duties and obligations that went with it that are now the business of government not the sovereign.

In 2014, the estate's capital value was £9.9 billion – another 14 per cent rise over the previous year – and the surplus of £267.1 million went to the Treasury.[38] In place of this, £37.9 million was passed on to the royal household to pay for the running costs of the monarchy. This is the Sovereign Grant which finally replaced the Civil List in 2012. The Civil List, with its clutter of different funding sources from various government departments to pay for royal travel (latterly paid by the Department for Transport) and the upkeep of the royal palaces (Department for Culture, Media and Sport) was replaced after 250 years by the single grant, which is currently based on 15 per cent of the revenues from the Crown Estate: £37.9 million, a five per cent increase on 2013–14 – the percentage to be reviewed once in every five-year parliamentary term. This appeals to both sides: from the palace's point of view it gives a continuity, flexibility and degree of independence to the royal income, enabling better and more consistent planning in the allocation of resources with a built-in hedge against inflation, and as far as the government is concerned it is a simpler and more streamlined calculation. The Sovereign Grant takes in the cost of royal duties, the upkeep of the palaces and the cost of royal travel. Whereas before government grants-in-aid had to be spent where they were allocated – the travel grant went only to travel costs – now part of it can be diverted to, say, building repairs if they are more urgent.

The change to a single source of government funding was the result

---

38 The Crown estate has paid more than £2 billion to the Exchequer over the past ten years.

of a two-and-a-half-year campaign by Reid to persuade the Treasury that it would be a more efficient use of resources to bundle up the various grants and, if there was an underspend, would enable a reserve (they are currently aiming at five per cent) to be built up. He told me: 'I went to the Treasury and said one grant from one department made sense. It is actually a very small amount of money in government terms and it is a system that treats us as mature adults. The National Audit Office examines our books every year, the public accounts committee can summon me whenever they want and the size of the grant is decided once every parliament. We never spent up to the travel budget in any year but the property services budget was always short: coming from the Department for Culture which was always having its funding cut, heritage funding for buildings was an easy target – that is one reason why we have a backlog of repairs to most of the palaces.'

As it happened, Reid's proposal came at exactly the right time. When it was first presented to Chancellor Gordon Brown he had been suspicious of anything that smacked of extra funding for the royal family or independence from government – and particularly Treasury control, as he could not see the votes in it. But George Osborne, coming into office in 2010 was open to a more decentralised system and quietly brought Labour's shadow chancellor Ed Balls in to give cross-party agreement to the deal. The palace had hoped for more flexibility to account for inflation and a longer time frame of seven years instead of five. But essentially they got what they wanted – and Osborne even threw in an extra million pounds in the first year to pay for the Queen's diamond jubilee. What did the Queen make of the change to a sovereign grant? 'She thought it was an excellent proposal,' said Reid.

It was all so much easier in the old days. Medieval kings carried their treasure round with them and their household servants were their ministers. The revenues from the King's lands paid for all the costs of the government, the household and the monarch's personal expenditure and if more money was needed to fight wars it was raised in taxes and loans. Gradually the landed classes through parliament gained control over the King's powers to levy money from them. The Glorious Revolution of 1688 had its downside for the new Dutch king William of Orange in that, although he was granted £600,000 a year to cover his expenses, his military expenditure (which he wanted mainly to defend Holland from the French) had to be voted annually by parliament, which thus controlled the size of the army and what the monarch could do with it – in other words, not use it against the gentry or the Commons in Britain as Charles I had done.

The £600,000 annual grant was called the Civil List – to pay for the government's civil expenditure: the King's official duties and the royal household – and it was received from specific taxes, voted by parliament for the lifetime of the King. By limiting the King's resources and authorising how the money was spent, parliament gained a measure of control over the monarch and further legislation also prevented him from securing other sources of revenue by, for example, selling off Crown property. Out of the Civil List, which was increased to £700,000 in 1697, the King was expected to pay not only the costs of government but also the salaries and pensions of officials such as judges and ambassadors. Parliament eventually took control of the King's debts and Prime Minister Walpole ensured his continuing usefulness to George II by increasing the Civil List to £800,000 with the King allowed to keep any surpluses above that figure. By controlling the amount of money the King received, the country gentry who went to parliament ensured that they kept their taxes down, too.

When George III succeeded in 1760, there was a further power grab by parliament which took advantage of the new King's precarious finances and debts to gain more control over royal spending. The government took over the monarch's hereditary revenues from the Crown's estates and in return provided an agreed fixed sum to the King each year, initially £800,000, for his official expenditure. The economically minded young King agreed to this arrangement, which was intended to last for as long as he reigned. It ensured that if the King needed more, George would have to beg parliament for it. He indeed did need more, to pay the cost of the coronation (he even had to buy back the royal jewels which had been bequeathed by George II to the Duke of Cumberland who sold them back to him for £54,000), to subsidise his marriage, support his three brothers and two sisters and, eventually, sustain his growing family. Parliament clearly did not expect the King to live for sixty years and, as the grant became inadequate (made worse by inflation and the costs of first the American War of Independence then the Napoleonic Wars), it took over increasing areas of civil and then military expenditure directly. As the King's debts increased because of the inadequacy of the grant – by 1769 they were already more than £500,000 – so parliament gained increasing powers of scrutiny over how the money was spent, including the King's disbursement of pensions and bribes to his political supporters. George III still had a private income from the Duchy of Lancaster, at the time £48,000 a year, but even that was not enough for all the miscellaneous grants he distributed. There was considerable waste, too: members of the court expected to be housed and fed at royal expense, and holders of ancient offices continued to be paid from the Civil List even if their sinecures entailed no duties and had no purpose, such as the housekeeper of the no-longer-habitable royal palace at Newmarket who still received £150 a year for her lack of trouble. Parliament (and the King) did little about such conspicuous waste, but each time he applied for an increase in the civil list it was a struggle to get the money. And as parliament took over more government expenditure, so ministers became more accountable to MPs than they did to the King.

Until 1800 such was the suspicion of monarchical power that, although the King could buy private estates they were not then his to dispose of: they became Crown land and as such would be controlled by the government. Similarly, the King could not make a will because he did not have private property. The monarchy was not able generally to spend extravagantly on royal palaces or indulge in conspicuous expenditure: there was to be no royal Versailles in England.[39] Indeed when a builder bought a large plot of land on which he planned to build housing next to Buckingham House, which George III had bought in 1761 as a private residence, the King pleaded with the government to allow him an extra £20,000 so that he could buy the land for himself and preserve his privacy by preventing the possibility of occupants of the new buildings peering out of their windows to watch him wandering in the palace grounds. But the request was refused. The King's legal status was changed by an act of parliament in 1800, which allowed him to own property and make a will, but in return parliament insisted that he would be taxed on it as if 'it had been the property of any subject of this realm'. This was a considerable departure: kings had not had to pay taxes before, because the money would merely have gone into the Civil List. As the legal advice had it: 'It can never be intended that His Majesty should take money out of

---

39 This was entirely a good thing: as the historian Linda Colley points out in her book *Britons*, whereas Versailles accommodated 10,000 servants, officials and courtiers, and had plenty of space for plotting, intrigue and lavish entertainments, the English royal household was much smaller – accommodating about 1,500 in the case of George I, not all of them present at any one time – and much more restricted for space. English kings by and large could not afford to be too publicly extravagant, though George IV did his best. His father and mother, George III and Queen Charlotte, were carried to the coronation in sedan chairs and Samuel Johnson complained that the crown was 'worn out of sight of the people'.

one pocket to put it in another.' Now kings were private persons as well as public ones.

George himself was abstemious and lived relatively cheaply, but his sons were not and when the Prince Regent's only child died and a new heir needed to be bred quickly they haggled over what they should be paid when they were required to marry. In 1830 William IV's Civil List grant was reduced from the £845,727 his predecessor George IV had received to £510,000 because by then the grant was intended to cover only royal household expenditure, for the King's 'dignity' and personal comfort, not the whole cost of the civil government, even though it was still called the Civil List and would be until its final abolition in 2011.

In 1816, the year after the Napoleonic Wars finally ended, the Tory government had abolished income tax as surplus to requirements, so the King like the rest of his subjects, no longer had to pay it. But when Sir Robert Peel reintroduced the tax in 1842 the young Queen Victoria was persuaded by the prime minister to volunteer to show an example to the public by making a contribution from her own income and that of the Civil List. In return for the sacrifice, the Queen and her husband harried the government to pay annuities to their children and lobbied ultimately successfully for the extension of Buckingham Palace. Albert himself pressed the government to more than double his own annuity from £30,000 to £80,000. The Prince Consort insisted that the money was needed to enable him to live with 'the ordinary establishment and pursuits of an English gentlemen', which he decided required stables for his hunters, a pack of hounds, a breeding stud, shooting establishment, a moor or forest in the Highlands of Scotland and a farm. He was told to wait by the then prime minister Lord John Russell, but the royal family was effectively receiving a bonus anyway by not having to pay out £100,000 as a pension to William IV's widow Queen Adelaide, who had recently died. That money went straight into the privy purse. Out of savings from the Civil List and the sale of the Royal Pavilion in Brighton, the royal couple were able to afford to acquire land on the Isle of Wight and to build the large Italianate Osborne House, so that the Queen would no longer be jostled by tourists and errand boys when she went on holiday. Such expenditure – Osborne cost £200,000 by the time it was finished – at a time of the Irish famine crisis earned public ridicule.[40] A *Punch* cartoon of the period entitled 'A Case of Real Distress' shows a woebegone royal family going cap-in-hand past an emaciated group of shoeless beggar children, but the royals managed to get away with it and shortly to buy Balmoral too. Prince Albert was apparently a keen negotiator on top of his other skills and contrived to beat down the price – and it was bought in his name too so that the property would not be swallowed up into the Crown estate. The couple's redevelopment of their Scottish castle was helped along by a large legacy – the thick end of half a million pounds – from a Chelsea miser called John Camden Neild, who saved all his life only to leave his fortune to the Queen. 'Such things only still happen in England,' her uncle King Leopold of the Belgians wrote to her enviously.

The royals paid tax but repeatedly moaned about having to do so like ordinary people. Victoria's successor, Edward VII was not allowed to rescind his mother's decision to pay income tax by the Conservative government that was in power when he succeeded to the throne in 1901. Despite his repeated protests, he was politely but bluntly told that he would be required to pay, with no concessions even though he was technically consenting to do so at his gracious pleasure. In the Commons the chancellor of the exchequer, Sir Michael Hicks-Beach pre-empted any negotiations by announcing that the government had advised the King that the same course as Queen Victoria had accepted

---

40 The Queen herself generously donated £2,000 to famine relief.

would be followed, giving him no option but to comply. He repeatedly grumbled privately to ministers and complained when he had to make economies in the royal household, such as when a parliamentary select committee recommended that ministers should decline to continue covering the salaries of some hangers-on in the Civil List. The King wrote back that he 'regrets and is surprised that in a country like England, so devoted to sport, the committee should have struck out from the Civil List the salary and wages of the Master of the Buckhounds and the Hunt Servants together with the expenses of the hunt...and have thrown the whole onus of their cost on the king.'

But Edward VII was canny enough not to complain too publicly at a time when the country was fighting the Boer War – that would have been disastrous for his public reputation, especially given his well-known history of extravagance and loucheness – though he certainly lobbied ministers and senior civil servants to find a way of quietly reducing his obligations. Even so, with income tax still only five per cent in the pound, the King probably paid about £18,000 a year in income tax on his annual Civil List allowance of £470,000. He was still able to live well and save money out of the government grant – more than £261,000 during the course of his nine-year reign, mainly from savings in staff wages and from astute investment of the money in stocks and shares. When he died, the King was probably worth £2 million in 1910 values. Successive governments fended off his demands for increased allowances (the Civil List was still settled at the start of every reign, to last for however long its duration) on the not unreasonable grounds that any variation would have to be publicly aired in parliament and would accordingly cause problems for the King.

Instead, there was always the possibility of milking favours in other ways, accepting presents from wealthy tycoons for charitable purposes, who might then find themselves awarded knighthoods or peerages.

Perhaps some of that money went to the King as well: the Harmsworth newspaper family certainly believed that their ancestor Alfred Harmsworth, the founder of the *Daily Mail* and owner of *The Times*, bought his peerage directly from the King when he became Lord Northcliffe.

Curiously, the tradition that the King paid income tax was swept away at the start of George V's reign in 1910 by possibly the most radical of all modern chancellors of the exchequer David Lloyd George with the acquiescence of the Liberal prime minister Herbert Asquith. It occurred after George succeeded to the throne just at the very moment when the government was engaged in a desperate political struggle to force its reforming People's Budget of 1909 through the adamant opposition of the Conservative Party and its in-built majority in the House of Lords. The peers fought the budget, which introduced pensions for working people for the first time, with an obduracy that endured almost to the last ditch and the government's thoughts were turning to overcoming the Lords' opposition by the mass creation of Liberal peers who would support the budget and swamp the Tories.[41] To do that Asquith and Lloyd George needed the new King's permission so the bait of lifting his income tax – while increasing the tax levies on

41 The proposals in the People's Budget were modest: five shillings (25 pence, about a sixth of a labourer's average wage – which would have bought much more than it does now, but was still meagre enough) a week for those over the age of seventy whose income was less than ten shillings and who had not been in trouble with the law. This was calculated to cost £13 a year each for half a million people: £6.5 million in all. The budget was the first in history to attempt a redistribution of wealth to the poorer classes. It did mean raising taxation, for this and increased defence spending, from the better off. The Tories objected to the three pence in the pound increase in income tax (from nine pence to a shilling and one and sixpence for the super-rich) and even more so to the land tax – 20 per cent on the profit made on the sale of land – to pay for it. They argued that pensions would indulge the idle and encourage indolence, and vehemently attacked Lloyd George and his radical colleague Winston Churchill. The Duke of Beaufort said he would like to set his fox hounds on them, the Duke of Buccleuch stopped his annual guinea subscription to his local football club and Lord Anglesey, who had just bought himself a new yacht, halved his five pounds' monthly subscription to the London Hospital.

the peerage in the budget – seems to have been a quiet quid pro quo. Nearly a quarter of George V's annual Civil List of £470,000 to meet his constitutional and public duties – £110,000 – went to the privy purse for his private expenditure and he also received revenues of about £80,000 from the Duchy of Lancaster lands for his private use. So although the tax payable would have been relatively marginal – about £25,000 – it was a significant concession by the government. Lloyd George announced that in return for not having to pay the tax, the Civil List would in future meet the costs of state visits and royal foreign trips, which would amount to much the same, though this was unlikely to have been the case. There does not seem to have been much fuss, or even close scrutiny of this, at the time in the midst of all the uproar and it did not stop George V feeling coerced by the government and Knollys, his private secretary.

George V was himself relatively frugal, a habit passed on to the agricultural workers on the Sandringham Estate who before the First World War were being paid only 16 shillings a week, about a third less even than other impoverished farm labourers in Norfolk, for the privilege of being an employee of the King, from which they had to pay rent on their estate cottages. Before the war, George was prevailed upon by Sir William Carington, the keeper of the privy purse, to increase their wages, perhaps to prevent their taking part in a pending national agricultural workers' strike. The Sandringham estate workers did not strike, though others in the area did. But instead of increasing their pay by a round pound a week as Carington suggested, the King seems to have insisted that he could only afford 19 shillings – an increase in the annual wage bill of £468 when the extra shilling would have cost him a further £156 (that also only went to able-bodied men, not the estate's disabled workers who were expected to be grateful because they were 'employed out of compassion'). This came at a time when the King was spending £50,000 a year on stocking Sandringham with game birds.[42]

George V's main personal extravagance was his philately, buying up the stamp collections of those whose own debts had mounted during the war, cadging local stamps from ambassadors and sometimes paying huge sums at auction. 'Did Your Royal Highness hear that some damned fool has paid £1,450 for a single stamp?' a courtier hoping to curry favour asked him one morning, only to be told: 'I was the damned fool.' The King had just bought the Mauritian Two Penny Blue.

The First World War was helpful to his finances: there were fewer wages to pay to the reduced palace staff, there were no foreign trips (except to the Western Front), no state dinners and few foreign visitors, and an ostentatious economy drive was instituted to show the public that even the King was making sacrifices: no wine was bought and meals were meagre. The King actually offered to resume paying tax, but this was turned down by the government on the grounds that it would add to the pressure on other wealthy inhabitants to follow his example and might lead to attacks from the press demanding that he should pay even more. In the end the King made a one-off gift of £100,000 to the Treasury in 1916 and continued to pay thousands more to servicemen's charities, but he still got off lightly, saving at the calculation of the author Philip Hall about £78,000 from the Civil List in the four years of the war.

---

42 The royal family have never been notably generous payers of their employees. There is perhaps more a sense of obligation on their staff's side than their own, with patriotic pride at working for royalty substituting for more lucrative remuneration. In March 2015, the lower-paid staff at Windsor Castle were balloted for industrial action for the first time ever by the Public and Commercial Services Union, over a dispute about being paid for undertaking extra work such as showing visitors round. The staff accepted an improved pay and conditions offer in May 2015, and the possibility of disruption was removed.

Unlike most other aristocratic families during this period, King George and his relatives did not face the increased death duties and super taxes, imposed to help pay for the war, that crippled and denuded many great estates and country houses across the country. The slow destruction of the great houses had begun in the agricultural depression of the 1870s but accelerated in the twentieth century. The aristocratic town houses in London and Edinburgh went first, then parcels of land from the family estates, then the second and third houses spread around the country were sold off, allowed to deteriorate or pulled down, without much regard for their architectural or historic merits. It has been calculated that one country house in six in England was demolished during the twentieth century: there was an incentive too in that if they were destroyed they could not be valued for probate duty. Very often the houses had become too inconvenient to keep up: too expensive and uncomfortable, worth more as a vacant site than an outsized mansion. The staff to run them could no longer be afforded or enticed to return after moving to better-paid jobs elsewhere. In 1940 death duties were raised from 50 to 65 per cent of an estate's value, the duties were raised again in 1946 and once more in 1949, and eventually reached 80 per cent. The game was up for all but the very richest, luckiest or most enterprising families – but the royal family faced none of this. Even when the Queen Mother died in 2002, leaving her daughter property and possessions worth an estimated £50 million – the will was sealed so the total is unknown – no inheritance tax was paid. The exemption was originally intended to ensure that the monarch's property, held for the nation, was passed on intact to the heir (no more having to buy back state jewellery as George III had to do), so it was at least questionable whether the Queen Mother's private property was taxable, but the issue was not pressed.

For the royals, appearances still had to be kept up. After the First World War, George V and his advisers made serious efforts to obtain an increase in the Civil List to cover increased wage costs and repairs to the royal palaces, and stave off the awful prospect of what his then keeper of the privy purse Sir Fritz Ponsonby described as 'the King going to open Parliament in a taxi cab'. He was granted a one-off £100,000 (the same amount as he had paid in 1916) , but at the cost of a Treasury inquiry into the expenditure of the royal household, which recommended drastic savings, including a 60 per cent decrease in the royal food bill, it being noticed that the leftovers and much of the produce was being eaten by the palace servants. The wage bill was also cut by seven per cent, by making some of the more menial staff, though not the more exalted placemen, redundant: Ponsonby's salary was increased by £500 a year and the new deputy treasurer was appointed on a salary of £2,200. The farriers and stable boys lost their jobs, to be replaced by chauffeurs and the live-in maid servants were required to vacate their rooms in the palace, with some being made redundant. By such means savings of up to £40,000 a year were achieved.

The King continued to be exempted from income tax but now so were several members of the royal family. On the bulk of the annuities paid to them by the government 80 per cent of their income was made exempt from tax. From 1921, the Prince of Wales's obligation to pay tax was drastically reduced (he had argued for this on the grounds of the increasing cost of his public duties). He paid tax on 20 per cent of his annuity from the government, compared with the 50 per cent paid by others in the same income bracket and was not required to pay income tax at all on his revenue from the Duchy of Cornwall. Instead he agreed to make a voluntary contribution each year to the Treasury which, at £20,000, was a considerable saving on the £35,000 he would have paid in income tax. This was little known about publicly since the duchy's annual accounts were no longer widely published, but merely placed in the library of the House of Commons – a practice which continued until 1982.

This creeping exemption from tax became custom and practice, with the royals pleading imminent poverty and increasing public duties involving expenditure. It was robust special pleading, which would effectively exempt the royals from paying tax on income and revenues from Crown estates for nearly three-quarters of a century, apparently on the basis that it had always been so. During the economic crisis of 1931, George V voluntarily reduced his Civil List by £50,000 as a one-off, as in the First World War, and also took it upon himself to reduce the Prince of Wales's annuity payment from the Civil List by £10,000 without informing him in advance. This understandably did not meet with the Prince's approval when he took a telephone call from his father to be told the bad news while he was in a French nightclub in Bayonne with his current mistress, Lady Furness. In fact, he was furious and, showing his well-known sympathy for the impoverished of the country, declared: 'The king and I are being had for a pair of mugs.' His younger brother, Prince Albert – the future George VI – was none too pleased either that the King was reducing his grant: 'It has come as a great shock to me,' he wrote to the master of the Pytchley hunt, 'that with the economy cuts I have had to make my hunting should have been one of the things I must do without and I must sell my horses too. This is the worst part of it all and the parting with them will be terrible.' Presumably he had not noticed that the country was in the middle of a depression. His hunters fetched about £1,000 at auction.

George V went further and suggested the royal staff should show solidarity by accepting a ten per cent reduction in their wages until it was pointed out to him by Prime Minister Ramsay MacDonald that since they were paid by the King that would only be a savings benefit to him. He did still gain from the crisis though, asking for and receiving the government's acceptance that he should no longer have to pay tax on the revenues of the Duchy of Lancaster: which saved the King about £20,000 a year.

Slowly and almost surreptitiously, the royals' payment of tax was drastically reduced in the years after the First World War, just as everyone else's in the country was rising sharply. Edward VIII was outraged when he succeeded his father in 1936 to discover that the old King had not left him any money[43] on the grounds that he had had plenty of opportunity to build up a surplus from the Duchy of Cornwall – which he had: more than a million pounds. He effectively hid this money from both the government and his brother George VI when he abdicated a few months later, pleading poverty and demanding a pension to go quietly, threatening to disclose his financial affairs to MPs. The new King eventually had to buy out his elder brother's ownership of Sandringham and Balmoral (they cost the new King £300,000 to buy outright, put in a trust to pay Edward £10,000 a year) and George VI provided him with a pension of an additional £11,000 a year on the condition that he never returned to Britain without the monarch's approval. The Duke of Windsor was not required to pay income tax on this annual £21,000 and he was later even granted tax-free status by the French government when he retired to Paris. But it had all been an unseemly private wrangle which further embittered relations between the brothers.

At some point after George VI's accession, the government quietly removed the entire remaining income tax levy on his private income, a considerable advantage since general taxation was again raised steeply to pay for the Second World War. While the royal family advertised their privations to show they were sharing the country's hardships, and that they were undoubtedly brave, it was perhaps as well the King's

43 The King left his £3 million fortune to his other four surviving children.

subjects did not know that he was not sharing their financial privations. George VI at this time was left having to pay tax only on his income from rents paid by tenants on his estates at Sandringham and Balmoral: a very small part of his revenues. He did make the same one-off payment to the government as his father had during the First World War: £100,000, but not until 1948 when he was asking for more money for his daughter Princess Elizabeth on account of her marriage to Prince Philip. Part of that money was turned into an annuity for the Princess so that her annual grant rose to £40,000 a year, £10,000 of which went to her husband to supplement his Royal Navy salary.

On her accession in 1952, like her predecessors, the Queen received a Civil List settlement, in her case of £475,000 with additional annuities of £160,000 going to other members of the royal family including her then two children, but the Conservative government also included for the first time a provision for inflation of £70,000 in the total which was meant to build up reserves which could be drawn upon as prices and wages rose. This was followed in the 1960s by the government's assumption of other costs which had previously been paid from the Civil List, including the royal train, upkeep of the royal palaces, visits abroad and entertainment during state visits. By the late 1960s though, the palace was complaining once more that it could not cope, particularly with the rise in staff wages. Payments to those working below stairs were so low that the household was now filling the shortage of local recruits by recruiting abroad and the palace kitchens were now largely staffed by Spaniards. Indeed, part of the monarchy's sudden increase in openness to publicity – the *Royal Family* documentary and the Prince's investiture in Wales – was to demonstrate its usefulness and value for money.

Instead of being dealt with privately and discreetly as previously, the negotiations all came to public attention because Prince Philip spoke on American television of the hardships the family was having to endure. 'We go into the red next year,' he jocularly told the NBC programme *Meet the Press* in November 1969. 'Now inevitably if nothing happens we may have to – I don't know – move into smaller premises, who knows? For instance, we had a small yacht which we've had to sell and I shall probably have to give up polo fairly soon, things like that.' If it was an attempt to influence the negotiations with Harold Wilson's Labour government of the day rather than, as seems more likely, a maladroit outburst of what was really on his mind – an early gaffe perhaps? – the remarks, which the palace tried unsuccessfully to suppress, certainly provoked a reaction back in Britain. The idea that the Prince might have to sell his polo ponies at a time of national economic stringency and that he had pleaded poverty in front of the Americans of all people was not well received. A group of dockers in Bermondsey even volunteered (at the behest of the *Daily Mirror*) to club together to buy him a horse.

It caused a tizzy in the cabinet, too. Harold Wilson certainly did not want to provoke accusations of being mean to the Queen a few months ahead of an election. 'The nearer the Queen they get the more the working-class members of the cabinet love her and she loves them,' sniffed the notably patrician Wykehamist Richard Crossman in his diary. The public row was headed off by the setting up of a cross-party select committee, which had a Tory majority but included the vociferously anti-monarchist Labour backbencher Willie Hamilton. The committee eventually decided to allow an increase in the Civil List, endorsed by parliament, but the MPs discovered that, despite the growing criticism of royal lifestyles – Princess Margaret with her spoilt friends and penchant for holidaying at public expense on Mustique was a particular target of the press – the Queen was not prepared to give up her tax-free status. That took another twenty years to achieve. In the meantime, she and her advisers argued against being required to pay tax, using the same grounds as her predecessors always had: how burdensome it would be with all the duties she had to perform. In this she was strongly supported by her mother. As one official told the biographer Robert Lacey: 'Not paying tax was one of the things her father told her to fight for. Her mother felt just as strongly and kept reminding her not to give in.'

The system was increasingly labyrinthine as various government departments had taken over elements of the Civil List's previous responsibilities while at the same time the funding of the royal family was shrouded in secrecy: where did official duties begin and end? As Philip Hall noted, when a valet walked the corgis was that paid for privately or was that part of official responsibilities? Hall's diligent researches showed that it was a myth that the royals had never paid tax but was merely a practice that had developed with government acquiescence. The public might not mind too much during royal celebrations: at the silver jubilee and the wedding of Charles and Diana four years later, but by the end of that decade criticism was increasing and spreading. There were critics on the Conservative as well as the Labour side of the Commons that, at a time of public austerity – the start of the Thatcher era – and pressure on budgets, the royal family seemed impervious, their state-funded income sacrosanct.

By the early 1990s, the palace's own private polling showed a large majority believing that the royals should pay tax. The secrecy was even counterproductive since it created more interest as well as increasing confusion as to who paid for what. Even Prince Charles suggested to his mother that the time might have come to make a contribution. He had been making voluntary payments to the Treasury himself in lieu of tax since the age of twenty-one and from now on would pay income tax, too. But negotiations which do indeed appear to have started in a fairly stately fashion between the Queen's private secretary and the government in early 1992 suddenly became urgent with the catastrophes of the royal marriage breakdowns and the Windsor Castle fire later that year.

Court officials have always given the impression that the negotiations had concerned the Queen herself paying tax but this is being economical with the truth: the discussions actually centred on *her successor* being asked to pay tax, not her. The intention was still to shield her from the change, for the duration of her reign. Since her reign has gone on for nearly a further quarter of a century, such a surreptitious agreement would have saved her many, many millions and cost the public purse very dearly.

The decision that the Queen would pay tax herself was rushed through within days in response to the fire. As with so many other developments and innovations of her reign, the Queen neither initiated nor objected to the change herself. Inevitably the hurried announcement that the Queen would start paying tax appeared to be a reaction to public pressure – which is exactly what it was: 'a victory,' as the *Sun* said, 'for people power' – for which the tabloid inevitably claimed credit. The announcement was made within a week of the fire. When the news was broken to her mother, her reaction was to call for a stiff drink.

In retrospect the decision marked a considerable turning point in the monarchy's relationship with government and the public. It came without a murmur after nearly a century of private lobbying and wrangling by the most powerful closed shop in the land against a long succession of government ministers inclined to reach the best settlement that could be achieved as quietly as possible, without alarming the country and provoking a nest of republican hornets. It was a strategic retreat and not a very dignified one. The Queen – and Charles – would pay income tax on their personal income, but their estates did not pay corporation or capital gains tax (the Treasury decided that the estates were not corporations), nor would her successor have to pay inheritance tax, so the private fortune and property would remain intact for the next monarch. Part of the deal was a slimming down of the number of recipients of the government's annuities, from eleven, to three: the Queen, the Duke and the Queen Mother. In future the Queen herself would pay the allowances of her daughter, her younger sons and other members of the cousinage who carried out public functions. There would be no more additional annuities, any support for the hangers-on[44] would have to come out of the Queen's Civil List, which now became a ten-year settlement.[45]

The tax negotiation was actually the culmination of a series of changes to the royal household initiated by Lord Airlie, who became lord chamberlain, responsible for running the palace, in 1984. The 13th Earl of Airlie, almost an exact contemporary of the Queen, had known her since they were both children and he had grown up on the extensive family estates close to Balmoral. By his own admission he knew nothing about the workings of the royal household before his appointment but he was precisely the sort of aristocrat with whom the Queen felt at ease – '... immensely grand ... he looks wonderful when

---

44 A trifle unfair: some of the extended members of the royal family, such as Princess Alexandra, the Duke and Duchess of Kent, and the Gloucesters were popular and assiduous in carrying out public duties, and Princess Anne is one of the hardest-working members of the family, her grumpy public image long dissipated.

45 The younger, more distant members of the royal family do now work for their living. Prince Andrew's daughters, Princesses Beatrice and Eugenie have had paid jobs, albeit of a fairly grace-and-favour kind: the former worked for Sony as a junior production assistant for a time, the latter helps to run benefit auctions. Princess Anne's son, Peter – the Queen's eldest grandchild – and his sister Zara have both foresworn royal titles: the former works in sports management and Zara is an equestrian rider. Meanwhile, in March 2015 it was announced that Prince William was to work for Bond Air Services as an air ambulance pilot in East Anglia, at least when royal duties permitted. Prince Harry left the army in the summer of 2015 and was volunteering to help wounded and disabled ex-servicemen.

dressed up in ceremonial garb. Cecil B de Mille would describe him as being a bit too much' as a courtier told the historian Ben Pimlott. The office was an ancient and stately one – but now there was a difference. Airlie had just retired from a career in merchant banking and he arrived at Buckingham Palace with a self-made brief to make efficiency savings. Now in his late eighties, and still strikingly erect and handsome as befits a former Guards officer, when I saw him at his apartment in Chelsea he told me: 'I formed the opinion that the royal household was operating in a bit of a time warp and it was not adopting best practice. In particular, expenditure was exceeding revenue provided by the government and something had to be done fairly quickly. I advised the Queen that we needed to carry out an internal review from top to bottom.' When he outlined what he wanted to do, the Queen's sole question was to ask why she had so many footmen. But it was not footmen who were the problem: it was lax management, tweedy inefficiency and outdated and complacent traditions. People came in at 10 a.m. and broke for dry Martinis at noon, as the courtier told Pimlott. Expenditure was lax, insufficiently supervised and running out of control: like an ancient family heading for ruin outgoings exceeded revenues and the capital funds were keeping the institution going. Airlie brought the accountant Michael Peat – two old Etonians together – in from Peat Marwick, the royal auditors, to compile a report into how the place was run and what savings could be made. In 1986 Peat produced a document running to nearly 1,400 pages, making 188 proposals for change, nearly all of which were adopted over the coming years. There were efficiency savings, a rationalisation of staff and departments. New, more business-like, approaches were adopted: everything from the introduction of portion control at banquets and receptions, to reductions in overheads and privatised transport contracts. Airlie saw himself as a company chairman, working alongside the private secretary as chief executive, both answerable to a single shareholder, the Queen. This new approach went some way to heading off criticism of a lax and luxurious palace and they were in keeping with the new business ethos of the Thatcher years. Many such old-fashioned firms went to the wall, but that was not going to happen to the monarchy, even under a Tory government dedicated to privatisation, and, thanks to Airlie and Peat, by the time the tax question came up, the palace was ready and acclimatised to take it. The more conspicuous items of expenditure were going – even the ageing *Royal Yacht Britannia* would soon be decommissioned by the government, much to the Queen's chagrin – and the royal collections and state rooms at Buckingham Palace and Windsor Castle were opened to the paying public during times when the Queen was not at home. The changes, in some respects more cosmetic than real, had the political effect of reducing the regular rounds of public controversy about exorbitant royals.

The fear was that if the palace did not put itself in order the government would do so for it – and that had to be avoided for fear of the stringency that would be involved. Airlie said: 'The government was getting too closely involved in the running of the royal household, particularly the Treasury.'

The Civil List settlement arranged at the time the Queen agreed to pay tax ran out in 2000 and to show that the institution was providing value for money for the first time, Peat organised the publication of an annual report from then on. Just like any other company, there would be an effort at least to show what the Civil List was spent on and where the money went. It has since become an annual event at the end of June each year. A glossy booklet like a company report is produced, complete with a photograph of a smiling Queen on the front, and Sir Alan Reid backs into the limelight to announce at a press briefing that the palace is providing better value for taxpayers than ever before. For some years, the price comparison was that the cost of Her Majesty's public duties amounted to the equivalent of a loaf of bread (60 pence in 2003), or two pints of milk (61 pence in 2004), two first-class stamps (2007) or 56 pence in 2014 (the best Reid could manage for this calculation was 'just over a penny a week') for everyone in the country, though this has come to seem too risible as well as inaccurate. There are significant omissions, the cost of security, paid by the Home Office, being the most obvious. What that costs is anybody's guess, never revealed and hard to calculate since, if they were not guarding the Queen, the police royal protection squad would presumably be protecting someone else.

Since much of the report was bland and relatively uninformative, media interest tended to focus on two separately published annual reports, on the royal travel grant, which documented the cost of all official trips amounting to more than £10,000 and on the upkeep of the royal palaces. For the first time the extravagance of taking helicopters and charter flights as opposed to trips by road or scheduled flights was documented. Prince Andrew became a particular source of ridicule – 'Air Miles Andy' – for the frequency and indulgence of his travel schedules: why had the Ministry of Defence spent nearly £8,000 to whisk him up to St Andrews Golf Course twice in 2003 so he could fulfil engagements as honorary captain of the club; and why had it been necessary to spend a further £3,000 on a helicopter to take him from Kensington Palace to Oxford for a lunch and back again for an evening engagement, when most people might have taken the train? He seemed impervious to such details, year after year, and was still at it in 2013 when the annual report showed that £14,692 was spent chartering a flight to take him from Farnborough to Scotland to visit the Royal Highland Fusiliers, an occasion which conveniently coincided with the

Open Golf Championship at Muirfield. There is a touch of the Marie Antoinettes about the Queen's second son and the insouciant sense of entitlement that he habitually shows has rubbed off severely on his public image. 'It always tends to be Prince Andrew,' sighed Margaret Hodge, the Labour MP chairing the Commons public accounts committee in October 2013 as she asked Reid who had paid for a three-week trip the Prince had made to Indonesia, Vietnam and the United States, during which he had undertaken three engagements – opening a British embassy, opening a trade fair and attending a dinner. 'There was quite a lot of holiday,' she suggested. 'How do you ensure that it is right for the state to pick up his bill for the air fare and expenses?' The answer was that the Indonesia trip was paid for out of the sovereign grant, another tranche was paid by the Royal United Services Institute and 'a proportion' was met by the Prince privately.

Royal officials struggled each year to justify such costs and there was a significant reduction in the number of private charters, but they still played into the old image of a profligate monarchy. Why was it necessary to spend £351,000 to fly Prince Charles to India and Sri Lanka by charter plane[46] or nearly £250,000 to fly him to South Africa for Nelson Mandela's funeral in December 2013? Because, it was said, in the latter case that was the only way of getting him there in a hurry, because there was a security recommendation that it should be a chartered flight and because Mandela's burial site at Qunu in the Eastern Cape was so remote. 'It is noticeable that the younger generation are taking more scheduled flights,' said Sir Alan. 'We try to

---

46 In fairness, part of the cost is incurred by pre-trip staff reconnaissance missions. Part is also, however, down to the size of the retinue that Charles and Camilla take with them on official trips: secretaries, valets, dressers, a hairdresser, private secretary, press officer – up to a dozen staff. At least when Prince Harry went on an official visit to Estonia in 2014 he flew by EasyJet.

persuade members of the royal family to take scheduled flights.'
Evidently with limited success.

On the ground, the royal train – an ancient set of carriages, equipped
in the early 1970s, furnished with Spartan G-Plan fittings and single
beds and usually kept in sidings in the Midlands – was another source
of criticism. It is generally used about ten times a year, as often by the
Prince of Wales as by his parents – the only ones allowed to commandeer
its use – and each time it rolls on to the tracks it costs up to £20,000; the
annual cost is the thick end of a million pounds a year. In 2014 the train
was used nine times, with the cost of one journey by the Prince from
Windsor to Worcester and back to Kensington coming in at £19,578,
evidently without the use of a senior railcard. This figure of course is
somewhat magnified to include the cost of storage and maintenance
of the train. It is kept at Wolverton, outside Milton Keynes, and, if they
want to use it, the train comes to the royals – it chugs quietly into
Euston late in the evening, long after the rush hour, and the Queen and
Duke, or the Prince, are driven over to meet it. Then it heads off into
the night en route to the next morning's destination and pulls into a
rural siding to enable its occupants to get some sleep. The following
day, it can beat the rush hour and deliver the royal party on time into a
station at a city-centre location. The palace justification for the train is
that it is secure, convenient and can be used for sleeping and work,
ready for early-morning appointments without the risk of getting
caught in traffic. The promise is always that the train is reaching the
end of its natural life. Then what to do about it will come under
scrutiny, with the implication that it might not be replaced. But this is
an argument that has been used for some time – somehow the train is
always ten years away from the end of its natural life.

Overall, transporting the royals costs more than £4 million a year, a
figure that has not significantly changed in the past decade. Reid

acknowledges the bad headlines the royal travel costs provoke, but maintains that the introduction of the sovereign grant gives him increasing control over how they get to where they are going. 'We can look at the whole grant holistically. Is it OK for Harry, say, to go to Australia or should the money be spent on an extra garden party? If a certain member of the family wants to go to a golf match, is the best way of going to charter a helicopter or are there cheaper options available? We do not have an unlimited budget for travel abroad and members of the royal family only travel at the government's request. The sovereign grant is an aid to saying no – yes, that is correct. I have more weapons at my beck and call now.'

Foreign trips are decided by a royal visits committee consisting of officials from Downing Street, the Foreign Office, government trade and business departments, and the private secretaries of the Queen and Prince of Wales. Charles tends to travel by chartered flight for security reasons and because of the size of his retinue, but all trips now have to be submitted in advance to the palace travel office which researches the most cost-effective way of attending the engagement and forwards its suggestions to Reid. The provision of helicopter transport has also been updated after officials discovered that the helicopters previously used on contract were not being maintained in their opinion to a satisfactory standard: which begs the question of what might have happened if one had come down while carrying a member of the royal family. The palace now has a Sikorsky 76 on a ten-year lease and a smaller AgustaWestland on a minimum hours contract.

The Queen personally has to sign off on the final cost of trips. Reid said: 'I think the royal train still has some way to go before it gets to the end of its life. For the Queen and her consort at their ages it is a very appropriate way of travelling and actually, when it comes to it, that would be an argument that could apply with justification to the Prince of Wales too.'

The upkeep of the royal palaces was also a source of constant complaint at Sir Alan's annual briefings in Civil List days: the backlog of repairs to the assorted buildings was stretching ever further into the future. The lead on the roof of Buckingham Palace needed replacing, the wiring was sixty years old, the boilers were at the end of their useful life, a piece of masonry falling from the pediment had narrowly missed Princess Anne, and Queen Victoria's mausoleum at Frogmore, which she shares under marble effigies with her beloved Albert, was in imminent danger of disintegration. The Sovereign Grant was intended to ease the spending constraints for repairs, but some things are more urgent than others. Sir Alan and his deputy Mike Stevens were given a hard 20 minutes by the Commons public accounts committee in the autumn of 2013 because they still had not costed the schedule of what needed to be done. The mausoleum was still in danger of falling in on the old Queen and her consort's tomb, and the boilers and wiring were still waiting to be replaced. The latest estimate for the cost of the backlog of repairs is £50 million, though that will certainly rise: 40 per cent of the properties are estimated to need repairs. Reid told me: 'At least fifty per cent of every increase in the sovereign grant will go on property repairs in future but it has to be done even if it is never going to make the royal family any more popular. You could spend the money to allow the Queen to dish out free ice-creams to everyone instead, I suppose . . .'

Meanwhile, the royal accounts for 2014 show £3.4 million was spent refurbishing an admittedly large – twenty-room – apartment at Kensington Palace for the Duke and Duchess of Cambridge. The apartment was formerly Princess Margaret's, which since her death in 2002 had been used for offices and had not been renovated for fifty years. But, even so, it was a large amount of money, particularly as Sir Alan said it had been a simple redecoration, done to 'a very comfortable but ordinary level'. The young couple had been at pains, an aide said, to bear down on the public costs and had been 'extremely sensitive to the fact that public funds were paying for a lot of this work.' They themselves had paid for the renovation of the smaller of two kitchens and evidently received a sub from the Prince of Wales for carpets and curtains. 'Young couples setting up home receive some help from their parents or grandparents. Some assistance may have been provided,' said William Nye, Prince Charles's private secretary, dryly.

The royal accounts are now scrutinised by the National Audit Office each year and the Commons Public Accounts Committee keeps an eye on the figures, MPs on the latter enjoying the light public grilling they give Reid and his deputy Stevens from time to time. It is a process that would have been considered effrontery only a few years ago: hard to see Fritz Ponsonby or George V's banker friend and adviser Sir Edward Peacock[47] submitting to it. How much of the building repairs had been costed, how much were the three hundred students forming the catering staff at royal garden parties paid, why if there was a wages freeze on all salaries above £21,000 did the top five officials, earning more than £100,000 a year each, get pay rises? Perhaps mild embarrassment is the best that can be achieved. The daylight has certainly been let in on that particular magic. Denying that Prince Charles was lavish, Nye said: 'The Prince of Wales lives a life of an heir to the throne.'

---

47 The man who had advised the King during the 1931 national government crisis.

Chapter 11

'A spirit of loyal enthusiasm'

(Mrs Biggs suggests the first royal jubilee, 1809)

*I*t's a clear spring morning in central London. The sky is blue, the clouds are scudding, the daffodils are out and on the Mall, and large red, white and green Mexican flags are fluttering in the breeze to welcome the country's president, his excellency Señor Enrique Peña Nieto, and his former soap opera actress wife Angelica to Britain on a state visit.

In front of an admittedly scattered crowd of tourists, mainly French and German teenagers on school outings, the band of the 1st Battalion of the Welsh Guards hoves into view in the distance. They are playing 'Green Grow the Rushes, O' as they tramp steadily up the Mall led by a drum major in full ceremonial rig, from jockey cap to eighteenth-century engraved tunic in gold and red, maroon cloak and white knee-length gaiters. It is too cold for the band and the troop of guardsmen marching behind them to be in scarlet tunics alone today: they are all wearing grey military greatcoats. The wind is ruffling their bearskin helmets, their step is perfect, their boots gleaming and they have a certain swagger to them. This is the army – and the monarchy

– putting on a bit of a show for the guests. Not that the tourists particularly notice – don't they march down the Mall every day? No, even the French teenagers seem impressed by the postcard picture of an archetypal British scene: they stop arguing and momentarily put down their sandwiches and bottles of Coke. There is even a little awe: 'Can you smoke here, or not?' asks a German schoolgirl. 'Yes,' replies a friendly bobby, 'But it's not good for you, you know.'

The guardsmen are very young, hardly more than teenagers themselves, but as they march it is as if in your mind's eye you can see earlier guardsmen in similar uniforms storming the heights of the Alma and forming infantry squares against Napoleon's cavalry at the Battle of Waterloo. The battalion banner, embroidered with the names of battle honours is carried reverently.

The kids are getting bored in the cold, Londoners are just mildly aggravated at being prevented from crossing the road to get to their lunch dates: 'Frightfully sorry, Fiona,' says one into a mobile phone. 'I may have to call off our meeting: the road's blocked and I can't get across. They say I'll have to go all the way round by Victoria...bloody annoying. Yes, it's something to do with the Queen...'

'Don't worry: she'll be through soon' a policeman tells another onlooker. 'You'll just have to wait or go round Westminster. It will only be twenty minutes.'

And there she is, in a maroon Bentley whizzing at some speed up the empty Mall, followed by security in a Range Rover and a white people carrier. There is a definite frisson, even from jaded City-types frustrated in crossing the road for the lunch appointments, at the sight of the small white figure, barely seeing over the sill of the car's side window. In the distance, on Horse Guards Parade, the Household Cavalry, resplendent in glittering breastplates and plumed helmets can be seen lining up as the band plays on. A short pause and then there are shouted commands, martial music – both national anthems – and the muffled, distant sound of a forty-one-gun salute echoing across the capital like thunderclaps from a clear sky. On the parade ground, the president, a diminutive and distinctly unmilitary-looking figure is inspecting the guard of honour, accompanied by the Duke of Edinburgh, still upright and beady eyed, sprightly and walking unaided three months short of his 94th birthday – later in the day at the state banquet he will read the menu and follow the text of the speeches without the aid of spectacles, too.

Then, inspection over, it is back to the palace for lunch, but not by the transport they came in: this time the royal family and their Mexican guests will return in a line of horse-drawn carriages of a sort that would not have surprised Queen Victoria herself. Leading the way, the Queen and president are in the Diamond Jubilee state coach, which is drawn by six grey horses. The high slung coach, with the royal crest painted on the side, gold-painted wheels and roof mountings, topped with a crown, looks as though it has been around since before the era of the horseless carriage, but in fact was only delivered to the Queen from its Australian builder in 2014. It does however have some mod-cons: button-controlled heating and electric windows. Next, the Australian state coach – this one is slightly less ornate but built by the same firm thirty years ago – has the Duke of Edinburgh and Señora Rivera, less than half his age, chatting away animatedly inside. These two carriages are accompanied by the detachments of the Household Cavalry – the Life Guards and the Blues and Royals – breastplates gleaming in the sunlight, the plumes on their helmets fluttering and their horses skittishly clattering down the Mall at a fast trot, as if ready for a charge across a nineteenth-century battlefield: one unlucky rider already off, his mount still keeping pace with the rest as if it was in the Grand National. Trailing behind, seemingly straight out of a Sunday afternoon classic serialisation, comes a series of black landau carriages carrying ladies-in-waiting, Mexican ministers and ambassadors from both countries. From out of the open window of one of the landaus a hand stretches out, bearing a cellphone, snapping pictures. All this is picturesque of course: a passing pageant, a little bit of a spectacle, a treat for those taking part and for those who happen across it while wandering through St James's Park towards the palace. They could just as easily have travelled by car. But only those baulked from crossing the street to their lunches, or the joggers whose accustomed route is blocked seem to be impatient with the sight. I thought of what a former royal official had said to me a few weeks earlier: 'I think the vast majority of the people are attracted to the traditions of the institution. They don't want a parade of Mondeos. They like the music and the fuss and the shouted commands and the uniforms. You want to see the state performing in public, don't you? Everyone recognises what is happening, in a dignified way.'

Inside the palace, after lunch in the blue drawing room – an intimate affair, just a smattering of Mexicans, senior members of the royal household in uniform and members of the royal family turning up for a meal – there is a traditional little ceremony in the Queen's picture gallery next door. Most people have holiday snaps and souvenirs, the Queen has gifts and items from the archives to show off. There is indeed showmanship in this as part of the palace's promotional strategy. In the past any such display would have been shown off privately to a visiting head of state. Now it is done in front of the cameras, with the choicest items on display on a table right in front of them so that the Queen and her visitor can be seen full-face admiring the treasures. 'You need,' says a former adviser, 'For the cameras to be able to see the twinkle in her eyes. It is all part of showing the institution at work and what that means.'

In May 2011, when the Obamas visited, they were shown handwritten letters by George Washington, George III ('America is lost! Must we fall beneath the blow?') and Abraham Lincoln, from the middle of the Civil War sparing time to send his condolences to Queen Victoria on the death of Prince Albert. Nothing quite that historic for the Mexicans, but there was a lavishly embroidered white sombrero, given to the Queen by a previous Mexican presidential visitor in 1973 (sadly, she did not try it on), a leather saddle complete with lariat presented to the Duke on a visit to Vera Cruz in 1975 and a map of Mexico City in a book dated 1606, not long after the Spanish conquest, which has been lurking in the royal library since the reign of William IV in the 1830s. Impressive enough for most visitors. The visiting politicians and their wives lingered long enough behind the artefacts to have their photographs taken by the Mexican photographers accompanying the trip, ready to beam back the evidence of their success to the media back home.

Then in the evening came the state banquet, with 170 white-tie-and-tailed and evening-dressed guests in the palace ballroom, overpoweringly scented floral displays lining the tables, gilded centre pieces and silver and gold ornaments all around the room, and 140 staff brought in to serve them, half palace employees and the others on contract. Those on the guest list represented the British establishment, dressed as they might have been a hundred years ago (except that most of the women's costumes, such as the off-the-shoulder scarlet number worn by the president's wife, would have scandalised and titillated the Edwardians). David Cameron, Nick Clegg and Ed Miliband were all there in white tie, as if harbouring the guilty secret that this was their normal wear and their daily suits are just a disguise to hide their true natures. There too, Mark Carney, the governor of the Bank of England, and other bankers including Douglas Flint, chairman of HSBC, in altogether more congenial company than that of the MPs on the Commons

Treasury committee who had given him and his bank's tax-evasion practices a roasting the week before. The archbishop of Canterbury was on the top table chatting genially to the prime minister whose economic policies he and his fellow bishops had denounced as heartless only a few days earlier – two more old Etonians together. Then there were the American and Saudi ambassadors and various Mexican ministers and their wives, dotted around the ballroom, gossiping informally while a military band played in the balcony above. As they settled in their seats, there were flattering speeches from the Queen and the president and toasts to the continuing amity between the two countries. Speeches come before the meal these days, at the Queen's preference, a tradition begun at the time of her *annus horribilis* speech in 1992 when she had thought her heavy cold meant her voice would not last out the meal. Señor Pena Nieto larded the praise: 'During more than six decades of accelerated global transformation, you have led their emblematic constitutional monarchy with admirable devotion, temperance, wisdom and dignity...you have presented to the world the positive image and influence of the United Kingdom,' he said in rousing Spanish, while the Queen, next to him, unconcernedly studied the English translation, routine compliments not a sufficient cause for a smile or even a nod.

Then it was her turn to speak of two countries linked by ties of family, friendship, commerce and international cooperation, based on a remarkable similarity of views and values – natural partners on so many pressing issues. Not too similar of course, it went unmentioned that Britain does not quite have powerful drug cartels massacring civilians at will, or kidnapping student teachers with the aid of the police. Those inconvenient truths were left to a smattering of demonstrators far away outside the palace gates. Instead there was a powerful emphasis on mutual trade and business links, in the interests of prosperity for both countries and hopes for more student exchanges. Then they all sat down to fillets of *sole diplomate, noisettes d'agneau de Windsor* and *tarte au chocolat*, with New Zealand chardonnay, a rather nice-looking 1999 premier cru and Mumm champagne, while the band played on and Pipe Major Ross McCrindle of the Scots Guards limbered up to essay a short programme on the bagpipes. The following day the president's party would hold talks with business leaders before flying up to Aberdeen for meetings with the oil industry about matters of mutual interest. That was the trip's hard edge and real purpose, oiled with cold-eyed realism by the state folderols of marching bands, carriage drives and the state banquet. Goodness knows how many the Queen has given in the past sixty-four years, but gamely she continues.

The Court Circular, daily list of royal engagements, is now available on the monarchy's website, which is another innovation – the Queen even supposedly tweets inoffensively these days[48] – shows a pretty constant routine. In March, the royal family came together for the Mexican state visit, then the Commonwealth Day service at Westminster Abbey followed a few days later by another service at St Paul's Cathedral to mark the end of British military action in Afghanistan. Then the family fanned out: Prince Charles and the Duchess of Cornwall to the US for five days, Princess Anne on a visit to the Philippines, the Duchess of Cambridge to Margate and the Duke of York to Shropshire and Sevenoaks on visits. Meanwhile, the Queen herself ploughed on: naming a new ship called *Britannia* at Southampton, touring Battersea Dogs' Home, visiting the Battle of

---

48 Or allegedly tweets. When with some fanfare the media were called in to witness her first attempt at using social media at the Science Museum in October 2014, the man from the *Wall Street Journal* was unsporting enough to notice that the tweet had actually come from an aide's iPhone not the iPad the Queen was using. Well, she was eighty-eight at the time – and that did not stop her immediately having 724,000 followers.

Britain memorial on the cliffs above Dover, then unveiling a statue at Canterbury Cathedral, and all the while meeting new ambassadors and saying farewell to old ones – Qatar, Venezuela, Nicaragua, Austria – sparing time to go through the hallowed ritual of 'pricking' out the names of new high sheriffs for the Duchy of Lancaster, holding investitures, attending receptions and dinners and meeting the new president of Sri Lanka.

If this all sounds banal, perhaps it is but it is part of the routine currency of being a head of state. Not everyone could do it: the cheap jibes on social media about the royals not having a job, or doing a job that anyone could do, are not actually true. These are public obligations and duties which can't be undertaken lightly or negligently, or only if you feel like it – there is a responsibility behind them. At eighty-nine, the Queen has been doing it for sixty-four years. It is in fact a conscious working out of the commitment she made in a famous radio broadcast on her twenty-first birthday: possibly the most substantial setting out of her future role and duties that she has ever made. 'I declare before you all,' she piped, 'That my whole life, whether it be long or short, shall be devoted to your service and the service of our great Imperial family to which we all belong, but I shall not have the strength to carry out this resolution alone unless you join in with me, as I now invite you to do…God help me to make good my vow and God bless all of you who are willing to share in it.' The speech was not actually hers; it was written for her by her father's private secretary Tommy Lascelles and was delivered while she accompanied her parents on a tour of South Africa in April 1947. Its cadences were old-fashioned and rather courtly even then and the sentiments were maybe not couched in the sort of language someone just coming of age would routinely use. They were also addressed to an Empire that would shortly disintegrate. Yet they touched a public emotion by their seriousness and by the evident sincerity of the young woman who solemnly said them – and evoked God in doing so. And, more importantly, she believed the words then and has followed them strictly ever since. Are we serving her, or is she serving us? It does not really matter: she has implicitly followed her idea of service as a compact with the nation for nearly seven decades. Furthermore, the nation knows it and appreciates it: it does not want a frivolous, *It's a Royal Knockout* Queen. On the boat back from South Africa, Lascelles noted 'the remarkable development of P'cess E': 'Not a great sense of humour but a healthy sense of fun...never spares herself in that exhausting part of royal duty. She has got an astonishing solicitude for other people's comfort; such unselfishness is not a normal characteristic of that family.'

Nevertheless, the palace routines she inherited and did not question five years later were not ones that would work today. The sense of duty remains the same but it has been moulded and reshaped to modern realities. At the palace they call it the 'Marmite Jar' strategy, as in the small pot of brown, sludge-like, salty savoury spread, made from the remnants of yeast left over from the brewing of beer, which was first concocted in Britain in 1902. The brand and its oval label showing a small ovenware cooking pot – a French marmite – and lettering on a red banner is self-consciously slightly archaic and meant to indicate a traditional 'heritage' product: the same now as it has ever been. But that is not strictly true. The label may be much the same but the wording and the typeface have evolved and so has the shape of the jar: you can get large jars or little jars, squeezy plastic jars, upright round jars, upside-down jars, teapot-shaped jars and cricket ball shaped jars, Marmite Gold, Marmite flavoured with Guinness and they even periodically on special occasions muck about with the brand name: at the diamond jubilee the labels read 'Ma'amite'. Even the ingredients have changed a bit over time. Well, as one courtier explained to me (over a lunch which did not include Marmite): the monarchy is a bit like that – it has subtly changed and evolved, but slowly and discreetly so that no one notices. That is the aim anyway and with the monarchy, too, the product stays the same to all appearances, but subtly changes. The sorts of rituals the Queen was used to when she first came to the throne sixty years ago are inappropriate now and the assumptions have also changed; had they not, the monarchy would have gone the way of curds and whey.

The evolution revolves around changes in accessibility and, to a lesser extent, informality, but also in the way the palace runs things. The Queen no longer needs to wonder what her subjects think as she gazes out of the window at Buckingham Palace – she meets them more often, tours a wider range of places and anyway has private polling to assess what the public feels about her, the royal family and the institution of the monarchy. They certainly – though they would never divulge this – know what the public attitude is to Prince Charles becoming King and how acceptable it will be for Camilla to be Queen as opposed to consort. And they know this not just for Britain but for the main overseas realms as well.

Even in her mid-eighties, the Queen was still open to unexpected, even bold, new initiatives. In May 2011, there was her official visit to the Irish Republic: the first by a British monarch for a hundred years. In view of the troubled history during the twentieth century of relations between the two islands, it was a courageous step and one which was vociferously opposed by some in Ireland as untimely and unwelcome, but it still went ahead with the encouragement of the Fine Gael government of Enda Kenny and the Irish president Mary McAleese. There had been semi-private visits before by Charles, Andrew, Anne and Edward, and by their father for informal or unofficial events, and more official visits to Britain by Irish prime ministers and presidents, but none to Ireland by the Queen herself. The four-day visit was something that most politicians and diplomats on both sides of the Irish Sea would have thought might occur one day but not so soon and probably 'not in this reign', as the Queen might have said herself. But the visit confounded all expectations and the sour voices of Sinn Féin were left sounding churlish and dated. It was not as if the itinerary stuck to safe events: the Queen visited the Garden of Remembrance to Ireland's past heroes – most of whom had died fighting against her ancestors – stood, head bowed, in silence and laid a wreath. She also went to Croke Park, the home of the Gaelic Athletic Association, a modern sports stadium but one whose name still carried bitter memories of a lethal attack on spectators by British troops during the war of independence in November 1920. This time, they gave the Queen a hurley stick as a present. That evening at a state banquet, she started her speech with a brief burst of Gaelic: 'A Uachtarain agus a chairde' – 'President and friends' – a common enough courtesy of the sort she had made in speeches around the world in similar circumstances, but one which here was greeted as if she had kissed the Blarney Stone. Mrs McAleese was seen to mouth: 'wow!' three times in surprise and pride. The speech that followed, more significantly, expressed graceful remorse for the violence both sides had perpetrated on each other: 'With the benefit of historic hindsight we can all see things which we would wish had been done differently, or not at all.' Perhaps she was thinking of the Croke Park massacre and perhaps her audience were thinking of the IRA's assassination of Lord Mountbatten in the harbour at Mullaghmore in County Sligo in August 1979[49]. By the time the visit finished three days

---

49 The Queen was introduced to Martin McGuinness, the former Provisional IRA commander, now deputy first minister of Northern Ireland, in 2014. In May 2015 Prince Charles met Gerry Adams of Sinn Féin in Galway during a public visit to Ireland, before visiting the site of his great-uncle's assassination for the first time: old hurts not forgotten, or necessarily forgiven, but realpolitik prevailing.

later, the Queen was shaking hands with a Sinn Féin councillor and taking part in a walkabout in the streets of Cork. The visit was a triumph – a turning of the page – which cemented the good relations between two neighbouring mature and friendly states and set them on a new course. Of course the Queen was advised to do it and her visit was carefully choreographed by both sides, but she need not have done it, and it was her skill and openness which made it so successful.

A year later there was another coup of a different sort: her participation in a film at the start of the London Olympics which seemed to show her parachuting into the Olympic arena. No one, apart from a closely restricted circle, knew *that* was going to happen. One former communications secretary told me: 'I was sitting watching at home and I thought: "It can't be her . . . it *is*!"' Game for a laugh at eighty-six, utterly unexpected – and dignity unaffected.

There has been an opening up – somewhat – in the circle of personal advisers to take in a slightly wider cross-section of views and backgrounds: more with university degrees, many more secondments from Whitehall and particularly the Foreign Office, fewer from the ancient, posher regiments or the landed aristocracy and more with relevant qualifications – though, fortuitously, Sir Christopher Geidt, the current private secretary, has both a military (Scots Guards) and diplomatic background (and a public school and Oxbridge education). Sir Alan Reid, the keeper of the privy purse, for instance, went to Fettes and St Andrews, but also had a long career with KPMG. He said: 'This was the last job I ever expected to do because I was a management consultant rather than an accountant and I wondered whether I would have to roll up my sleeves to do the accountancy, but fortunately this job is one where human resources skills are important. I had a tense twelve months hoping I was doing it right but fortunately my style seemed to suit the Queen. This place is not full of Etonians and former

Guardsmen any more, as it was perhaps twenty years ago.'

Certainly the personnel are recruited for having more relevant skills than their predecessors once had. Sally Osman, director of communications at Buckingham Palace since 2014, is a former journalist who moved into public relations and headed the media teams at Sky TV, the BBC – an institution of comparably high-profile and as defensive as the palace – and Sony, before moving to be Prince Charles's press secretary the previous year. Her deputy Kristina Kyriacou moved up to take charge of the Prince's media relations, having joined Clarence House after a long career representing music stars such as Gary Barlow, George Michael and Cheryl Cole, and working for the Comic Relief charity. Commander Colville must be revolving in his grave. Few these days make their entire careers in the royal service, but having done so is an excellent mark for the CV.

Communications remains a source of some friction between Buckingham Palace and Clarence House. At the start of 2014 the plan was to merge the two communications teams in one operation at the palace, which was why Osman moved across. It was a proposal presented as an attempt to improve coordination and as an indication that the prince was assuming more charge of day-to-day operations. But the merger ultimately did not happen because Charles changed his mind, seemingly fearing a loss of control of a key part of his private office. A palace adviser said smoothly: 'He took the view that he wanted the press office focusing on his agenda and amplifying his core messages – it is quite a specialised area. I think he felt the operation would become disjointed – there is a geographical pull, to be part of the hub in Clarence House where he spends significant time.'

Since Clarence House is all of 300 yards from Buckingham Palace, it would seem that control is indeed the right word. The adviser made light of it: 'They were absolutely right to suck it and see. Obviously it just did not feel the right thing to the prince. If he wants his team there and feels cut off without them, he pays their wages...'

In the spring of 2015, Catherine Mayer's biography of Prince Charles caused controversy when the book's serialisation in *The Times* focused on a comparison, made by an unnamed source, that the two courts were like *Wolf Hall*, Hilary Mantel's novel of intrigue at the court of Henry VIII, which was then coincidentally being serialised to great popularity on the BBC. The idea of rivalry was promptly disavowed by Clarence House with a gratuitous sideswipe at Ms Mayer implying – erroneously – that she had not had much access to the Prince. Since Mayer had scrupulously detailed her meetings with Charles during the course of researching the book, including a lengthy on-the-record interview, sitting next to him at dinner and accompanying him on a hike round the Dumfries House estate – and had the recordings to prove it – this seemed either a particularly maladroit and fatuous assault, or implied that the anonymous source of the criticism had not actually read the book before slagging it off. There are some signs that the paranoid spin-doctoring days of the Bolland era are returning to the Clarence House court, now that Peat and Harverson have left. There are indeed strong rumours of divisions in the household – the still influential Fawcett and communications secretary Kyriacou are said by insiders not to get on – and it is unlikely that the attack on the book would have been undertaken without the Prince's approval. Royal biographers, even sympathetic ones, do tend to find themselves frozen out after their books appear. Mayer is said to have received congratulatory telephone calls from Buckingham Palace staff and commiserations from dissident sources at Clarence House following the attacks on her integrity.

A contact of mine, who has worked closely with the prince for more than twenty years – and who may even have been the source of the *Wolf Hall* quote – said: 'There are separate courts – of course there will be rivalries and people of ambition trying to make their mark. I don't think it's so much *Wolf Hall* as *Downton Abbey*. A hundred years ago there were plenty of people who had lifestyles like that, now very few do. Charles is one of them. William and Kate are much less *Downton* than Charles is.'

The re-orientation of the royals really took place in tandem with the household reforms initiated by Lord Airlie and Michael Peat, with the formation of what was slightly grandiosely called the Way Ahead group, at which senior members of the family met their advisers on a regular basis, not only to coordinate and plan future events, to avoid clashes and ensure the country was adequately covered by royal visits, but also to discuss strategy and formulate positions for likely future constitutional changes. That too was an Airlie initiative: 'It seemed desirable to address the longer-term issues facing the monarchy,' he said. 'Way Ahead' was chosen because Airlie felt that the alternative, 'strategic review', sounded too corporatist and would scare people off. Those attending meetings of the group from the mid-1990s included Airlie, Fellowes, his successor Janvrin, and Sir Michael Peat and the Queen, Duke of Edinburgh, Prince Charles, Andrew, Edward and Princess Anne would also attend. These were highly confidential meetings at private secretary level only – Bolland's lobbying for attendance was resisted. Among the issues discussed were the slimming down of the royal family to its central core – 'There are just too many of us,' the Queen had remarked, thinking the palace balcony was getting crowded – and changes to the succession rules, years ahead of when the coalition government in 2011 eventually legislated to allow equality of the sexes, not male precedence. Even the flying of the Union flag from Buckingham Palace flagpole and its lowering to half-mast on special occasions in future was hammered out.

There could be a refocusing of the priorities for royal visits, too, to take in a broader spread of the nation: more focus on housing (hence the somewhat unrelaxed pictures of the Queen taking tea with Mrs Susan McCarron at her housing association home on the Craigdale estate in Glasgow in July 1999) more visits to state schools, to hospices and to youth clubs, fewer visits to launch battleships (there were fewer to launch) and more to galleries. The commemorations of war were not missed: in March 2015 the Queen and Duke visited the Battle of Britain war memorial and visitor centre at Capel-le-Ferne on the cliffs above Dover, speaking to the last remaining pilots from the battle seventy-five years on – a battle both the royals could themselves remember. The Queen also attended the 70th anniversary VE Day commemorations in early May 2015: an event which could not have failed to bring back memories of her night out in the Mall all those years before; such anniversaries still have meaning even though the dwindling numbers of veterans turning out are a sure sign of her contemporaries' mortality. But for the centenary of the outbreak of the First World War the previous August, it was noticeable that the younger members of the family were in attendance, almost as if the baton was being passed to a new generation. These changes of focus were not accidental, but calculated.

In the private secretary's department at Buckingham Palace a team of young researchers, led by Caroline Creer, was set up in 2009 not only to draw up a matrix of visits to ensure a spread of geographical locations and royal personnel, but also matching interests to locations. The Queen and Duke will go and see veterans and attend the church services, Prince Charles will visit the farmers and the agricultural projects, Camilla, hospices, the osteoporosis and other medical centres, the Duchess of Cambridge the art galleries and studios, William the military and Harry the sports fields. Creer's team is also responsible for monitoring the media – both in Britain and across the Commonwealth – flagging up stories and issues that ought to require a response and alerting the private secretaries to looming controversies such as, for instance the row in Australia in early 2015 when Prime Minister Tony Abbott awarded the Duke of Edinburgh an Australian knighthood. The decision, which the prime minister took without consultation, quickly roused touchy local sensitivities – should not the knighthood go to a local person, rather than an ancient British Duke far away who already held a number of similar honours? The palace knew about it as soon as the Australian public did, though not before. The unit also analyses and advises on constitutional issues and alerts the private secretaries about the possible implications of forthcoming legislation. It liaises with the Cabinet Office and there are regular meetings with departmental private secretaries and the prime minister's diary secretary to coordinate engagements. 'We are watching the waterfront to see in advance if anything impinges on the royal household,' said a member of the team. The information is condensed down onto one side of paper – 'the golden rule' – to be passed to the private secretaries.

In choosing royal events now and reconnoitring locations, the Queen and Duke's ages have to be taken into account: is there a steep or potentially slippery slope involved? How great are the distances: would it be better to use a golf buggy, or pop them into one of the royal limousines and drive slowly; it is always imperative that the public should get at least a glimpse if they have taken the trouble to turn up. Opening parliament now has to be carefully managed because the crown and robes are so heavy. But one assistant secretary says: 'She's still pretty fit. In the summer of 2014 she did a garden party – eight thousand people at Buckingham Palace – and then went straight off to France, another garden party in the Paris Embassy, then on to

Normandy for the D-day commemorations, then back the following day in time for the Derby. She was on her feet for hours. It exhausted me, I can tell you.'

What drives this is a sense of duty as outlined in that speech when she was twenty-one, but also a feeling of obligation to an annual routine: it is what she has been doing for decades. There are still royal visits abroad, a three-day state visit to Germany in June 2015, for instance, but gradually some of the burden is being shared with the Prince of Wales and with Prince William. Charles does some of the investitures now and, in 2013, attended the biennial meeting of Commonwealth heads of government in Sri Lanka in place of the Queen; it was a visit judged to be too far, too hot and too controversial, given the human rights record of the then host government. The Queen is expected to attend the next CHOGM at Malta in November 2015, however – it is not only much closer to home, but was also the island where she spent much of the early part of her married life between late 1949 and early 1951, while her husband was stationed with the Mediterranean fleet and is the nearest the couple have ever come to an ordinary married life; ordinary a comparative term as she was still a princess – but it was also where she was accordingly extremely happy. This will probably be her last visit to the island.

Does this conscious (and self-conscious) engagement with the public and this ceaseless round of conscientious duty mean that the Queen and her children have truly become a family in touch with their people? Evidently not – nor would that actually have much appeal: it is the glamour and prestige that does it and always has. Where the royal family is at its weakest is when the public think that they are taking an advantage, deploying an unfair sense of entitlement and privilege: in short, the 'Air Miles Andy' approach. Prince Andrew perhaps left the Navy too soon, aged forty-one in 2001, with the rank of commander

– subsequently promoted to honorary rear admiral on his fiftieth birthday – for he has struggled since to find a worthwhile occupation. He once expressed a wish that he might have become a plumber – have learned a trade – unfortunately out of the question for a member of the royal family of his generation. Instead for a while he became a trade ambassador for Britain, a somewhat vacuous job, extolling British companies and export potential to foreigners and stimulating inward investment. But any good he did was obscured by the difficulty of demonstrating which orders or investment had indeed been won by his efforts except where his title gained privileged access to heads of government. It did not help that some of his missions seemed to be in aid of weapons manufacturers.

A former palace official sighed: 'Andrew is passionate about wanting to contribute. The trade role was perfect for him because he felt he was having an impact. The problem with Yorkie was that he can be very arrogant and petulant. I think that's down to insecurity.'

He seemed to spend a great deal of time in some of the remoter countries of the steppes: with the relatives of unsavoury local dictators in Azerbaijan and in Kazakhstan, whose president's billionaire son-in-law became sufficiently friendly with him to buy Sunninghill Park, the mansion the Queen had paid for on the occasion of his marriage to Sarah Ferguson, built between Ascot and Windsor Great Park. The house, known as South York in homage to *Dallas* because of its vague resemblance to a Texan oilman's ranch, had been empty and derelict for some years and was then bought by Timur Kulibayev for £15 million in 2008 – £3 million more even than was being asked for it, paid for through offshore bank accounts, though he did not subsequently move in. Even then the deal was on the generous side. Andrew's official expenses were lavish: £620,000 in 2010, including £154,000 on entertainment and the rest on travel. But what ultimately

brought his ambassadorial career to an end was a friendship with
Jeffrey Epstein, a wealthy American financier who had served a prison
sentence for procuring underage girls for prostitution and had given
money to help pay off Sarah Ferguson's debts. Epstein and Andrew
had holidayed together in Thailand in the past and the Prince was
photographed strolling with him in New York following his release
from prison in 2011. Publication of the association and the adverse
publicity it created finally persuaded the Prince to resign his
ambassadorial role and concentrate on supporting domestic good
causes such as education and training instead. Compromisingly, there
was also a photograph of Andrew with a young woman called Virginia
Roberts who subsequently claimed to have had sex with him while
under the age of consent: a charge the Prince strenuously denied. In
April 2015 a judge in Florida ordered that Roberts' allegations should
be struck from a court case in which she was attempting to join two
alleged victims of Epstein who were suing the US government over
the plea bargain prosecutors reached with him. 'These lurid details are
unnecessary,' the judge told her

The trail of mishaps and misjudgements effectively undermined the
public image of the sixth in line to the throne. It has been that insouciant
sense of entitlement that has chiefly done for him. When that happens
every little thing seems to count against you, as any miscreant politician
could have told him. In September 2013, the Prince was strolling
innocently by himself in the grounds of Buckingham Palace when he
was stopped by two armed police security officers who did not
recognise him. An altercation apparently followed before the officers
realised their mistake and apologised, but there was shouting and
bawling out. Andrew's *amour-propre* took a knock. Did they not realise
who he was? In fairness, the officers were on edge because an intruder
had indeed got into the palace a couple of nights earlier – not as far as

the Queen's bedroom as the vagrant Michael Fagan managed in 1982, but still a security embarrassment. Andrew, reputedly the Queen's favourite son, graciously accepted the police apology a day or so later.

Perhaps it is unfair to harp on about such events when the royals unexpectedly brush up against the hassles of ordinary life, but it does seem to take them by surprise when they do so. It is a very separate, sheltered life. The former palace official said: 'They have circles of influence surrounding them and fawning. No one ever says no and very few tell them when something is not a good idea. Look at world leaders such as I have had dealings with, or seen close up: Thatcher, Reagan, Blair, Bush: after eight years in power you are bonkers: you lose touch with reality. Charles can be a bit like that. The remarkable thing about the Queen is that, after sixty-odd years, she is more grounded, far more in touch with what is going on than people give her credit for.'

The Queen does seem remarkably unfazed by modern society, more so than her anguished son. Sir Alan Reid said: 'If you press to get things changed here, that does not work, but if you work on it you can make progress without tears. Very often resistance comes from advisers who are worried about what the Queen might say, rather than the Queen herself. She does not block change. I was responsible for drawing up the palace's first equal opportunities policy and it contained a reference to sexual orientation. I was told that phrase could not possibly stay in but she passed it without batting an eyelid.'

The image is of an essentially passive figure who does not initiate change herself but accepts it. Perhaps this has been her stance for so long on major issues that it follows into minor ones too. Reid has an example. The Queen is a debenture holder for the royal box at the Royal Albert Hall. She does not go very often herself but the box, which seats twenty, is permanently available for her use and so when the royal family does not want it, it can be used by palace staff. They have to buy the seats – the royals are not *that* generous – but it does give them access to events that the Queen would never go to herself: concerts by Eric Clapton or the Killers for instance. The rule always was that they should dress smartly in suits and ties, until Reid pointed out that this was scarcely appropriate when the rest of the audience was in jeans and T-shirts. 'She said to me: "I wondered when you were going to get round to changing that silly rule." So we did.'

Reid, who sees the Queen at least twice a week, added: 'I think it is part of her leadership skill. She does not intrude herself. People who are delegated tend to work better and be happier. If it goes wrong she does not need to do much more than raise an eyebrow.' Lord Airlie – who after all has known her for so long that he attended her fifth birthday party – said: 'Following a worrying and difficult conversation with the Queen, you invariably find that she has made you feel better.'

Things are perhaps a little stiffer at her son's court. A close acquaintance of the Prince of Wales over many years said to me: 'I cannot say it was friendship. There was all this etiquette stuff. You can easily find yourself bowing to him – at least nodding the head like he was Henry VIII. I never did that in my life but you know, he called me by my Christian name and I called him Sir. I would have felt odd calling him Charles, because that was what his wife would have called him, but there are not many other options to choose, are there? There was certainly formality. It would be pretty fatal to cross the line from colleague to friend. Has he ever been round to my house? Good Lord, no.'

He mused: 'It is a strange life. He gets some things wrong, you know, just little things which show he's not on quite the same planet. Like the time he visited a house, I was told by someone who was with him, and noticed a row of tea towels hanging on the radiator to dry. You need to know that tea towels are what the royal family use to dry their dogs. After they left and got in the car, the prince said: "Dog towels everywhere . . . extraordinary." He had no idea what their usual use was.'

My contact added: 'They are living in a very rare place now. Do I feel sorry for them? No. They have nice long holidays. They don't have to put the kids to bed or cook a meal. It is a privileged existence. Can you expect anyone to be entirely normal if they have never had to queue for anything and everyone always says yes to them? When a royal comes to visit, he is visiting them and he gets a lift to go there. He doesn't have to take public transport. Life is made easy: it is all arranged.

'The family is a business – that's worth remembering. Relations within the family are all conducted and engineered by officials. Their daily life is not like other people's. Their diaries are fixed six months in advance and rarely changed. There is no spontaneity. Would I swap with them? No fear.'

Chapter 12

'Safer not to be too popular. You can't fall too far'

(Duke of Edinburgh, 2003)

In late March 2015, the royal communications team issued routine guidance for the media in preparation for the birth of Prince William and Duchess Kate's second baby at St Mary's Hospital Paddington. A large pen would be set up on the pavement opposite the hospital: 30m long and 5m deep for cameramen, photographers and journalists in readiness for the big event a month hence. Those wishing entry had to apply for accreditation by the first week in April in the knowledge that the pen would only be set up by the Metropolitan Police once the Duchess had been admitted: television cameras in front, photographers on their stepladders behind, reporters squeezing in where they could. The scene was set for the royal event of the year. All they could do was wait, as expectantly as any family and meanwhile, unlike other families, speculate on the baby's names: a £300 bet on Alice as a girl's name, placed at a betting shop in Royal Tunbridge Wells successfully rocketed that name up the list. But would it supplant the bookies' favourite: Elizabeth? By mid-April the bookmaker William Hill proudly announced that betting on the prospective baby's names, gender and birth date had passed £250,000.

The palace's practised crowd control measures teed up the world for the next turn in the royal tale, ready for the latest episode in the everyday story of regal folk. Where once the birth of a new prince or princess was attended by the home secretary to ensure authenticity – no smuggling in of an infant in a warming pan – now the proclamation comes from the massed ranks of the world's heaving, sweating media perched outside the front door (although it is also later posted, according to tradition on a blackboard in the front courtyard of Buckingham Palace for the crowds to peruse). And so it came to pass: Her Royal Highness Princess Charlotte Elizabeth Diana of Cambridge was duly born on the morning of 2 May, weighing in at a decent 8lb 3oz and instantly becoming fourth in line to the throne behind her grandfather, father and older brother, and almost as instantly having her own Wikipedia page. The names were obvious in retrospect, not least because the Duchess's middle name is also Elizabeth. The Queen pronounced herself delighted: 'We love having another girl,' and Tower Bridge, the London Eye, Trafalgar Square and Ottawa's Peace Tower were bathed in pink light. In far-off Washington DC where I happened to be staying that weekend, the royal birth was the second item on the television news (after demonstrations in Baltimore following the death of a black man in police custody). All conversation ceased in the bar where I was having lunch and eyes swivelled to the screen as the royal couple came out of the hospital with the baby ten hours after the birth. 'Oh my God: look at *her*!' squealed a woman. 'I can't believe that – get me her stylist,'; meanwhile, the reporter on screen was burbling obsequiously: 'What a beautiful, beautiful family. This is a historic day. London is celebrating tonight.' Well, maybe it was: two days later as I boarded my plane to come home, the Delta air hostesses were handing out pink candy lollipops inscribed with 'It's a girl!' to every passenger.

The Windsors have fulfilled the first obligation of a royal family in ensuring the succession. They have an heir, an heir to the heir, and now an heir and a spare for the generation yet to come. All being well and with the power of modern medicine and the resilience of the family's genes, the royal house is secured into the next century. Considering the ups and downs of the past hundred years, that is a remarkable achievement. The monarchy's popularity now seems at least as great as at any time in the Queen's reign.

Not everyone thinks it should continue like that. In the predominantly white countries of Canada, Australia and New Zealand, there are vocal groups campaigning for their nations to become republics – in Australia they nearly succeeded in 1999 – and they have a potent argument in calling for their head of state to be one of their own citizens rather than an aristocratic figure from far overseas, reminding them of their colonial legacy. If they are looking for a row though, the republicans can't quite make one happen since the royal position from Buckingham Palace is that if they want to become republics, the British monarchy won't stand in their way: it is up to them. The same would be true in Britain: as the Queen says, if that is what the people want, 'we'll go quietly.' They learned their lesson with George III.

The tipping point in the realms overseas has not yet been reached, but it may be when there is a change of sovereign. Similarly, the Queen has been head of the Commonwealth throughout her reign and there has been no appetite from the fifty-three countries to change that while she lives. It sometimes seems that she is the single most unifying force in the organisation and its most enthusiastic supporter and she has attended more of its biannual conferences than anyone else, missing only two. Although the Commonwealth was actually founded in 1949, three years before she came to the throne, it was still a quasi-imperial organisation of colonies and former colonies and it is only during her reign that the Empire was finally dismantled, across Africa, the Far East and the Caribbean.

She has respect and loyalty. But will Charles have the same? How will Commonwealth leaders feel about having an hereditary white man imposed on them? While he may not be a divisive choice – and it may not be possible to gather a consensus around any of the organisation's political leaders – Jacob Zuma anyone? Or Tony Abbott? – what seems certain is that the independent states will want to assert that independence from what no one calls the mother country any more and choose their own titular leader for themselves, even if the choice is made by whoever are their leaders at the time. If Charles follows his mother as head of the Commonwealth it is likely to be only because the members cannot agree a democratic alternative among themselves: a precarious position that will change as soon as a charismatic figure comes along.

Those are all powerful arguments for change, but in Britain republicanism remains the obsession of a small minority. Republic, the main campaigning body, has only four thousand paying members, contributing on average £20 a year each to meet its £100,000 running costs, though it claims an additional 30,000 supporters and the sympathies of maybe between a quarter and a third of the public. Republic feels itself puny against the power of the palace and struggles to get a hearing in the media, though that is partly because its views and arguments have been made in similar terms for many years. Its chief executive officer, Graham Smith, a former IT specialist who lived in Australia for seven years, tends to pop up like the bad fairy to pour predictable scorn and contempt on all royal occasions – even happy ones – without discrimination or good humour, which may hearten supporters but does not make the alternative sound terribly positive, persuasive or beguiling. The negativity crowds out the message. He clearly feels he has to shout in order to get heard at all, but perhaps he is too much the organisation's lone voice, a variety of spokespeople might have more impact and give more light and shade to the argument.

When I met him at a café in St Pancras station, en route to his home in St Albans, Mr Smith conceded it was a struggle to get the republican voice across. 'It is an uphill battle. We are David against Goliath, but we can keep on going,' he told me intensely. 'If you think about the process we would have to get forty per cent plus on our side, plus MPs. Then I think if Australia and New Zealand start to move in our direction it would be a fairly strong signal that support is moving our way. Monarchies unravel... there's an emperor's new clothes aspect. There will be a moment of national realisation. Getting rid of the monarchy would be an enormous step. It is do-able in my lifetime. Look at the Scottish referendum: ten years ago no one would have predicted it would be that close. We are getting more organised, more campaigning. That is our challenge: building a strong campaign, ready for change happening quite quickly.'

And how would it work? There would be a referendum and then unravelling the monarchy and its web of constitutional powers and wealth would be quite straightforward, he says. The head of state at the time might get a pension and could keep their personal property – Balmoral and Sandringham – but the rest would have to make their own way. Buckingham Palace and its treasures would be opened to the public throughout the year and paying visitors would be able to see the parts that are now closed to them, like the bedrooms – that would solve the argument that the royal family attracts tourism to the country.

'We don't owe them anything. The head of state would get a salary the same as the prime minister and they could have a house somewhere in London. We'd be saving the taxpayer £300 million. Our position is, even if the monarchy was free, we should still get rid of it because it is secretive and anti-democratic. It is helpful to have a head of state who is above the political fray but they should have an activist role as a facilitator and appointer of the prime minister, like they do in Italy or Greece. In Ireland the presidents are former politicians but they are inspirational and can genuinely represent the Irish people.'

This does not take much account of the history and evolution of Irish independence. Then he said: 'You see, the Queen is not inspirational. I don't think people can remember anything she has said all these years. We could have a charismatic head of state. They should not be silent, but be able to speak to and for the country. They can do that without getting into party political debates. The Queen is not prepared to speak in any meaningful way.'

That is her whole point, of course. It would certainly be a change to have a vociferous and opinionated head of state, especially given that whenever the Queen does speak, or Prince Charles, they are attacked by Graham Smith of Republic for saying anything. So who would be elected: a former prime minister? 'No, ex-prime ministers are usually ex for a reason. I don't think it would appeal to them...it would not be a powerful post. We will not find it difficult to get people.'

Mr Smith is sure that the great day is coming: 'Every time there is a royal event, our membership goes up. We had five hundred new members at the time of the royal wedding in 2011. We get more with each royal baby. The thing is, for all its good public relations, the institution has not changed: they had a shock in the 1990s and changed the way they managed their PR but the fundamental issues: cost, secrecy, the dilution of democratic values have not changed. It is not fit for purpose; it is wasteful of the public treasury and it operates to different standards than the rest of the population. Monarchy allows power to be concentrated in the hands of the executive. When you start explaining this, people change their views. That is our challenge up against their formidable machine.

He added: 'I think things will change when Charles becomes king, especially if he becomes political. With the Queen there is nothing to latch onto. I don't think she's a good head of state but it is hard to attack her. Our chance will be with what happens next. Charles would be a good thing for us: he does not play the media game particularly well and I think people will quickly become quite tired of him. The thing is, they want to play a celebrity game but it should be all about the politics. They should be treated like politicians – invite Charles on to defend his positions and if he won't come on, say so. We've said this to the BBC several times…'

Has he ever met them? 'No, but I was in the same room as the Duke of Edinburgh once, to get my Duke of Edinburgh's award. I was a republican even then but I went along just for the novelty.' I don't think Mr Smith is obsessed, but then he added: 'I have met people who have met the Queen. They found her socially awkward. She expects everyone to conform to her customs and standards of etiquette. She does not seem to be able to cope with normal people. I think she jars with people.'

With that, he was off to catch his train and to continue fighting the good fight. It may be that the Queen understands better that people might disagree with her more than he does that they might disagree with him. It is very hard indeed to see what the Queen could do, or say, that he might possibly agree with, short perhaps of saying that she is abdicating. For him it is an uphill struggle: as I made my way back to the Tube, the walls were festooned with posters for *The Audience*, the hit play about the Queen's relations with her prime ministers: more fun and unquestioning of the constitutional settlement.

When the *Guardian* mounted its republican challenges in the early years of the millennium, its object was to provoke a debate about the sort of head of state Britain should have. It argued cogently that when the time comes there will not be any opportunity even for a discussion. In keeping with the old medieval precedents, when kings were proclaimed as soon as possible to forestall challengers, on the morning after the Queen dies, the heralds will be out at St James's Palace proclaiming King Charles III. The mechanism will roll smoothly into place and it will be a *fait accompli*, as it will be when King William V succeeds his father and King George VII follows him. It is worth remembering that in the past two hundred years the original heir apparent has not succeeded to the throne more often than not: Edward VII and, briefly, Edward VIII are the only princes of Wales to become King since George IV two centuries ago, but these are quirks of history and successions have been peaceful and unchallenged for more than three hundred years.

There is little evidence that the majority of the British public mind this, particularly. They are not obsessive about the royal family and it rarely impinges on their lives, except perhaps when there is a particular celebration or an extra bank holiday. The number of obsessives who camp out before a big royal event or who collect every detail of their lives is not very great and is harmless. But many more people rather like the idea of Britain having a monarchy. It sets the country apart from many of its neighbours and helps to give it a sense of itself: they quite like the tradition and the quirky history of the dynasties and the marching bands and the jingling brasses on the horses' bridles. Maybe it does bring in a bit of tourism: not so much the chance of seeing a royal but of experiencing their palaces and castles, the Changing of the Guard and Westminster Abbey. Anyone who has fought their way through the crowds outside Buckingham Palace to see the troops swapping over duties and the band playing at 11 a.m. knows that it is an attraction. There is a compelling and easily explicable historical story too, full of extraordinary dramas and striking personalities and a sense that it has all been going on for a very long time, even if much of the ceremonial is not as time-hallowed as they think. The tourists might well still come for all that, but the point of the rituals would be missing: why bother guarding the palace if there is no one there? Or why parade for a president in a grey suit who lives in another house 'somewhere in London'? It all seems a bit dour. And, of course, any head of state would need security protection from terrorism, so that would be a cost whether for a president or a monarch.

Even at times of royal crisis, the monarchy's essential stability has remained firm: in 1871 when the Prince of Wales nearly died, in 1936 after the abdication and in 1997 following the death of Princess Diana there was a rallying round. You can say it was sentimental or misconceived, especially in the last case, but the princess's funeral was followed within five years by the Queen's golden jubilee, within eight by the Prince of Wales's remarriage, within fourteen by Prince William's wedding and within fifteen by his grandmother's happily unexpected participation in the Olympic Games' opening extravaganza – all widely celebrated. To blame the public's gullibility is joyless, patronising and counterproductive. But, conscious of their precariousness if things go wrong, the royals take keen note of every show of public support. As Prince Philip said fatalistically to Gyles Brandreth at the time of the golden jubilee: 'Safer not to be too popular. You can't fall too far.' It keeps them on their toes.

The chief weakness of the republican case is that there is no compelling narrative to explain why it should happen, what it would cost or how it could come about in a country with no recent tradition of contesting the nature of the state. The Ireland analogy does not really work here: the Irish have a different history and inevitably set themselves up constitutionally in contradistinction to the British state. To the question of what sort of figure a president should be there is no uncontested answer in a country which has never seen the need for an elected head of state before. Despite Mr Smith's contention that the president does not need to be a senior politician – which is undoubtedly true – the fact remains that it is likely to be just such a figure and one elected by at best half the electorate. It would be someone too, of views and with an agenda; not passivity, otherwise there would be no point in electing them. Mr Smith wants an activist president, but not an activist monarch, and at least probably he would want someone sharing his views: how awful to be stuck even for a few years with a head of state you could not stand! The questions of who it might be – or at least what sort of person – and why have to be answered. What would they do that the British monarchy does not and why would they necessarily do it better? The democratic argument is fine but when you have a monarch who does not interfere in the democratic process in any dynamic or contentious sense, what is essentially gained?

The British public in their cheerfully complacent way do not seem inclined to challenge the status quo if it ain't broke, for they see very little reason to fix it with something more ostentatiously political and inevitably partisan, especially given the low standing of politicians. And those politicians are certainly not inclined to change the system. There is no anti-monarchist Willie Hamilton in the Commons any more and no party espouses republicanism as any sort of priority. It is a faddish cause, not a populist one. I chatted about this to a very senior Labour former cabinet minister in his office at the Commons. If anywhere in the current political set-up, change would have to come from the Left. He gazed out at the Thames: 'I think there's no case. The institution is working pretty well and there are more important issues to be concerned about. I don't see any virtue in changing it whatsoever. Most republics cost a lot more. No, there's no appetite in the Labour Party whatever. The monarchy does not hold any unacceptable power. There would have to be a compelling reason to make change a priority.' Then the clincher: 'And it would be a terrible vote loser. There's no way you could make the case...

'William and Kate came to my constituency, solid, working class, urban, and they electrified the town. No, I think people should give Charles a chance. And William and Kate are a class act, especially given the traumas of his childhood. He's remarkably well-balanced.'

Sitting in his firm's office in Somerset House (which makes him a tenant of the Crown Estate) Mark Borkowski, a public relations executive and publicist with an interest in the royal family, said: 'The traditions that the royal family upholds are popular because the country is safe. They stand for history and stability, the heritage industry and Rule Britannia: we take all that for granted but it is lusted after by other countries. No one does it better do they? They create an idea of strength and security, but they cannot rest on their laurels. They have got to keep evolving. I am not necessarily a huge fan of the monarchy but they have neutered the republicans.'

All that could change, of course, if Charles is maladroit or seeks to change the monarchy disruptively, if he becomes overly partisan or faddish, or succeeds in overturning how the British regard the institution, because in doing so he would be changing part of their sense of their country. If he is an old king in too much of a hurry, he will be in danger. That would undermine the conceit that the monarchy floats above politics because it is a timeless institution. But it is likely at his age to be a short reign: time limited by age. And there lies a possibly even greater problem. It is actuarial. Britain has got itself not only a middle class monarchy, but it is likely also to have at least a middle-aged one for decades to come. An ageing society may not mind that too much, but it does mean that the institution may also become more hidebound and sclerotic. What may change the nature of the state in coming years is the possible break-up of the United Kingdom, if Scotland eventually opts for independence. Both Alex Salmond, during the 2014 referendum, and Nicola Sturgeon have maintained they would wish to keep the monarchy in an independent Scotland. There are precedents with the Commonwealth monarchies but inevitably there would be a diminution and in a diminished and truncated state, anything might happen. The fact that Salmond felt the need to reassure Scottish monarchists indicates that the Queen still has a pull north of the border, but does the duke of Rothesay? (Prince Charles's title when in Scotland.)

The royal family do not believe in abdication, but change is inevitably coming. The Queen will be ninety in April 2016, her husband is ninety-four. Will the Queen soldier on her whole life long as she once pledged to do, when the Duke of Edinburgh dies? Surviving partners often give up. Officials insist the Queen will not abdicate and would continue to reign after her husband's death. Would there in that case be a regency, as there would have to be if she became incapacitated? Buckingham Palace has given this thought and had a look at the relevant legislation just in case. There were four regency acts in the twentieth century, all passed at the beginning of reigns when the new sovereign's children were under the age of eighteen, but for any current purposes the procedure is contained in the 1937 legislation allowing the lord chancellor, the speaker of the House of Commons, the lord chief justice of England and the master of the rolls to step in if 'by reason of infirmity of mind or body [the Sovereign is] incapable for the time being of performing the royal functions'. In order to make and sign that declaration to the Privy Council they would of course need firm medical evidence. Such a provision has not been required since poor George III was recognised to have declined into his final madness beyond hope of recovery in 1811. Let us hope for all concerned it does not come to that.

In any event, at some time in the not too distant future, Charles will succeed his mother if he is fit to do so and, when he does, he will be already well past retirement age: he is considerably older than any previous monarch who has ascended the throne. He has waited all his life for that moment and it will not pass him by if he can help it. But beyond him, Prince William is already in his mid-thirties, in the press photographer's words, 'another bald bloke in a suit'. It is becoming a rather staid family: comforting, respectable, but ever-so slightly frumpy. Not many fairytales, not much magic. Camelot it ain't. The grind will go on; the soap opera may continue: Prince George and Princess Charlotte will grow up, go to school and then look for partners, but will people become bored with a never-ending royal Groundhog Day?

This book has argued that the institution of the monarchy has survived and flourished because it has quietly evolved to meet changing circumstances and expectations within a framework of dignity, pragmatism and inherent conservatism. Its success is not very mystical, though it has a spiritual element: it survives because it is unthreatening and gives the British people a sense of solidarity and stability, a symbol of their country and its heritage. It has even pulled off the trick – fortuitously – of floating above class and its wealth has not been an impediment to its popularity despite the tenacity with which it has protected its coffers. Most importantly it has enabled the British (and populations across the world) to identify with it, in solidarity with a family which is not like them at all...

On the Thursday before Easter 2015, the Queen and the Duke

visited Sheffield to distribute the Royal Maundy: the annual ritual that dates in its present form, so far as the sovereign is concerned, all the way back to her grandfather in 1932. When medieval kings, starting with John in 1210, distributed alms and washed the feet of the poor they were following the *mandatum* – Christ's command to love one another. But these days instead the Queen distributes specially minted coins in two purses, red and white, to worthy pensioners – the same number as her age: so in 2015 to eighty-nine. The red purse contained a £5 coin and a five pence coin notionally to cover an allowance for clothing and food and the white held two pence, three pence and four pence coins adding up to 89 pence. The coins are legal tender, though they would perhaps receive funny looks on the tills, not to mention being a prodigal waste of their actual as opposed to their face value. But it is a mistake to think that they represent the sovereign's own largesse, in distributing her own wealth. In fact, the Royal Mint bears the cost of designing and producing them.

The ceremony itself was full of the sort of show that bespeaks a timeless tradition, powerful and sentimental enough to bring a catch to the throat. The Queen was followed by a phalanx of clergy and trailing Yeomen of the Guard in their scarlet Tudor uniforms, some bearing the large alms dishes on which the purses are carried. The procession was accompanied by local primary school children carrying the towels that would once have washed the feet of the poor – the last symbolic remnants of the medieval act of sovereign obeisance, together with the nosegay posies of herbs and Spring flowers the Queen and clergy carried as a reminder of how smelly a ritual it must once have been. Slowly up and down the Nave, first down one side and then down the other, round and into the side aisles, the group wound to the sound of the rhythmical slow tramp of the Yeomens' feet amplified by the rapping of the staff of their sergeant major on the flagstones: a clump that would be like something out of Gilbert and Sullivan were it not so ponderous: every step an echo from a distant past.

This too is royalty at work, a gesture to an ancient order of things when kings felt a paternal need to fulfil Christ's command at least once a year, Here, in what was once known as the People's Republic of South Yorkshire the elderly worthies, dressed in their best suits and bonnets – definitely no smelly feet – bowed their heads graciously as the Queen smiled vaguely at them, handed over their purses and wordlessly moved on. Any conversation would come later at the reception in the Town Hall. This was the first time that the Royal Maundy service had come to Sheffield – the ceremony used to be held only at Westminster Abbey but in the current reign it has been taken to Anglican cathedrals around the country and, with nearly fifty to choose from, most have only been visited once. The Queen has missed just four services in sixty-four years, twice when heavily pregnant or having just given birth and none since 1970.

The recipients had all been chosen, as they always are, for their long-standing worthiness in their churches and communities. The duke apparently likes to bark facetiously these days: 'Why are they getting it? They're all at least twenty years younger than I am.' The hardy elderly folk of south Yorkshire might have appreciated that particular blunt sally but they were, it is fair to say, bowled over just to have met the Queen. 'It's been absolutely wonderful,' said Betty Brockman, the former deputy head of a comprehensive school in Doncaster, 'it's just fabulous to meet the Queen. I've never done it before.' Nearby, ninety-two-year-old Bruce Wyatt and his wife Christine were similarly thrilled. Bruce spent thirty-four years down the local pit at Pilley near Barnsley, ending as an overseer, but had also piously kept his local parish church going, almost single-handed – a different image indeed to that often conveyed of a South Yorkshire miner. It is fair to say that Bruce is more a fan of the Queen than of Arthur Scargill. 'It's been marvellous,' he said, coming over all emotional and breathing hard. 'I haven't slept properly since I was told I'd been chosen to be here today. I was so worried about it going well and it has, hasn't it? She's a wonderful lady. If anyone had ever said to me I'd be standing as close to her as I am to you, well, I'd never have believed them.'

Outside the cathedral in the spring sunshine the crowds were ten rows deep and dourly enthusiastic in their Yorkshire way. Inside, the congregation had been overwhelmingly white and at least middle-aged. Outside, the crowd was much more ethnically mixed and younger: mothers and dads with young babies and toddlers, Asian Muslim men and women, African mothers in hijabs and chadors, Chinese youngsters, most with local accents. Outside the town hall, where the Queen and duke and the Maundy recipients had moved for lunch, a large crowd several thousand strong had gathered expectantly. Two white lads wearing tracksuits and trainers were considering the situation and whether to wait for the royal party to come out and watch them get into the limousine.

'At least you can say you've seen the Queen,' said one.

'Naw, I can see her any time on t'telly, at the Grand National and that,' said the other

'Yeah, but in the flesh like . . . '

'She's not that important . . . '

'Aye, she is.'

'Shall I get on your shoulders when she comes out?' said the more enthusiastic one.

'Naw, I'll climb up one of them drainpipes to see 'er.'

When an eighty-nine year old still has such pulling power the monarchy is certainly safe – for now.

Source Notes

Chapter One: *'I have to be seen to be believed'*
The biographical information about the Queen is taken principally from the royal biographies cited in the bibliography by Ben Pimlott, Robert Lacey, Sarah Bradford, Andrew Marr and Robert Hardman. Jeremy Paxman's discomfiture at the prospect of meeting the Queen can be found on page 22 of his book *On Royalty*. Pope Benedict's meeting with the Queen is drawn from personal observation, as I reported in the *Guardian* on 17 September 2010. The royal gifts were detailed in a palace press release on 14 January 2015. The ComRes poll on royal popularity was commissioned by and published in the *Daily Mail* on 11 April 2015.

Chapter Two: *'It is a great inheritance — and a heavy burden — on the girl who becomes Queen'*
Sources for what Britain was like in 1952 are taken from David Kynaston's *Family Britain 1951–57*, from Peter Hennessy's *Having it so Good: Britain in the Fifties*, from Sarah Bradford's *George VI*, from Roy Jenkins' *Churchill* and from Philip Ziegler's description of contemporary Mass Observation surveys in *Crown and People*.

Chapter Three: 'Do you come here often?'

The Duchess of Cambridge's visit to Margate took place on 11 March 2015. Roy Strong's book details royal coronations, as do the biographies of individual monarchs cited: On Elizabeth I: J.E. Neale's biography and Penry Williams' *The Later Tudors*; on the royal pictures, Jerry Brotton's *The Sale of the late King's Goods;* John Brooke's *King George III*; Fanny Burney's *Journals and Letters* on meeting the King; Christopher Hibbert and Saul David's biographies of George IV; Elizabeth Longford and A.N. Wilson on Victoria; Kenneth Rose's on *King George V*; and Sarah Bradford on George VI. Linda Colley's *Britons: Forging the Nation 1707–1837* is outstanding as is her husband David Cannadine's groundbreaking essay in *The Invention of Tradition* by Hobsbawm and Ranger. John Prebble and Hugh Trevor-Roper had fun with King George IV's jaunt to Edinburgh in 1822. For Charles Greville's diary on the King's burial and William IV's attempted walkabout, see the entries for 9 July and 20 July 1830. *The Times*'s devastating obituary of the King was published on 30 June 1830 and its welcome for George VI on his coronation 107 years later was on 12 May 1837. The very early newsreel footage of Queen Victoria's diamond jubilee in 1897 can be viewed on YouTube. David Starkey's entertaining essay on the modern monarchy is in Smith and Moore's *The Monarchy: Fifteen Hundred Years of British Tradition*. John Plunkett's fascinating research on Queen Victoria and the media is in his book *Queen Victoria: First Media Monarch*. The Queen's Irish trip in 2011 was covered in all media including myself in the *Guardian* between 17–22 May.

Chapter Four: 'Our great problem is democracy'

For an account of the Queen's intervention in the Scottish referendum campaign see the *Guardian*'s report on 17 December 2014. For European royal families see Peter Conradi's *The Great Survivors*. The monarchy is famously discussed in Walter Bagehot's *The English Constitution*, chapter two.

Chapter Five: 'An entire effacement of self'

Kenneth Rose discusses the House of Windsor's First World War name change in *King George V*. His gossip about the private secretaries is also in his entertaining *Kings, Queens and Courtiers*. Walter Monckton's role in the abdication crisis is in Frances Donaldson's *Edward VIII* biography. Pimlott is good on the secretaries of the 1960s–90s and Robert Lacey on the Diana crises.

Chapter Six: 'A sphere beyond politics'

My interview with Richard Chartres was on 27 November 2014 and my book *A Church at War* gives the background to the church's crisis over homosexuality. Monica Furlong's *C of E: The State it's In* is a fine background study of the church. The Victorian church is discussed in Owen Chadwick's magisterial work of that name. The Coronation Oath is outlined on the monarchy's website and the Declaration is to be found on the Catholic Encyclopaedia's New Advent website. Queen Victoria's visit to a child's bedside is in Plunkett, *Kilvert's Diary* for 3 January 1872 describes the reaction to the Prince of Wales's illness and Roy Jenkins's *Sir Charles Dilke* biography describes his ill-fated republican campaign, while Frank Prochaska's *Royal Bounty* describes royal charitable efforts. The Queen's Christmas broadcast transcripts are on the monarchy's website. My interview with Ian Bradley – my former tutor at Oxford and an old friend – was on 12 November 2014 and his book *God Save the Queen* is – of course – essential on her spirituality.

Chapter Seven: 'You have mosquitoes, I have the press'

Plunkett is hugely entertaining on the royals' relations with the Victorian press. The 1723 quotation about loyal newspapers is in Colley's *Britons*, page 201; Kenneth Baker in his book on George IV, caricatures and writes about the King's attempts to stop them. The *Daily Mail*'s disobliging article on the fashionability or otherwise of Prince William and his wife was published on 10 December 2014. Rose's courtiers book is scathing about Commander Colville. Pimlott quotes Ronald Allison about updating the royals' media presentation on page 380 and he and Lacey's biographies on the Queen discuss the *Royal Family* documentary.

Chapter Eight: 'I think we're a soap opera'
Prince Charles's upbringing and career are discussed in Jonathan Dimbleby's thorough biography *The Prince of Wales*. The tabloid side of the war of the Waleses is very enjoyably told in Peter Chippindale and Chris Horrie's *Stick it up your Punter!* The Charles and Diana palace kiss is described in Lacey and *Punter!*, and Lacey and Pimlott are also the sources for the Barry Askew story. Pimlott outlines the *It's a Royal Knockout* programme in all its grisly detail on page 525. Al-Fayed's evidence at the Diana inquest was reported by me in the *Guardian* on 18 February 2008. The best source for the Princess's death is Martyn Gregory's *Diana: The Last Days*: fine investigative journalism at the time which was never contravened in the lengthy inquest nine years later.

Chapter Nine: 'Speak to us Ma'am'
The extensive media coverage of the aftermath of Princess Diana's death dates from the first week of September 1997. The Queen's broadcast is detailed in Lacey's fine, updated biography *Royal*. The *News of the World* exposure of Prince Harry's drug taking was published on 13 January 2002, its 'Edward is not gay' interview with the Countess of Wessex was published on 1 April 2001. Prince Charles's leaked letter

about the Countryside March was published in the *Mail on Sunday* on 22 September 2002 and the same paper's account of the Prince's Chinese thoughts was published on 13 November 2005. Mark Bolland's interview with the *Guardian* was published on 25 October 2003. Coverage of the Prince's second wedding was on 9 April 2005. The Burrell trial's collapse was reported in all media on 1 November 2002 and the withdrawal of the case against Harold Brown was reported on 4 December 2002. The Peat report was published on 13 March 2003. Broadcast coverage of the royals was analysed in the two-part BBC documentary *Reinventing the Royals* in February 2015. The entire course of William and Kate Middleton's romance is described in loving detail in Robert Jobson's *The New Royal Family*. The *Melbourne Age*'s assessment of the Prince's first independent visit to Australia was published on 21 January 2010.

Chapter Ten: 'What does she do with it?'
The royal accounts and the annual report of the Prince of Wales are available online and there are also websites for the duchies of Lancaster and Cornwall which detail their activities. The *Sunday Times* published an interview with Alison Nimmo, who runs the Crown Estate, on 5 April 2015. The most substantial investigation into the royal family's tax avoidance was Philip Hall's *Royal Fortune: Tax, Money and the Monarchy*. My interview with Sir Alan Reid took place on 7 April 2015. Colley discusses the British royal family's palaces compared with Versailles on page 199 of *Britons*. George III's finances are discussed in Brooke's biography. George V's stamp collection and his exchange about extravagance with a courtier is in Rose's biography, on pages 41–42. Prince Philip's American interview is discussed in Pimlott's biography of Elizabeth II, on page 394, and Crossman's quote about the Queen is in Andrew Marr's, on page 219. Lacey reports the quote on the royals not giving in on tax on page 236 of *Royal*, Pimlott's

description of Airlie is on page 532, and Reid's evidence to the Public Accounts Committee took place on 14 October 2013.

Chapter Eleven: 'A spirit of loyal enthusiasm'
The Mexican president's state visit began on 3 March 2015. The Lascelles quote on the Queen's twenty-first birthday broadcast is cited in Pimlott, page 119. Clarence House's attack on Catherine Mayer's biography of Prince Charles surfaced in rival papers which had secured serialisation rights, such as the *Daily Telegraph* on 1 February 2015. On the state of Sunninghill Park, see my report in the *Guardian* on 1 March 2009 and the *Daily Mail's* account of the still-dilapidated mansion on 8 October 2014. The decision of the Florida judge Kenneth Marra to remove Prince Andrew's name from a federal court case was reported in the *Guardian* and other papers on 7 April 2015.

Chapter Twelve: 'Safer not to be too popular. You can't fall too far'
My interview with Graham Smith of Republic was on 10 March 2015. The Maundy service in Sheffield was on 2 April 2015.

Bibliography

Bagehot, Walter. *The English Constitution,* Collins Fontana, 1973

Baker, Kenneth. *George IV: A Life in Caricature,* Thames and Hudson, 2005

Bates, Stephen. *A Church at War,* I.B. Tauris, 2003

Bates, Stephen. *Asquith,* Haus, 2006

Baylis, Matthew. *Man Belong Mrs Queen: Adventures with the Philip Worshippers,* Old Street Publishing, 2013

Beaken, Robert. *Cosmo Lang: Archbishop in War and Crisis,* I.B. Tauris, 2012

Bogdanor, Vernon. *The Monarchy and the Constitution,* Clarendon Press, 1997

Bradford, Sarah. *George VI,* Penguin, 2002

Bradford, Sarah. *Queen Elizabeth II: Her Life in Our Times,* Viking, 2012

Bradley, Ian. *God Save the Queen: The Spiritual Heart of the Monarchy,* Continuum, 2012

Brendon, Piers and Whitehead, Philip. *The Windsors: A Dynasty Revealed 1917–2000,* Pimlico, 2000

Brock, Michael. *The Great reform Act,* Hutchinson, 1973

Brooke, John. *King George III,* Panther, 1974

Brotton, Jerry. *The Sale of the Late King's Goods,* Pan, 2006

Burney, Frances. *Journals and Letters,* Penguin Classics, 2001

Chadwick, Owen. *The Victorian Church,* A and C Black Ltd., 1966

Chippindale, Peter and Horrie, Chris. *Stick it up your Punter! The Rise and Fall of the Sun,* Heinemann, 1990

Clarke, Christopher. *The Sleepwalkers: How Europe went to War in 1914,* Penguin, 2012

Colley, Linda. *Britons: Forging the Nation 1707–1837,* Yale University Press, 1992

Conradi, Peter. *The Great Survivors: How Monarchy Made it into the Twenty-first Century,* Alma Books, 2012

David, Saul. *Prince of Pleasure: The Prince of Wales and the Making of the Regency,* Abacus, 1999

Darter, William. *Reminiscences of Reading by an Octogenarian,* British Library Historical Collections, reprint of 1889 edition

Dimbleby, Jonathan. *The Prince of Wales,* Warner Books, 1994

Donaldson, Frances. *Edward VIII,* Futura, 1978

Fraser, Antonia. *Perilous Question: The Drama of the Great Reform Bill,* Phoenix, 2013

Furlong, Monica. *C of E: The State it's In,* Hodder and Stoughton, 2000

Gilmour, David. *Curzon,* John Murray, 1994

Gregory, Martyn. *Diana: The Last Days,* Virgin Books, 1999

Hall, Philip. *Royal Fortune: Tax, Money and the Monarchy,* Bloomsbury, 1992

Hamilton, Alan. *The Times Royal Handbook,* Piatkus, 2002

Hardman, Robert. *Our Queen,* Hutchinson, 2011

Harris, Kenneth. *Attlee,* Weidenfeld and Nicolson, 1995

Hennessy, Peter. *Having it so Good: Britain in the Fifties*, Penguin, 2007

Hibbert, Christopher. *George IV: The Rebel Who Would Be King*, Palgrave Macmillan, 2007

Hobsbawm, Eric and Ranger, Terence. *The Invention of Tradition:* articles by Cannadine, David. 'The Context, Performance and Meaning of Ritual: The British Monarchy and the Invention of Tradition' and Trevor-Roper Hugh. 'The Highland Tradition of Scotland', Cambridge University Press, 1983

Jay, Antony. *Elizabeth R: The Role of the Monarchy Today*, BCA, 1992

Jenkins, Roy. *Churchill*, Pan, 2001

Jenkins, Roy. *Gladstone*, Macmillan, 1995

Jenkins, Roy. *Sir Charles Dilke: A Victorian Tragedy*, Collins, 1958

Jobson, Robert. *The New Royal Family*, John Blake, 2013

Junor, Penny. *Charles: Victim or Villain?*, HarperCollins, 1998

Kenny, Mary. *Crown and Shamrock: Love and Hate between Ireland and the British Monarchy*, New Island, 2009

Kynaston, David. *Family Britain 1951–57*, Bloomsbury, 2009

Lacey, Robert. *A Brief Life of the Queen*, Duckworth Overlook, 2012

Lacey, Robert. *Royal: Her Majesty Queen Elizabeth II*, Time Warner, 2002

Leapman, Michael. *The World for a Shilling*, Headline, 2002

Longford, Elizabeth. *Victoria*, Abacus, 2011

Lorimer, David. *Radical Prince: The Practical Vision of the Prince of Wales*, Floris, 2003

Marr, Andrew. *The Diamond Queen: Elizabeth II and her People*, Macmillan 2011

Mayer, Catherine. *Charles: The Heart of a King*, W.H. Allen, 2015

McIntyre, Ian. *The Expense of Glory: A Life of John Reith*, HarperCollins, 1994

Merck, Mandy. *After Diana: Irreverent Elegies*, Verso, 1998

Middlemas, Keith and Barnes, John. *Baldwin: A Biography*, Weidenfeld and Nicolson, 1969

Morton, Andrew. *Diana: Her True Story – In her own Words*, Michael O'Mara, 2003

Nairn, Tom. *The Enchanted Glass: Britain and its Monarchy*, Verso, 2011

Neale, J.E. *Queen Elizabeth I*, Penguin, 1971

Nicolson, Nigel. *The Queen and Us: The Second Elizabethan Age*, Bedford Square Books, 2003

Olechnowicz, Andrzej. *The Monarchy and the British Nation: 1780 to the Present*, Cambridge University Press, 2007

Paxman, Jeremy. *On Royalty*, Penguin, 2007

Pearce, Edward. *The Diaries of Charles Greville*, Pimlico, 2006

Perkins, Anne. *Baldwin*, Haus, 2006

Pimlott, Ben. *The Queen: A Biography of Elizabeth II*, Harper Collins, 1997

Plomer, William, editor. *Kilvert's Diary*, Penguin, 1978

Plunkett, John. *Queen Victoria: First Media Monarch*, Oxford University Press, 2003

Prebble, John. *The Highland Clearances*, Penguin, 1963

Prebble, John. *The King's Jaunt: George IV in Scotland 1822*, Fontana, 1988

Prochaska, Frank. *Royal Bounty: The Making of the Welfare Monarchy*, Yale University Press, 1995

Purkis, Diane. *The English Civil War*, HarperPress, 2006

Rennell, Tony. *Last Days of Glory: The Death of Queen Victoria*, Penguin, 2001

Richards, Jeffrey, Wilson, Scott and Woodhead, Linda, editors. *Diana: The Making of a Media Saint*, I.B. Tauris, 1999

Rose, Kenneth. *King George V*, Macmillan, 1983

Rose, Kenneth. *Kings, Queens and Courtiers*, Weidenfeld and Nicolson, 1985

Smith, Robert and Moore, John, editors. *The Monarchy: Fifteen Hundred Years of British Tradition*, Smith's Peerage Ltd., 1998

Starkey, David. *Crown and Country: The Kings and Queens of England*, Harper Press, 2010

Strong, Roy. *Coronation: A History of Kingship and the British Monarchy*, HarperCollins, 2005

Straw, Jack. *Last Man Standing: Memoirs*, Macmillan, 2012

Trevor-Roper, Hugh. *The Invention of Scotland: Myth and History*, Yale University Press, 2008

Uglow, Jenny. *In These Times: Living in Britain through Napoleon's Wars 1793–1815*, Faber and Faber, 2014

Vizetelly, Henry. *Glances Back through Seventy Years, Volume 1*, Kegan Paul, Trench Trubner and Co., 1893

Ward, Yvonne. *Censoring Queen Victoria: How Two Gentlemen Edited a Queen and Created an Icon*, Oneworld, 2014

Weir, Alison, Williams, Kate, Gristwood, Sarah and Borman, Tracy. *The Ring and the Crown: A History of Royal Weddings 1066–2011*, Hutchinson, 2011

Williams, Penry. *The Later Tudors: England 1547–1603*, Oxford University Press, 1998

Williams, Richard. *The Contentious Crown: Public Discussion of the British Monarchy in the Reign of Queen Victoria*, Ashgate, 1997

Wilson, A.N. *Victoria: A Life*, Atlantic, 2014

Ziegler, Philip. *Crown and People*, Collins, 1978

Official reports

'The Sovereign Grant and the Sovereign Grant Reserve Annual Reports and Accounts 2013–14'

'Duchy of Cornwall Financial Statements 2013–14'

'The Prince and Wales and Duchess of Cornwall Annual Review 2014'

'Duchy of Lancaster Report and Accounts 2014'

Public Accounts Committee 2013–14: '39th report: The Sovereign Grant'; witness session 14 October 2013

Newspapers and magazines

Guardian

The Times

Daily Telegraph

Sunday Telegraph

Sunday Times

Sunday Times Rich List 2015

Daily Mail

Mail on Sunday

News of the World

The Economist, 'The still centre', 9 June 2012

Macleans 2011: The Firm's Got Buzz

Broadcasts

Goodman Elinor: *The Royal Activist,* BBC Radio 4, 29 June 2014

Hewlett Steve: *Reinventing the Royals,* BBC2, 19/26 February 2015

Websites

Oxford Dictionary of National Biography: www.oxforddnb.com

The Official website of the British Monarchy: www.royal.gov.uk

Catholic Encyclopedia: www.newadvent.org

Kent reference library: www.kent.gov.uk

Dissertation

Preston, Natalie. *Brand Monarchy: Political Marketing of the British Monarchy 1997–2014*, Royal Holloway, University of London

Interviews

The Earl of Airlie

Mark Borkowski

Very Revd Dr. Ian Bradley

Rt Revd Richard Chartres

Lord Hennessy

Robert Lacey

Sir Alan Reid

Graham Smith

And 20 others, who were interviewed anonymously during 2014–15

Acknowledgements

*T*he people I interviewed for this book gave their time both freely and generously, and spoke frankly about the royal family. Unfortunately the quid pro quo was that many of them either did not wish to speak on the record, or would agree only to their most inoffensive statements being attributed – a compromise I decided not to deploy since naming them in one context would inevitably lead to them being identified or misidentified in another, or at least suspected, of being the source of their more contentious remarks. I appreciate that this use of anonymous quotation will be unsatisfactory to many readers, but it was the price paid for their frankness. In recompense I have tried to indicate in general terms their seniority and the positions they have held within the Royal Household. All those I interviewed for this book have been senior members of that household, usually in close daily acquaintance with members of the royal family, for a number of years and in several instances for decades. They have served either the Queen at Buckingham Palace or Prince Charles at Clarence House – in some cases both – or have been closely associated with them as advisers on their private interests or public duties. Almost all the interviews took place within the past year. I thank both them and the interviewees who were prepared to be identified for their help with this book and I hope they will agree that I have reported their views fairly.

James Roscoe, David Pogson and Laura King at Buckingham Palace were most helpful and considerate in assisting me with information, answering queries and securing my accreditation to attend events. They may not agree with everything in this book but its contents are no reflection on them at all.

I also wish to thank Alan Rusbridger and the *Guardian* for assigning me to cover the royal family, and allowing me to do so in Britain and around the world for twelve years. I suspect my appointment owed something originally to the paper's perceived need to have someone to cover stories originally broken in the Sunday tabloid papers of record, but the job did allow me also to report on many royal events: royal weddings and a royal funeral, two jubilees, scandals and celebrations, trials and tribulations. If the paper thought it slightly risible given its republican stance to have a royal correspondent – I was never actually billed as such in a byline – that is what I was to all intents and purposes. It is a tribute to the paper's editorial integrity that, although as this book will have made clear, I am rather more in support of the institution than the *Guardian* is, I was never pressured to toe a different line, or censored in what I wrote.

Contrary to popular opinion, covering the royal family is neither glamorous nor usually particularly exciting. Indeed it is often very tedious and enervating because of the constraints of writing about an institution which is ultimately largely inaccessible and theoretically without opinions. That the job was at all tolerable and enjoyable was in large part due to the help and camaraderie of fellow correspondents to whom I offer my thanks, including especially: Caroline Davies and

Rob Booth of the *Guardian*, Valentine Low and, before him, the late Alan Hamilton of *The Times*, Gordon Rayner of the *Daily Telegraph*, Richard Palmer of the *Daily Express*, Rebecca English and Robert Hardman of the *Daily Mail*, Duncan Larcombe of the *Sun*, Robert Jobson of the *Evening Standard*, Roya Nikkhah of the *Sunday Telegraph* (now with the *Sunday Times*), the late Chris Morgan of the *Sunday Times*, Laura Elston and Alan Jones of the *Press Association*, Phil Dampier, the late James Whitaker, Peter Hunt and Nicholas Witchell of the *BBC* and Judy Wade of *Hello!* magazine. All errors of taste and fact are of course mine!

My agent Charlie Viney is largely responsible for my writing this book and, as ever, has been a great supporter of it, and I also wish to thank Melissa Smith at Aurum for guiding it to publication and Emily Kearns who edited the text. My wife Alice, as always, has been a pillar of support and kindness, and this book is accordingly dedicated to her, with much love.

Stephen Bates
Deal, Kent
June 2015

Index